A WONDERFUL THII
FOR CAMBRIDGE

'The existence of the Home we owe to
Mr Agnew's pious benefaction;
the name of the Home to Mrs Agnew'

A WONDERFUL THING FOR CAMBRIDGE

The Evelyn Hospital – 1921 to 2003

SHEILA MANN

GRANTA EDITIONS

Published by Granta Editions, 25–27 High Street,
Chesterton, Cambridge CB4 1ND
Granta Editions is a wholly owned imprint of Book Production Consultants plc

ISBN (hardback) 1 85757 085 5
ISBN (paperback) 1 85757 084 7

Designed by Jim Reader
Design, editorial and production in association with
Book Production Consultants plc, 25–27 High Street,
Chesterton, Cambridge CB4 1ND
www.bpccam.co.uk

Printed and bound by Kyodo Printing Co (Singapore) Pte Ltd.

Contents

About the author

Sheila Mann trained as a nurse at University College Hospital, London, qualifying in 1964. She worked at Addenbrooke's Hospital, Cambridge, between 1964 and 1968 and from 1972 to 1981, specialising in ENT surgery. From 1968 to 1972 she studied at the University of Essex, receiving a BA in the History of Art and an MA in the History and Theory of Architecture. Agency nursing during the vacations inspired a return to her chosen profession. She worked at The Evelyn Hospital in Cambridge from 1983 to 2004, where she specialised in surgery until 2000. Subsequent experience on the medical/oncology and radiology units and in the outpatient clinics provided valuable experience in fields not previously encountered. She was inspired to write the history of The Evelyn after discovering, when producing a pamphlet to celebrate the Hospital's seventy-fifth birthday, that a complete and untapped archive existed in the Hospital's attics.

Acknowledgements

My thanks are due, first and foremost, to Julian Agnew, Chairman of The Evelyn Trust for giving me permission to write this book and for allowing me access to the Hospital's archives and to his great-grandfather's diaries.

I am also indebted to the following individuals, some of whom have not lived to see the fruit of their and my endeavours:

Aileen Adams, John Agelasto, John Allen, Mary Anderson, Dona Armstrong, Mildred Beechner, John Belsted, Edward Beresford-Davies, Julian Bland, Brenda Bott and Peggy Leonard (née Hobbs), Derek Bown, Sue Colquhoun, Hereward Cooke, Joan Cooper, Anthony Craigen, Elizabeth Dadley, Heather Dixon, David Dunn, Peter Finlayson, Geoffrey Fisk, Mary Gardner, Sheila Gillies, Audrey Gregg, Angela Haines, Elizabeth Hawkins, John Heffer, Evelyn Holland, Sylvia Horwood-Smart, Sarah Inman, Michael Lindop, Ann Mathias, Lynda Mills, Pat Mitchell, Peri Mundell, Isobel Nourse, Lavinia Nourse, Francis Pemberton, Kathryn and Graham Petrie, Betty Prior, John Randle, Morwenna Rendle-Short, Oliver Rowell, Steve Sallaberger, Charles Sharp, John Shaw, Alistair Smellie, John Stevens, Robert Swindlehurst, Bob Verney, Edith Whetham, Robert Whitaker, Dorothy and Percy Willis, Kenneth Wilsdon, Jenny Wilson, Athene Withycombe, Charles Woolf.

The following institutions have also been most helpful:
The Alexander Archive at the
   University of Texas at Austin, USA;
Applecourt Residents Association;

Cambridge City Council Department
of Architecture and Planning;
The Cambridge Evening News;
The Cambridgeshire Collection at the
Central Library, Cambridge;
Cambridgeshire Heritage at the
County Record Office;
The Royal Academy of Arts;
The Royal Institute of British Architects;
Trinity College, Cambridge.

My gratitude also goes to past and
present colleagues and patients, too numerous to mention, who have
shared their memories of The Evelyn
with me, entrusted me with precious
documentary evidence, and taken so
much interest in work in progress.

Finally, my heartfelt thanks go to
my husband George Mann, research
assistant and word processor
extraordinaire, without whom this
book might never have reached
completion.

Sheila Mann

Evelyn and Charles Morland Agnew.

CHAPTER 1

A Thank-offering for his Wife's Recovery

THE STORY OF The Evelyn Hospital begins with a lady and gentleman called Evelyn and Charles Morland Agnew. In 1918 they were 58 and 63 years old respectively, and they divided their time between a country house in Hertfordshire and a flat in London. A residence in the metropolis was required because Morland Agnew was head of the family firm of Thos Agnew & Sons Ltd of Old Bond Street; indeed, he had been largely responsible for the firm's development from contemporary art dealers in Manchester into internationally known fine-art dealers in the capital. A Trinity man, Morland Agnew maintained close links with Cambridge and the surrounding countryside, his visits having been more frequent of late because Gerald, the eldest of his five sons, had been invalided back from

France in 1916 and was currently training officer cadets at his and his father's old college.

In January 1918, Morland Agnew recorded in his diary that 'Mother' (as he called his wife) was suffering from 'intransigent dyspepsia – or whatever it is'. Her GP recommended that a medical specialist's opinion be sought. In February she saw Thomas Horder, consultant at St Bartholomew's Hospital and future royal physician. He thought there was some 'ulceration', and after X-ray investigations decided that surgery was 'absolutely necessary'. The choice of surgeon was easy: Arthur Cooke FRCS (usually styled Dr Cooke in recognition of his erstwhile career as general practitioner) was honorary surgeon at Addenbrooke's Hospital in Cambridge. He was also a close friend of, and

Arthur Cooke, FRCS, *honorary surgeon at Addenbrooke's Hospital.*

relative by marriage to, the Agnew family through his wife Vivien (Viva). Mr and Mrs Agnew decided that her operation must be performed in Cambridge so that she could be under Arthur Cooke's immediate care.

On 1 March, the Agnews moved to the University Arms Hotel, where Morland lived during his wife's stay in hospital. After dinner he took her to the Nursing Hostel in Thompson's Lane. Initial impressions were favourable – her room, though cold enough to warrant an open fire, was 'large, airy and quiet'. Evelyn's operation began at 1 p.m. on 3 March and was over by 3 p.m. Arthur Cooke was assisted by his general practitioner colleague William Wingate, shooting companion of Morland Agnew. Morland worried that 'the operation must have been a great strain on Arthur', but fortunately for all concerned 'Mother took it very well'. Morland, on the other hand, called 3 March 'the most trying day of my life'.

During the weeks following his wife's operation – her recovery was prolonged and it was not until late the following month that she was well enough to go home – Morland spent much time at the hostel. As Evelyn's condition improved, Morland's worries were removed from her to focus on her surroundings; these he described in his diary as 'wretched in many respects, not to say disgraceful'. He went on to add that the hostel was 'wretchedly equipped, a poor house, and in a poor situation'. (Evelyn's visiting grandson Geoffrey, then a schoolboy at St Faith's, remembered it as 'a black hole … with no daylight'.) Morland was greatly relieved when, on 29 April, 'we got Mother out of the Home'. He decided that what Cambridge needed was a 'really good nursing home' and that he himself would provide it.

In fact, it was within days of his wife's operation that Morland Agnew asked her surgeon to 'think out a

1. At this period the colleges made very poor provision for the care of sick undergraduates. Those with minor illnesses were cared for by their tutors or sent home to be looked after by their family. Were the hostel to close, members of the University requiring more than basic nursing care or without a family to care for them would not even be able to use the public wards at Addenbrooke's; they did not qualify because they were not poor enough. Undergraduates whose family circumstances were such that they could not afford admission to a private nursing home could invoke Crane's Charity for a grant-in-aid.

2. Edith Grace Cracroft trained at the Bolingbroke Hospital in south London. Her first post, at University College Hospital, was followed by war service in France as matron of Fécamp Hospital. On returning to Britain, she worked in Scotland and Huntingdonshire before joining the Thompson's Lane Hostel.

scheme' for a replacement for the hostel, and discussed financial provision for it with the manager of the local branch of Barclay's Bank, Edward Mellish Clark. He also went to look at possible sites. *His* nursing home would be everything that the Thompson's Lane Hostel was not: modern, well equipped, peaceful, light, spacious, and pleasing to the eye.

In fairness to the hostel, it is necessary to say that the Agnews had not seen it at its best. In 1911, Miss Young, its foundress and director, retired. As it was thought to be of 'very pressing importance to the Colleges that the benefits of the hostel should not be discontinued'[1] the hostel was taken over by the Cambridge Nursing Association (CNA); the arrangement was regarded by the latter as a temporary measure so as not to deprive 'the University and the neighbourhood of the only Nursing Hostel large enough to supply public needs'. From 1911 to 1914 the hostel was run on a rather *ad hoc* basis by the CNA, its committee members reiterating that they could not be expected to undertake more permanent responsibility. In 1914, overall management was transferred to a committee consisting of representatives from the colleges and the Cambridge

medical fraternity (including Arthur Cooke), with Edward Mellish Clark acting as treasurer. Lady members of the CNA committee (of whom Mrs Mellish Clark was one) acted as House sub-committee with responsibility for the house-keeping arrangements. Representatives and lady members alike were unpaid, philanthropic people busy in other spheres of public and private life who were expending considerable amounts of time and energy on the running of the hostel. Nursing care was organised by a matron, whose 'ability and zeal' were rewarded by a half share in the net profits – if any. The matron at the time of Evelyn Agnew's operation was a Mrs Miller who, luckily for Evelyn, had recently had 'considerable experience as a Surgical Sister in France'. In 1920, she was replaced by Miss Edith Cracroft, who to 'fully justify her appointment' became the first Matron of Morland Agnew's new nursing home.[2]

Between 1911 and 1918, the hostel's financial position was precarious. In spite of the colleges collectively guaranteeing £600 towards renovation and working capital, the medical users' annual donations of between £25 and £100 (the latter being Arthur Cooke's portion), regular

The Nursing Hostel in Thompson's Lane, 1918. Its shortcomings inspired Morland Agnew in his initiative to create a new nursing home

rent remissions from its landlord, Magdalene College, and two loans of £300 each from the funds of the CNA-administered Fitzwilliam Street Nurses' Home, the hostel was perpetually short of funds. To make matters worse, between 1914 and 1918 it was badly affected by 'the decrease in the numbers of resident members of the University, the high price of materials ... the great rise in the cost of provisions ... and other difficulties caused by the war', tending to run at a loss even when practising strict economies.

In 1919, the hostel entered a period of greater, though still modest, prosperity. Even so, the hostel's management committee was keen to give up its responsibilities, hoping that the hostel could be established 'on a more permanent basis, whether in ownership, by transferring it to an independent person or association, or in locality by removing it to some more suitable spot than Thompson's Lane'. They also asked from whence the necessary funds for any or all of these arrangements were to come, adding that provision of 'adequate nursing accommodation for Cambridge' should not devolve solely upon the University but also upon 'the public at large'. The committee's desire

for change received added impetus from Magdalene's desire to repossess the hostel in order to help accommodate the post-war boom in undergraduate numbers.

It was at this point that a member of the public sufficiently well-off, and an alumnus of the University to boot, provided a solution to the committee's problems. In a statement dated 22 May 1919, the committee was happy to report that 'a friend of the University ... had offered to assist in establishing a new Hostel in Cambridge ... This kind offer came from Mr C. Morland Agnew, of Trinity College, who has most generously expressed his willingness to build and equip a new Hostel ... for the benefit of Cambridge and the neighbourhood.' Plans made independently at his wife's bedside were about to be realised: 'I said I would find money to start it up, up to about £20,000 ...'.

Within days of the first anniversary of 'Mother' having undergone 'that dreadful operation at Cambridge', her husband's plans for 'a really good nursing home', began to bear fruit. 'In finding a site for his home', wrote his grandson Geoffrey in a 1985 memoir, 'my grandfather was lucky. An old house, The Orchard, with a 4 acre garden, in Trumpington Road, had

The Orchard standing in its extensive garden, 1918.

been lived in by Dr Joseph Prior, a Fellow of Trinity. He died in 1918, leaving his property to Trinity.' On 11 March 1919, Morland Agnew wrote in his diary, 'went with A. Cooke to look at Prior's old house … with a view to the site for the nursing home'. On 14 March he 'took Mother to see The Orchard'. On 25 March Arthur Cooke met future medical users: 'they approve of the proposed site'.

The Orchard as it stood was not, however, suitable for conversion to a nursing home. In spite of this, and notwithstanding problems already encountered in a similar situation in Thompson's Lane, the hostel's management committee's initial suggestion was that, 'owing to the great difficulty of building in present circumstances and the delay which would be caused by an extensive building scheme', it would be better 'to adapt an existing house and make such additions as are immediately necessary', even though the cost of altering and updating would be considerable. But because the proposed house 'does not contain so many rooms as the present Hostel, … Mr Agnew has asked the Committee what further accommodation is necessary'; there was no point in moving to a more salubrious site if that site was smaller than its predecessor. Luckily, both problems could be solved with the help of Mr Agnew's donation, the amount of which would allow both for the renovation of The Orchard and for an increase in accommodation by means of the erection of a new but separate wing. Thus, although 'the expenses of maintaining a better equipped building must necessarily be greater … it [was] hoped that with a few more rooms, a more general use of a better building by the neighbourhood, and perhaps a slight rise of fees', the new nursing home would be self-supporting.

The Orchard's biggest asset – its enormous garden – was initially regarded with suspicion. Dr Leathem, Bursar of St John's, cautioned that 'the extensiveness of the grounds … may be a source of profit but only if they are judiciously managed'; their scale is indicated by his proposing as gardener 'someone who understands market gardening'! Morland Agnew thought the situation pleasant but 'very swampy'. Both worries were unfounded; the gardens would be a source of pleasure and produce for the future nursing home.

The Orchard's grounds were trapezoidal in shape, being approximately 400 yards long and 50 yards wide (370 metres by 45 metres). They were entered by two gates (a main and a servants' entrance) opening from Trumpington Road. The house, encircled by a gravel drive, stood close to the northern boundary of the site and, in spite of its size, took up only a small part of the total area. From the house, lawns edged by flower borders punctuated by stone urns swept out to the south and east. Mature trees stood along the edges of the grass. Along the southern and eastern boundaries ran the kitchen gardens, while also to the east – sandwiched between the lawn and that part of the kitchen garden which bordered Vicar's Brook – were the fruit garden and orchard. Various brick or wooden sheds standing near the north and south boundaries were destined to become the dirty-linen store, mortuary, laundry, and bicycle and gardener's shed of the new establishment; the greenhouse was to continue its use after renovation.

In spite of Morland Agnew's desire 'to get a start made', The Orchard was not yet his. On 5 May, he wrote to the Bursar of Trinity making an offer for the house. But Trinity, as Geoffrey Agnew pointed out in his memoir, did not usually sell the properties that it owned, but merely rented or leased them. Luckily for an old alumnus – one who had recently written to the University Vice-Chancellor expressing

both his bitter personal experience of the Thompson's Lane Hostel's unworthiness and inadequacy and his desire to build what would be a benefit 'to his old University and to the town in which it stood' – Trinity was prepared to make an exception. The price, considering the size and situation of the site, was reasonable: £4,500. It was not, however, until 19 January 1920 that Morland Agnew signed an agreement for the purchase of The Orchard, the sale being completed the following month and the freehold conveyed to him on 8 May.[3] On 16 July 1920, the future nursing home's Committee of Management held its first meeting at which, optimistically –

but as it turned out, correctly – it was noted that 'there is reason to hope that the Home will have been handed over for occupation by July 1921'.

Morland Agnew's happiness, already evident in the autumn of the previous year at having The Orchard 'on the plan at last', was enhanced by his also having chosen his architect, as recorded in his diary for 14 May 1919: 'Spoke to Sir Aston Webb re Nursing Home at Cambridge and told him about The Orchard idea.' On 11 June he and Sir Aston visited The Orchard; on 12 June Morland obtained plans of the house from the Bursar of Trinity, forwarding them, together with a 'large Ordnance map' to Sir Aston's office in London. Later the same month, he and Sir Aston discussed the future home in person and by letter. On 10 August Morland wrote that Sir Aston 'has just sent plans of the Nursing Home', adding, with more than a hint of anxiety, 'Is it possible for me to build this!'

'In choosing as his architect Sir Aston Webb', wrote Geoffrey Agnew, 'my grandfather showed the impeccable taste and aesthetic judgment which had made him an unrivalled buyer of pictures.' Sir Aston Webb KCVO, GCVO, CB (1849–1930) was then President of

Sir Aston Webb, 1849–1930, one-time President of The Royal Academy.

3. There was, however, a restrictive covenant attached to the freehold, namely that no building was to be allowed within 100 feet (30 metres) of the boundary to Newton Road.

the Royal Academy and a talented painter of watercolours. His architectural practice, with its headquarters in Queen Anne's Gate, was the largest of its time. (By the time of his association with 'The Orchard idea' Sir Aston's son Maurice had joined the practice as a partner.) Although Sir Aston was no stranger to building elsewhere than in London,[4] much of his work was in the capital – for example, the main entrance of the South Kensington Museum (later the Victoria and Albert Museum) of 1899 and the remodelling of the east front of Buckingham Palace of 1913. He also took part in one of the London County Council schemes for rebuilding central London; this involved laying out The Mall as a processional way leading from the Victoria Memorial to Admiralty Arch (also designed by him), the ingenious curve of which not only disguised a bend in the road beneath but was also echoed in the curved façade of Morland Agnew's Cambridge creation.

Problems, albeit not of a personal nature, arose early in the edificial relationship between Sir Aston and Morland Agnew. On 21 December 1919, the latter's diary records a 'letter from Sir A.W. giving a quotation for building a Nursing Home … The suggested cost is more than I feel I dare contemplate. £27,000 for building alone.' On 22 December he wrote to Arthur Cooke, saying, 'we must modify our plans … or raise more money. I [am] not prepared to face a greater expenditure than £25,000.' No wonder Morland Agnew was worried: his original offer of £20,000 had already proved inadequate, and to this would have to be added £7,000 for building materials. As he was shortly to write in his diary, 'I am spending too much and fear I have been giving too much away!' On 23 December he 'wrote to Sir A.W., explained the financial situation'.

On 30 January 1920, Morland Agnew received revised plans, noting that 'to build 16 bedrooms instead of 20 brings the price down considerably'. On 31 January he forwarded the new plans to Arthur Cooke, who suggested further improvements; the latter also agreed to deal directly with Sir Aston over any doubtful points that might arise as building progressed. But, in spite of the plans now being 'good and feasible', even the lowest building estimate was still too high, Morland reporting that the original design had to be reduced further to twelve sets of rooms. Other

4. Sir Aston also designed the King's Building, fronted by the George V Gateway, at the Leys School, Cambridge, in 1913–14.

economies were also made, some of more consequence than others – there would, for example, be no verandah, and neither would there be an X-ray room. On 19 July architect and client met again: 'alterations in plans decided … he has been very good in … taking suggestions, improving them, etc.'. Sir Aston was now asked 'to go ahead as fast as possible', doing so to such effect that when Morland Agnew and Arthur Cooke visited the site on 21 November 1920 they were 'glad to see the building well advanced'. It is no small tribute to Sir Aston and to his chosen builders (Henry Martin Ltd of Wolverhampton) that the building designed and executed by them has lasted so well.

Well, that is, except for the roof. The roof, unfortunately for such an important aspect of the construction, was the part of the building that caused serious problems almost from the start. Of innovative design for its time, it also manifested a design fault which would belie the *Cambridge Chronicle*'s contemporary description of the Nursing Home as 'the most modern ideal of hospital construction' and 'the most perfect building of its kind in the Eastern Region'. According to Geoffrey Agnew, 'the roof was deliberately left flat in case it was necessary in the future to provide another storey'. The roof, usually described as flat – in fact it slopes slightly from south to north – was 'in concrete … 4 inches thick filled in between and around steel joists. The surface of the flats … to be floated with cement for asphalte.' Therein lay the problem.

Asphalt, otherwise known as tar or pitch, was then derived from naturally occurring sources like the Trinidad Asphalt Lake. Mixed with the appropriate aggregates to improve durability, it is used for surfacing roads and roofs. Its use on the latter is compromised by its responding to quite minor climatic changes by melting or becoming brittle and liable to crack. On a sloping roof, continual contraction and expansion combined with the effect of gravity may have deleterious consequences for the material's waterproofing capacity. So it proved here. As early as 1928, Coulson & Son, local builders associated with the Nursing Home almost since its inception, stated that the roof was 'faultily designed' and would always leak; they recommended annual resurfacing. Because of the expense that would be incurred, this was not done and only piecemeal repairs were carried out. From then

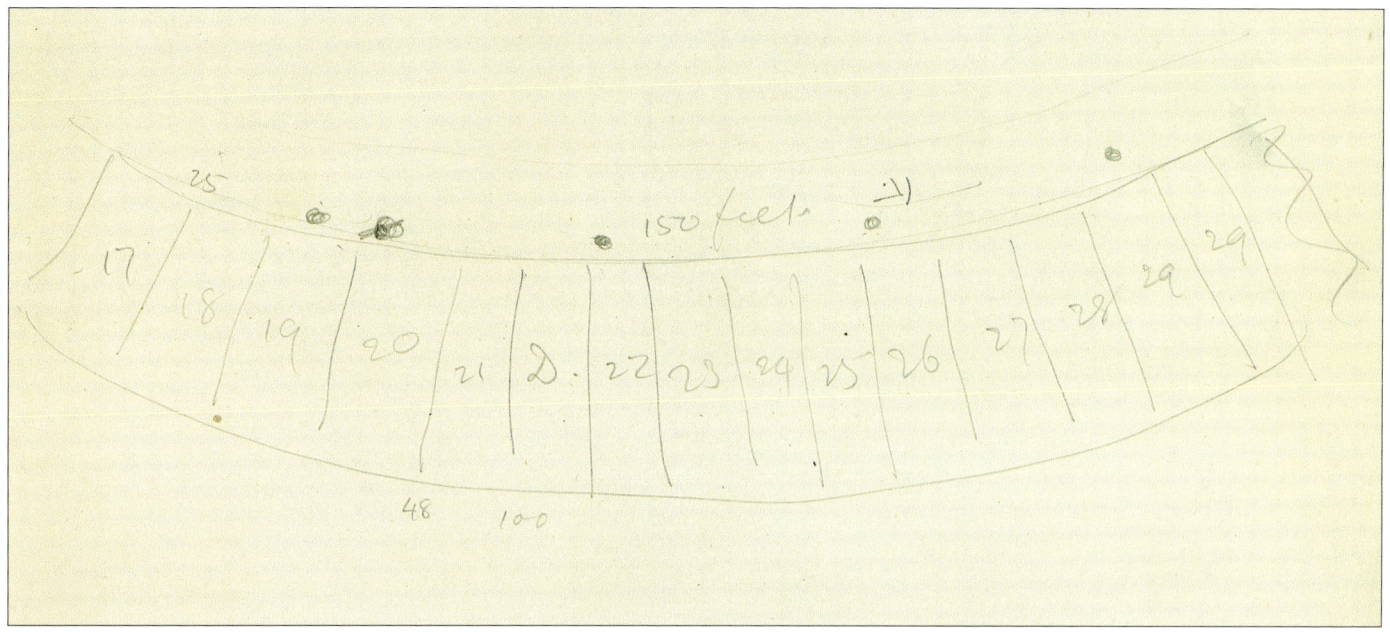

Sketch of the proposed new nursing home c.1920.

on, there is repeated reference to rooms on the first floor requiring repair and redecoration because of 'water damage caused by a leak in the roof'.

But worries of this kind were for the future. In spring 1921, the new Home proceeded apace, with Morland Agnew recording 'the building well advanced … the second week in July they say it will be finished'. He made frequent visits to the site, mainly to settle details of fittings and equipment such as fire appliances, sunblinds and the sterilising plant for the operating theatre. On 15 July he noted that although 'there is still a good bit to be done' – the

scaffolding was not finally taken down until 21 July – 'they talk of moving in in a week or so'. Somewhat later he noted, 'I consider that we are lucky to have the new building finished in such good time. I never expected it would be ready so soon.'

But just as the building neared completion, disaster struck. On 16 July Morland wrote, 'the lift has arrived and not at all the one wanted, and much too narrow; will not take a bed and barely a stretcher. This is annoying.' Next day, he 'wrote Sir Aston Webb a long letter … the lift [to be] much enlarged if possible'. With the building so nearly finished this proved

EVELYN NURSING HOME. CAMBRIDGE.

impossible. It is after the episode of the lift that a certain acerbity appears in Morland Agnew's diary entries referring to Sir Aston Webb.

On top of this, there were continuing financial worries – Morland had to realise stock in order to pay the many bills arising from the equipping of the Home, and there were the architect's and builder's bills still to come. He was therefore much relieved to discover that the final building costs (£19,589) actually came in below the revised estimate. This was just as well, considering that legal and administrative costs, the £4,500 already paid for the site, and the amounts due for work on The Orchard and for expensive items of equipment (theatre sterilising plant alone cost £700), would bring the total to £27,037 2s 9d. Although this was considerably higher than the £20,000 he originally proposed, it was also rather less than the £35,000 he might have had to pay. In a letter to Arthur

The first patients moved from The Orchard …

EVELYN NURSING HOME. CAMBRIDGE.

... to The Evelyn on 25 July 1921. The corner of The Orchard is just visible on the left.

Cooke, he wrote of how he 'had hoped that ... £25,000 would have seen it through, but entre nous it has not, by many hundreds ... I do not wish this to be known. However, if the building is satisfactory and if it proves a boon to Cambridge and vicinity I am content. I have done the thing as well as I could.'

On this note, let us join Mr and Mrs Agnew in exploring the boon they have respectively provided and inspired. Driving over from

Hertfordshire, we enter through the main gate and pass round the southern end of The Orchard to park on the gravel between the old and the new buildings. Here Matron waits to greet us, her little dog in her arms. As it is a fine day, she suggests that we first walk round the outside of the new building. The Agnews are happy to do this as they have not yet seen the façade without scaffolding.

The first thing we notice about the new building is that it is free-standing, a gap of over 56 feet (17 metres) separating it from the original house. Mr Agnew explains that the corridor originally designed to link the two buildings was a victim of the cost-cutting measures, but he hopes the old and new blocks will be joined some time in the future; it will be inconvenient, to say the least, to nurse patients (as is presently planned) in two separate buildings. Eventually all patients will be housed in the new block; this, Mr Agnew continues, will be extended as soon as the Home is in a financial position to do so. Arthur Cooke is already planning along these lines.

As we move out onto the lawn to admire the south façade we appreciate both its interesting curve and its clever design. Repeated groups of four windows (those on the ground floor being French windows; those above, casements) alternate with panels of cream roughcast standing on brick plinths. Towards the end of the building, but in a position which will be more central when the Home is extended, is a two-storey bay window in brick with smaller brick-surrounded windows flanking it. A French window leads from the ground-floor bay. We realise that the façade has been cleverly designed so that it invites addition of further elements as funds permit, and at the same time sympathetically echoes the garden front of The Orchard, which is clearly visible from where we stand.

As all the patients' rooms face south, the lack of a verandah has been compensated for by the installation of canvas blinds. These can be pulled down, on both floors, to shade the rooms from the sun. They also provide pleasantly cool areas on the terrace where patients' beds may be wheeled outside, or where patients may sit if they do not wish to take advantage of the sunlight on the lawn. A flowerbed runs the length of the 10-foot (3-metre) wide terrace to enhance the view. It is all a far cry from the noise and gloom of Thompson's Lane.

Rounding the roughly finished eastern end of the building, we find ourselves opposite the much plainer northern façade. Here a two-storey block projects from what will eventually be the centre of the block. It contains the kitchen on the ground floor and the operating theatre on the first floor. The theatre is lit by wide metal casements; it has a skylight, the pointed roof of which we can just see projecting above the deal cornice which edges the roof. The back courtyard also

THE BUILDING NEWS, JAN. 26, 1923.

THE EVELYN NURSING HOME, CAMBRIDGE.
SIR ASTON WEBB, P.R.A., AND SON, ARCHITECTS.

Feature from The Building News, *26 January 1923, showing plans and elevations.*

houses domestic offices such as the laundry, but Matron hustles us quickly past these as she is anxious to show off the interior of the Home.

Once round the north-west corner of the building, we find ourselves again outside the front door. This is centrally placed in the short west façade which faces The Orchard. Opening the half-glazed double doors, we enter the new Home, Matron's dog scampering ahead of us with a proprietorial air. The builders have just left, leaving everything 'neat and ready for occupation' – Matron has checked that the windows have been polished on *both* sides – and as the furniture has not yet arrived, we are able to see the interior of the Home without distraction.

Immediately to our left is the staircase to the first floor. At its foot a small lobby leads to Matron's rather poky office and a visitors' waiting room. Ahead of us stretches the main corridor, curved like the front, with patients' rooms to the right and ancillary rooms to the left. Brown linoleum covers the floor (Matron remarks that the curve of the corridor posed problems for the men who laid it) and cream distemper covers the walls. Brass door furniture gleams on the teak doors. Six patients' rooms open off the corridor, ranging in size from 12 to 15 feet wide (3.6 to 4.5 metres) and 13 feet (3.9 metres) long. Between the fourth and fifth of these rooms is a bay-windowed duty room for the nurses, its entrance flanked by linen cupboards. On either side of the duty room are rooms measuring 8 feet by 12 feet (2.4 metres by 3.6). These, Matron explains, are bathrooms, but as there is no plumbing on this side of the corridor two cast-iron wheeled baths have been purchased. These can be filled by means of rubber and canvas tubing designed to fit on to hot and cold taps across the corridor; they are emptied by means of draw-cocks, into a gulley on the ground floor and a floor sink on the first floor.

The first ancillary room we enter is the small ground-floor ward kitchen; this, like all the rooms on the north side of the main corridor, overlooks the back courtyard and the gardens of Brookfield next door. Next comes a WC (rather a small one at only 5 feet 6 inches by 5 feet – 1.6 metres by 1.5) with a splendid mahogany seat, a minuscule corner washbasin, and 'muffled glass' obscuring the window. Beyond this is a housemaid's closet with a sink for slops, and the ward sluice room containing two sinks with urine bottle jets, bedpan sprays and the wherewithal to fill and empty the patient' washbowls and jugs.

Between the sluice and the entrance to the kitchen, we discover the infamous lift – at this point the Agnews exchange rueful glances. On the far side of the kitchen door is the doctors' room, containing glass shelves and a scrub-up sink complete with hot and cold foot-action valves. Just beyond this is a second WC and closet. At this point the corridor ends in a doorway leading into the garden.

Retracing our steps, we enter the main kitchen. Immediately to our right is the servants' hall. Beyond it lie the scullery with its fire-clay sink, the slate-shelved larder, the china closet and a WC. The back door opens between larder and closet. The space left for actual cooking is comparatively small, with a gas-fired range set into an alcove; luckily this area is light and airy with two good-sized windows. The entire kitchen is walled to a height of 4 feet with white glazed tiles, and the floor is of mottled grey Marbolith terrazzo.

Returning to the staircase, we mount to the first floor. This follows much the same plan as the floor below but the functions of some rooms differ. For instance, the bay-windowed room is designated a robing room for the nurses working in the theatre opposite, Matron's office is replaced by a waiting room, the ward kitchen opens into a linen store, and there is a fire escape leading down from a door at the far end of the corridor. The patients' rooms lack French windows, but the beautiful view from their wide windows more than compensates for this.

The operating theatre, of the same overall dimension as the kitchen below (24 feet wide by 33 feet long – 7.3 metres wide by 10 metres long) is entered through a lobby which has the anaesthetic room to the right and the doctors' robing room to the left. As with the kitchen, valuable space is taken up by structures extraneous to the area – in particular, the lift. The theatre may also be entered via the doctors' wash-up (situated immediately above its twin on the ground floor), which itself opens into the anaesthetic room and thence to the operating area. This latter area, some 16 feet 6 inches wide and 18 feet (5 metres wide by 5.5 metres long) opens to the left on to a preparation room and a space occupied by the gas-fired sterilising plant and its attendant bowl and instrument sterilisers. The whole theatre complex is floored with green Marbolith. Walls and ceiling are distempered.

Between the doors to the lobby and the anaesthetic room stands a glass and metal instrument cupboard, although it is envisaged that the doctors will provide most of their instruments themselves. With much excitement, Matron now describes the theatre furniture – there will be, besides the adjustable operating table and a stool for the surgeon, stands for bowls, bottles, irrigations and dressing drums, a kidney-shaped instrument table and a three-tiered trolley.

With its wide north-facing casement window, glazed hipped skylight, and the six lamps suspended above the operating table from a metal frame (adjustable, Matron explains, to suit

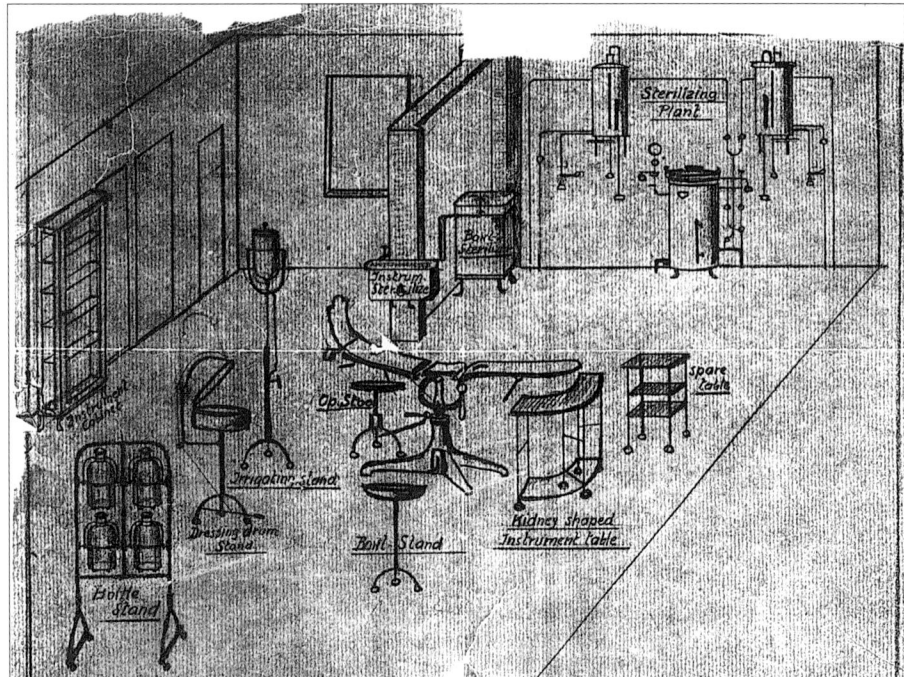

A detailed sketch of the operating theatre, 1921.

the need of the surgeon), the theatre is very well lit, though she rather fears that its proximity to the kitchen – combined with the positioning of the sterilisers within the theatre and the sun streaming in through the skylight – may cause the area to become too hot.

As we leave the theatre to return to the front door, Matron is keen to point out to us the modern conveniences which will make the Home so vastly superior to the Thompson's Lane Hostel: the electric bells in the patients' rooms, the speaking tubes between floors, the dirty-linen chute from the first floor to the ground floor, the dinner wagon, the wheeled stretcher and the telephone. She also adds how generous it was of the Cambridge Gas Company to connect the Home to the mains by providing and laying 60 feet of piping free of charge. Overwhelmed with information, Mr Agnew thanks Miss Aycroft (as he persists in calling her) and we take our leave.

What, in the meantime, had happened to The Orchard? Discussions between Morland Agnew, Arthur Cooke and Sir Aston as to 'things to be done to the old house' had taken place shortly after its purchase, with 'necessary work to the old house' costing £500 (£472 6s 3d by Mr Agnew's reckoning) appearing in the architect's Statement of Accounts of March 1921. Just over £900 in all was spent between September 1920 and payment of the final bills in February 1922 on work which seems to have been chiefly of a renovative and adaptive nature. Work was in fact begun on The Orchard even earlier than on the new building in order that, as Mr Agnew put it, 'the house might be used for undergraduates of Trinity College'; he was decidedly annoyed when, 'without any notice to me!!', Trinity abandoned the scheme 'after all arrangements had practically been made'. Other than undergraduates, it was obviously intended that The Orchard should house up to eight overflow patients until the new block was completed, ideally medical or convalescent patients who would not need to be stretchered across the gravel to and from the operating theatre; in practice, the old house continued to be used for patients until September 1923, by which time evacuation was necessary because of the poor condition of floors and ceilings.

The fact that building works were completed on schedule was fortunate, given that the Thompson's Lane Hostel had remained open pending completion of the new Home – the former's management committee was anxious that there should be no breach in continuity of patient care in Cambridge while the latter was built, but was at the same time responsible for the bills of both establishments. The dual responsibility and expense came to an end on 15 July when Morland Agnew collected the deeds of purchase of The Orchard, handing them over, together with his own deed of gift, to the Home's treasurer the following day. On 25 July, Morland's diary recorded: 'They moved from the old house, took 4 patients across.' On 2 August he received a 'nice letter from Arthur Cooke about the Home. He did an operation in the theatre on Saturday.' By 17 August, 'the upper floor rooms are all occupied'; a fortnight later the Home was 'full up with patients'. Miss Cracroft's only recorded comment concerning this exciting period of The Evelyn's history was a note made some time between 25 July and 11 August: 'Six operations in the Evelyn Home.'

The official opening of the Home took place on 5 October 1921, the *Cambridge Chronicle* sending a reporter to cover the event. His report, published on 12 October, was headlined

University's Hospital
Mr and Mrs Morland Agnew's Gift

and continued, 'The new hostel stands in spacious grounds … Specially designed for its purpose, the … hostel embodies … the most modern facilities for surgery and everything connected with it has been planned in accordance with the teaching of medical science … the operating theatre is the embodiment of the perfect arrangement of the Home and every facility is provided to assist the surgeon in his work.' Other modern facilities included 'heating … from a central heating system, supplemented by electric stoves' and a kitchen and service rooms which were 'models of convenience'. The contrast between The Evelyn and the Thompson's Lane Hostel was underlined by the Vice-Chancellor in a speech which drew attention to the fact that patients now had the chance 'of being awakened by the nightingale instead of the steam buzzer at the Electric Light Works adjacent to the hostel. The Master of Jesus, on the other hand, thanked Mr Agnew for his 'munificence', as a result of which sick undergraduates were to be relieved of the 'extraordinary

inconvenience and savage conditions' which resulted from their being nursed in college.

Mr Agnew, for his part, was modestly pleased, saying that although his original plans had had to be abridged, he looked on the new Home as a beginning and the building itself as both beautiful and inviting additions. For this he thanked his old friends Sir Aston Webb and Arthur Cooke, the former for his attention to the 'minutest details' of the building and the latter for providing so much inspiration and advice that he regarded him as 'joint donor with himself'. Mrs Agnew herself was thanked for allowing the Home to bear her name and 'for being ill … three years ago, as otherwise they would never have been there that day'.

At 3 p.m. The Evelyn Nursing Home was formally opened by the lady whose 'dyspepsia – or whatever it is' had been the start of it all, following which she was presented with a bouquet by Joan Mellish Clark, aged 5. Immediately the 'pleasant opening ceremony' was concluded, and with timing that could hardly be bettered, an undergraduate was borne through the crowd on a stretcher, the first official emergency admission to the 'University's Hospital'.

To provide a Nursing Home or Hostel

MORLAND AGNEW'S satisfaction with his new foundation was patent. On 16 July he wrote in his diary, 'I feel proud of the Evelyn Home. I do not believe there is a better, taking it all round, anywhere.' Later that same year, he received a letter from Arthur Cooke enclosing a missive from a lady 'praising up the Nursing Home ... it is gratifying to know ... that the management is so good'. This, he felt, was in no small measure due to his friend's active interest in the institution they had planned together.

His original idea in founding his nursing home was to present it as a personal gift to his wife's surgeon, stating that 'it would never have been started but for him' and that 'it is greatly owing to the high opinion and great regard which I have of him that I have undertaken this matter'. Arthur Cooke, however, felt unable to accept Mr Agnew's offer for both personal and professional reasons, although he was happy to be associated with the new Home in an administrative capacity. In agreeing to this, he fulfilled Morland Agnew's wish that 'so long as he is willing and capable of undertaking it, subject of course to the approval of the Committee, Dr Cooke should have an important share in the management of the Home'.

The Evelyn Nursing Home received its Certificate of Incorporation as a Limited Company on 1 May 1920. The *Memorandum and Articles of Association of the Evelyn Nursing Home* (a 'Company Limited by Guarantee and not having a Share Capital') was drawn up. The *Memorandum* began by stating 'the objects for which the Home is established'. First and foremost was:

> To provide a Nursing Home or Hostel into which primarily members of the University of Cambridge but also, when accommodation permits, any other persons (all of whom both members of the said University and other persons hereinafter referred to as patients) may (upon such terms as to payment and other matters as may be arranged between the Home and the patients) be received for the purposes of undergoing surgical and medical treatment at the hands of or under the direction of their own surgeons and physicians and to provide therein for the patients … such nursing attendance and board and the use of such furniture, linen and other things as are usually provided in a private nursing home and generally to maintain and carry on such Nursing Home or Hostel on the same lines as a private nursing home.

It went on to list the new Home's various aims: financial, proprietary, and what can be broadly termed 'co-operative'. In financial terms, the Home was to 'raise, expend, invest and accumulate funds and income', including the receipt of subscriptions and donations and, where necessary, the borrowing of money at interest on such securities (if any) as might be deemed necessary. Moneys thus raised were to 'be applied solely towards the promotion of the objects of the Home'; in this connection a condition was strictly laid down that no member of the Home's various governing bodies could profit financially from these moneys unless they had lent the Home money at interest or had out-of-pocket expenses in connection with their duties. The Home was also to pay the wages and salaries of its employees and to assist with their insurance and pension payments, and to 'remunerate any medical man or other expert for services rendered to the Home over and above those paid for by the patients themselves'. In proprietary terms, the Home was not only to 'purchase and acquire furniture, linen, plate, apparatus, books, periodicals, appliances, drugs and stores or any other thing necessary or expedient for use'; it was also to 'acquire, erect, furnish, adapt, and equip any building of whatever kind' for the Home's use. Having acquired the buildings, it was then to maintain them, insure them, and provide for the supply of the necessary services to them; it could also 'hire, sell, dispose of, let and manage' any property of which it was the owner. In 'co-operative' terms, it was to assist those 'associations having … objects similar to any of the objects of the Home … or … persons desirous of … working with the Home'; it was also allowed to make grants, loans or donations to bodies with objects similar to those of the Home and with broadly similar constraints on the distribution of profits.

As a limited company without share capital, The Evelyn could have no shareholders as such; what it had was 'members'. Membership began with the seven signatories to the *Memorandum of Association*; it was then extended to around fifty persons who became respectively 'life', 'subscribing' and 'nominated' members. A life member qualified by virtue of the 'payment at one time to the Home of the sum of £1' and a subscribing member by the annual payment of 2s 6d. Members were not allowed to profit directly or indirectly from moneys accruing to the Home; instead they were liable for a contribution of not more than £1 per head to go towards the payment of any outstanding debts in the event of the Home's being wound up during, or for

a year after, the period of their membership. The Committee of Management was responsible for approving applications for membership and could also remove members found to be unsatisfactory.

A Register of Members was opened to initiate the membership. A circular letter, enclosing a copy of the *Memorandum*, was sent to a list of 'town' and 'county' people selected by Arthur Cooke, asking them to contact the Company's Secretary if they wished to apply. The letter was dated 16 June 1920, and the first general meeting of members was promised for the middle of July, by which time thirty-five had been duly admitted. It was at this meeting, chaired by Morland Agnew himself, that the mournful announcement was made regarding the reduction in size of the proposed Home. A second meeting on 30 May 1921 was more optimistic: members' subscriptions amounted to £40 2s 6d, there being £38 7s 0d in the bank after petty cash disbursements.

Academia also appeared in the shape of nominated members. Nominated members were appointed as follows: 'Each College … in the University of Cambridge which shall for the time being guarantee at least £10 a year towards any loss or deficit in the current working of the Home shall have the right to appoint a Member of the Home.' If the 'Women's Colleges of Girton and Newnham' gave a like guarantee, they too could nominate a member; this they duly did. Nominated members had two privileges not accorded to life or subscribing members:

1. To nominate one member annually to the Home's Committee of Management – they could, if they wished, nominate themselves.
2. To send a substitute if unable to attend meetings; the rights of life and subscribing members were not transferable.

In agreeing to provide nominated members, the colleges recognised their obligation to support the new Nursing Home, for with the impending closure of Thompson's Lane there was really nowhere else for sick undergraduates to go. Before the advent of the National Health Service, the University needed The Evelyn as much as The Evelyn, initially at least, needed the University. Financial guarantees from the colleges provided immense support for the new Home, with member-nominating colleges subscribing sums which ranged from the suggested £10 to a more generous £50 annually for The Evelyn's first and, sometimes, subsequent years. Trinity, as the college most closely associated with Mr Agnew's foundation, went so far as to underwrite 25 per cent of total losses in the start-up period, provided these did not exceed £250 in any one year.

Having described the 'company' nature of the new Home, the *Memorandum* went on to describe how it was to be run. Initially there were to be three 'Executive Officers': the Chairman of the Home, the Treasurer and the Secretary. The Chairman of the Home was also the Chairman of the Committee of Management, which consisted of *ex-officio*, nominated and co-opted members – 'and during their respective lives' Arthur Cooke and Morland and Evelyn Agnew. Nominated members were, of course, college representatives; *ex-officio* members were:

the Lord Lieutenant of the County of Cambridge …
the Vice-Chancellor of the University of Cambridge …
the Mayor of the Borough of Cambridge …
the Regius Professor of Physic in the University of Cambridge …

The Professor of Surgery in the University of Cambridge …

Resounding titles indeed! Co-opted members 'shall be 18 in number, of whom three shall always be of the Medical Profession' – there was legislation as to length of tenure of office and potential for re-election. The Committee of Management was allowed to fix its own quorum and generally regulate its own meetings and proceedings. How often it was to meet was not laid down, though extraordinary meetings could be called if conditions warranted; in practice it met annually. There was, however, to be an Annual General Meeting of members with the Chairman of the Home presiding; at this 'a report … as to the State and Condition of the Home' was to be presented.

The Committee of Management then appointed three sub-committees to manage the day-to-day running of the Home. As the Executive Officers were also members of each of these committees, their numbers – even allowing for some overlap of members – verged on the unwieldy. The sub-committees were House, initially with seven members (10 with the Executive Officers); Garden with three (i.e. 6) members; and Finance and General Purposes (whose chief duty was 'to control expenditure'), with no fewer than fourteen (i.e. 17) members. The House and Finance sub-committees met on a regular basis, at monthly intervals; the Garden sub-committee 'when occasion required'.

But what of the 'Matron and Staff' who were to provide the 'attendance' required by the *Memorandum*? When the Home opened on 25 July 1921, it was staffed by the following:

Matron [Edith Cracroft];
an 'operating Sister' [Sister Ellis] seconded from the Thompson's Lane Hostel;
1 senior nurse and 3 junior nurses;
a probationer (the CNA had trained its own nurses);
a cook;
a house-parlour maid,[1] helped by a 'between maid' of all work;
a resident porter;
a gardener and a labourer.

The staff were supported by a Staff Sickness and Benefit Fund into which the Home paid £100 annually. When not required to pay out for sickness – for example, the cost of a member of staff being nursed in the Home itself or elsewhere – the fund contributed to staff amusements such as the nurses'

1. This was perhaps the Jane who, as a poem in The Evelyn archives puts it, 'comes in with her gay demeanour' to inform the patient that:

'I thought I'd bring you the vacuum cleaner, Because', she adds in her cheery way, 'The others are all too ill today.'

and domestics' Christmas parties, the purchase of a punt, and the building of a hard tennis court.

Miss Cracroft had the distinction of being the last Matron of the Thompson's Lane Hostel and the first of the The Evelyn Nursing Home. Aged 40 when she took over the latter, she was often commended in the early Annual Reports for the 'ability and zeal' with which she carried out her duties, stimulating her staff into giving loyal and efficient service. She did not attend meetings of the House or other committees unless specifically invited because a particular problem required her presence; instead she submitted a monthly report which she read out herself after the minutes of the previous meeting had been read. She then left before other items on the agenda were discussed. She was paid between £120 and £130 per annum, which included a uniform allowance. The nurses were paid substantially less.

The fact that even the senior nurse's pay was below nationally agreed levels was soon to cause problems. On 2 June 1922 the House sub-committee considered the question of the nurses' wages, reporting that 'for reasons of economy the Committee have up till now engaged the best nurses they

could and have been satisfied that they have carried out their duties conscientiously', although 'the standard of the nurses engaged so far has not been that of a first-rate nursing home because it had proved difficult to find suitable nurses at the offered salary of £65 a year'. The College of Nursing advised Matron that the fully qualified and experienced nurses the Home wished to employ should be paid at least £80 a year. As a compromise, it was agreed that 'as suitable nurses presented themselves the change to the higher salary should be made … but … in the case of younger nurses of less experience the Matron should be allowed to fix a suitable salary under £80'. At their third Annual General Meeting, on 16 June 1922, the Committee of Management noted their readiness 'to raise still further the already good quality of the nursing by employing nurses of a higher grade', who, they hoped, would be encouraged to apply by the improved rates of pay. Improved rates of pay meant a doubling of the nurses' salaries bill by March 1923, but that this was worthwhile was noted at the fourth Annual General Meeting, on 15 June 1923: 'The increased salaries to the nurses had been justified by the encomiums of the patients, endorsed by the doctors.'

That the nurses deserved their encomiums is evident from the poem quoted earlier, which also describes their activities:

> They sponge you down and they brush you up;
> They bring you broth in a feeding cup;
> They sew your buttons on tight as tight;
> They keep your chart as a sacred rite.

That together with 'Cotton dresses of soft smoke-blue' and 'Faces where kindness and fun show through', must have made The Evelyn a very pleasant place in which to be ill.

The Home's rapidly increasing popularity meant that the small number of nurses initially employed soon became insufficient. Throughout 1922 and 1923, there are references in the Finance sub-committee's minutes to bills for payment for nurses brought in from nursing agencies, some local, some as far away as London. By 1923, experience showed that the original plan of maintaining only a small permanent staff in the interests of economy was not working; indeed, augmenting their own staff with agency nurses was actually costing the Home money as fees recovered from patients were insufficient to cover the hired nurses' wages. Furthermore, it was noted that 'in times of pressure, when ... she has least time to give to their instruction, the Matron becomes responsible for nurses whose characters and powers are unknown to her. And these nurses themselves are often ignorant of the arrangement of the Home and of its method of work.'

At this juncture the Cambridge Nursing Association stepped in to provide a solution to The Evelyn's problems. On 12 July 1923, Mrs Mellish Clark reported that the CNA was being pressured by Addenbrooke's Hospital to sell the remainder of the lease of 13 Fitzwilliam Street, the CNA's headquarters and nurses' hostel, as the hospital was keen to expand onto the site. The CNA, however, also carried out the provisions of Miss Hutton's Benefaction, founded in 1875, which undertook, first, to nurse 'the sick and poor in their own homes' and, second, to provide 'private nurses for the University students and families in the Town and neighbourhood'. By 1923, the first provision had been taken over by the District Nursing Association, leaving the CNA to confine its activities to the second. The CNA's proposal to The Evelyn therefore involved the latter's adoption of the former's role; in this way the CNA's work would be continued 'with a good prospect of permanence', in accordance with provisions laid down by Miss Hutton. If the Home agreed to take over the letting-out of private nurses, the CNA would contribute £900 towards the cost of doing so. The Evelyn jumped at the chance. In agreeing to the CNA's offer, they could provide Matron with 'nurses enough to work the Home when full', *and* have nurses available for 'outside work' when the Home was comparatively empty. The scheme came into effect in October 1924, at which time 'fees paid in by private staff' first appear in the Home's accounts. From that date until the arrangement petered out during the Second World War, the Home would be described in Cambridge street directories as The Evelyn Nursing Home and Private Nurses Hostel.

Nurses who worked exclusively in the Home itself were termed 'inside' or 'home' staff, while those who worked chiefly in patients' own homes were called 'outside' or 'private' staff. Terms of work varied according to the post held. An inside nurse, for example, was resident in the Home and received a salary which included a monthly uniform and laundry allowance, but from which a small amount was deducted for board and lodging; whereas outside nurses were paid travelling expenses, received an annual uniform and monthly laundry allowance, and were resident when between cases – during which time their board and lodging was free. Outside nurses were paid according to the type of work undertaken ('ordinary', 'infectious and notifiable contagious' and 'maternity'), the number of hours the nurse was expected to be on duty (12 or 24) also being taken into account. The outside nurses' starting salary of £70 a year was lower than that of the average inside nurse, but it rose in annual increments of £5 to a maximum of £80 and was augmented by a bonus of 5 per cent (usually amounting to between 16s 0d and £3 a month) derived from the moneys brought in by the outside work overall. Income over and above this accrued to the Home. No agency fee was charged to the nurse or the patient. Outside nurses who were midwives commanded a larger fee and a higher percentage (up to 10 per cent) of their takings, while nurses prepared to look after infectious cases not deemed serious enough to be admitted to the Isolation Hospital were paid a 'quarantine fee' which started at a higher level than the top-rate weekly fee.

An offshoot of the outside staff was the college nurse. A college nurse (usually called 'Sister') presided over the sick bay in one of the seven colleges (of which Trinity and Magdalene were two) where such nurses were employed. Regarded as rather scandalous by some of the older male dons ('A *woman* in college!') their presence was much appreciated by undergraduates who had minor injuries or who, while not ill enough to be hospitalised, required nursing care of a higher standard than that previously provided by their own tutors. College nurses received a salary of £90 a year, but were expected to act as inside nurses during University vacations. They were resident at The Evelyn, whence they cycled to work, receiving a bicycle allowance during term. The college employing them was charged £5 2s 6d (later 6 guineas) a week for their termtime services – this was regarded as a good bargain by The Evelyn but as exorbitant by the colleges!

In 1936 a 'co-operative' nursing system was set up, with The Evelyn acting as agent. Nurses employed in a co-operative capacity nursed patients in the patient's own home and were paid by the Home after a deduction of 7 per cent from their earnings as an agency fee; the Home did not, however, pay the nurse until it had been paid by that nurse's patient. Co-operative nurses were non-resident and were responsible for finding and funding their own accommodation between cases. They were also responsible for reminding their current patient that they, not the Home, were to pay the nurse's National Insurance payments; when unemployed, the nurses paid their own contributions. The Nurses' Co-operative continued to provide the Home with a modest amount of extra income until the arrival of more commercial organisations early in the 1960s occasioned its demise.

That it possessed outside staff on whom it could call in times of shortage was, however, a boon to an institution whose inside nurses eleven years after its formation numbered fewer than twenty. In due course a deputy operating sister was appointed to cope with the additional workload in the Theatre, the senior nurse of the Top Floor Ward also being seconded to the Theatre as required; she was paid £10 a year more than her colleague in the Ground Floor Ward for her dual role.

In 1925 Matron was joined by an assistant matron who relieved her of a considerable part of the administrative duties, for besides acting as Matron's deputy when the latter was 'absent or engaged', she took on 'all matters in connection with the Outside Staff'; the inside nurses' off duty, holiday and sickness schedules; the dispensary and the ordering of drugs; distribution of stores of all kinds; supervision of the domestic staff; responsibility for the linen; distribution of patients' newspapers; and, last but not least, a daily inspection of the 'Surgeons' Washing Rooms'. Matron's attack of typhoid fever[2] and prolonged absence in 1935/6 provided the impetus for the appointment of the Home Sister (salary £90) 'with a view to increasing the efficiency of the working of the Inside Staff'; she also took over the running of the Home when Matron or her deputy were absent, one of her principal duties being 'to take charge of the office in the afternoon' in order that someone was available to answer the phone, talk to patients' relatives, and make bookings. The Home Sister's post was regarded by the House sub-committee as essential, but by the Finance sub-committee as an 'expensive luxury which the Home could not afford', and the post came

and went according to which sub-committee established or abolished it. In 1936, after 'prolonged discussions' by the House sub-committee, a sister in charge of each of the floors was appointed in order that 'there is always someone on each floor responsible for all the patients on that floor and … she shall know about their condition and treatment'.

What, therefore, remained for Matron herself to do? From the clinical point of view, she was to 'visit every patient daily and see that the nursing staff are performing their duties properly'; to this end, she did a round between 10.30 a.m. and noon.[3] She was to 'interview' the doctors when they visited their patients and to answer relatives' enquiries about a particular patient's condition. She was also to engage and dismiss nursing staff. Tasks of a non-clinical nature included the ordering of supplies and of the patients' meals. She was also responsible for delivering the patients' letters three times a day, at 8 a.m., 11 a.m. and in the late afternoon, and for being 'charming' to visiting 'friends and relations'.

In June 1937, a proposal to appoint a 'Lady Housekeeper' having come to nothing, the House sub-committee decided (in view, *inter alia*, of Matron's

2. In February 1933 an Evelyn nurse caught typhoid fever. Making inoculation against typhoid a condition of employment was decided against by both Matron and the House sub-committee. In 1935 Matron herself caught typhoid, spending 44 days in the Isolation Hospital and another 109 on sick leave and never fully recovering her health.

3. She did not come unaccompanied; as the poem quoted earlier put it:

And pattering in comes her small white Skye,
To cock his ears and wonder why
You're foolishly staying in bed like that
When you might be chasing the neighbour's cat.

Miss Edith Cracroft and staff, on her retirement as Matron, September 1938.

increasing incapacity) that the time had come for a further rearrangement of the duties of the 'Managing Staff'. As a result, 'the management of the kitchen, the arranging of menus, and all the ordering of the stores' was taken over by the Assistant Matron, and the sisters in charge of the floors were given 'additional responsibilities'. Although Matron concurred with the rearrangement, she found it so difficult to relinquish earlier responsibilities

that – as the Finance sub-committee ruefully noted in May 1938 – although initially the new proposals 'seemed to work ... this has not proved in the long run to be the case'. As there seemed to be 'no real chance of the Home doing better under the present Matron', Miss Cracroft was asked to retire on 15 September 1938. It was a sad end to a career in which much zeal and, in earlier days, much ability had been expended on the new Home.

The Maurice Webb extension, 1924–5.

A Fully Equipped Nursing Home

DURING MISS CRACROFT'S TIME as Matron, the Home had, as the Finance sub-committee noted on her retirement, become 'more than twice as large as when she joined the staff'. Indeed, long before Miss Nancy Puckle,[1] the Evelyn's second Matron, took up her post on 19 September 1938, the need to enlarge the rather limited amount of accommodation for patients had become pressing. It was this, together with the Home's desire to house the maximum number of nurses (and, to a lesser extent, ancillary staff) on site that led to the building schemes of the 1920s and 1930s. The latter desire was based not only on the Home's perceived need to provide on-site accommodation in the interests of efficiency and economy; it also stemmed from the statement in the *Memorandum of Association* of 1920

that one of the 'Objects for which the Home is established' was 'to provide houses or accommodation' for the 'nurses, attendants … and servants of the Home'. The impetus to begin work was provided by the impending arrival of outside nurses, who would have to be housed between jobs or when employed as inside nurses. Thus it was that on 28 July 1923 the Committee of Management considered both the offer of the Cambridge Nursing Association and 'plans for the necessary extension of the Home should the offer of the Nursing Association be accepted'. As the Finance sub-committee had already 'passed unanimously an expression of general approval of the offer', the Committee agreed that an extension should be added to the Home 'and the old house set free to accommodate the nurses'. Once completed, the Home

---

1. She had been assistant matron at Winchester Hospital. Trained at St Thomas', she subsequently became theatre sister there.

was to contain thirty-two beds, exceeding by seven 'those lost in the use of the whole of the old house for nurses'. This, the Finance sub-committee 'desired to state as their own opinion', would be a good thing, 'not only in the interests of The Evelyn Nursing Home but also in the interests of efficient nursing in Cambridge'.

But from where was the money to come? No further largesse was to be expected from Morland Agnew; the Home would have to find the necessary resources itself. The Finance sub-committee had already obtained an estimate from Sir Aston Webb 'whereby it appears that the building needed can be obtained for £7000', with Sir Aston prepared for economies if these were needed. A major contribution was to be the £900 promised by the CNA; to this could be added 'funds at the disposal of The Evelyn Nursing Home', it being a measure of the new foundation's prosperity that funds appeared to be readily available. The balance was to be raised by a loan from Barclay's Bank.

At this point 'efficient nursing' – at The Evelyn, at least – received a potential setback. The rateable value of the Home and its grounds was discovered to have gone up from £284

in November 1921 to £340 in 1923. An appeal to the District Valuer merely resulted in an even higher demand, for £500. This prompted Mr Mellish Clark to write to the local tax office: 'Your letter is so surprising a document that I am forwarding the whole of our correspondence to Sir William Joynson-Hicks, the Secretary of the Treasury' – Sir William had recently asked in the House of Commons that examples of 'automatic' rises such as the Evelyn's appeared to be should be forwarded to him – 'I think he will be curious to know how a property which is now valued at £500 was considered in November 1921 to be worth £284 and on the 30th May 1923 £340.' Mr Mellish Clark's letter bore fruit. After a lengthy correspondence involving the Treasury in Whitehall, the Inland Revenue at Somerset House and His Majesty's Inspector of Taxes in Cambridge, The Evelyn's rateable value was settled at £300.

With the rateable value established at a – to The Evelyn – satisfactory level, extension of the Aston Webb Wing was able to start. As early as December 1921, Sir Aston and Arthur Cooke had corresponded with regard to exactly what facilities were needed; they had also chosen their builder: Coulson & Son of Cambridge. Sir

Aston's plan involved the creation of four 'wards' on each floor; he also proposed to resite and enlarge the ward kitchens and to create a second staircase. Arthur Cooke's plan included two south-facing 'wards' of three beds each, but capable of containing a fourth 'in times of pressure',[2] two smaller double rooms, four single rooms and another duty room for the nurses. There was also to be 'an X-ray room' – the lack of X-ray facilities was already making itself felt. In fact, the extension as built was an amalgam of both men's ideas, with Sir Aston intent on delivering a building which would approach as closely as possible that envisaged by Morland Agnew, and Arthur Cooke on correcting gaps or impracticalities in the original design.[3] The extension was intended to match the existing building, joining the latter seamlessly in both design and execution.

It was not until after the building of the extension to the Home that work on The Orchard really got under way. Three areas of The Orchard required alteration: accommodation, office space, and conversion of the gas lighting to electricity.

Enlargement of the accommodation was, as we have seen, primarily required to house the influx of outside nurses. To this end, three of the larger rooms were divided by partitions to create cubicles for eight of these nurses, the Finance sub-committee announcing that 'There are at least twelve nurses' bedrooms in the old house which has now no patients in it but is used for the nurses' residence and Matron's flat.' That the cubicles were a somewhat less than perfect solution was noted almost as soon as they were completed, the Annual Report of March 1925 stating that 'The present arrangements cannot … be looked upon as permanent as the existing cubicles … should be replaced by bedrooms.' In fact, freeing rooms in The Orchard by removing the remaining patients to the new extension eased, but did not wholly alleviate, the accommodation problem. The House sub-committee, following the opening of the extension, urged that more nurses be employed to cope with the increased workload.

Office space was increased by building a small single-storey extension along the front of The Orchard at a cost of £400. So cleverly designed was this extension that one could be forgiven for thinking that it formed part of the original house, were it not for the plainer lintels over the windows. The office extension, like the

2. 'Wards' proved unpopular and were converted to single use.

3. Possibly the most exciting feature of the building scheme was the 'electric lift of adequate size'.

rest of the house, was wired for electricity. So excited were the inhabitants of The Orchard by their 'Electric Lighting' that 'extravagance' in its use (especially on the stairs) was noted; luckily, before matters got completely out of hand, 'steps had been taken to remedy it'.

No sooner had the Home completed one round of building than it prepared to embark on another. Once again, it was the need to accommodate more nurses that provided the impetus; this time, however, their accommodation was not to be of a temporary or an adaptive nature but was to be in a completely new, purpose-built block. On 28 October 1925, the Finance sub-committee raised the question 'of consulting an Architect over the layout of the future Nurses' Hostel'. On 2 December 1925, it noted 'the selection of a local Architect … had been made subject to Mr Agnew raising no objection'. None was forthcoming, and C.W. Long of Atkinson & Long, Trumpington Street, Cambridge, was appointed – the fact that he was a protégé of Sir Aston Webb probably counting in his favour.

Assuming, as everyone did, that the maximum number of nurses and ancillary staff were to be housed on site, the first question to be answered was where the hostel should be built. The possibilities were:

a) to the south of The Orchard;
b) an extra storey on the Home itself;
c) joining The Orchard to the Aston Webb building by a two-storeyed connecting block.

Options a) and b) were rejected, after more than three years of discussions and disagreements between the House and Finance sub-committees. Option c), though not without its disadvantages, was the one eventually approved, the Annual Report of 31 March 1929 agreeing that 'a block consisting chiefly of nurses' bedrooms should be erected between the two existing buildings'. It was to be called the Airspace Wing by reason of its occupying the 'air space' between the two parts of the Home.

The construction of a block connecting The Orchard with the patients' part of the Home meant, of course, that major alterations would have to take place to the east side of the former as well as to the west end of the latter. This gave the Home the opportunity of carrying out further alterations to The Orchard itself. These were of a substantial nature and

The Airspace Wing 1931. The Night Floor was added in 1937.

included redesigning a secondary staircase with the object of converting it into the main stairway, creating a large rectangular bay-windowed south-facing sitting room for the nurses, resiting the staff dining room, providing a dispensary and linen room, and adding a semicircular 'vestibule' to the front of the old house in order to create a new main entrance, whence a skylight-illuminated corridor led to the new connecting block.[4]

On 31 March 1931 the Annual Report was happy to record that 'The Inside Staff is accommodated in the old house and on the first floor of the new connecting block and consequently enjoy complete privacy.' The outside staff, whose 'uncomfortable sleeping accommodation' in The Orchard had been responsible for a drop in their number, found that the new 'Staff Block' more than made up for their previous discomfort. Furthermore, staff accommodation in The Orchard, which used to be so 'dreary, dingy and dark', was now 'bright, light and airy', for the 'outside of the old house has been painted for the first time in ten years and much internal decoration … held over pending the reconditioning of the old house has been carried out'. On 31 March 1932, the Committee of Management expressed their appreciation of the skill 'that their architect, Mr C.W. Long, has shown in reconditioning the old house and joining it up with the Nursing Block'.

4. A problem involved in the connection of the existing buildings was created by the ground floor of the old house standing higher than that of the Aston Webb block although there was no perceptible gradient in the land between them. Changes in level necessitated the construction of steps, the presence of which proved extremely inconvenient.

Contemporaneous with the building of the Airspace Wing was the Home's purchase of Brookfield, the house next door. The Evelyn's desire for *Lebensraum* had already caused it to cast covetous eyes on the land across its northern boundary, so far to no avail. However, the Annual Report of March 1930 noted that 'Trinity College has agreed, subject to the existing tenancy, to sell the Freehold of Brookfield to the Home.'

The Evelyn was allowed by its *Articles of Association* to 'acquire, purchase, hire, sell, dispose of, let, and manage' other properties; this it duly proceeded to do, the March 1930 Annual Report noting 'the Purchase of Brookfield' by the Home. The freehold was sold by Trinity for £4,500, the Home gaining for the same price as The Orchard nine years earlier a much larger house but with a much smaller garden: 2.6 acres (1 hectare) as opposed to The Evelyn's 4.5 (1.8). This brought The Evelyn's total land holding to just over 7 acres. The Home could not, at this point, make use of its purchase, other than charging rent, as Brookfield contained sitting tenants; indeed, it seemed at the time to be more interested in the possibility of creating an entrance to the Home from the north 'through the grounds of Brookfield' than in the possible physical expansion of the Home over its northern boundary. The Home did, however, have an idea of what it wanted to do with Brookfield once the tenants were no longer in possession, asking that Mr Long be notified regarding possible alterations to his plan for the Airspace Wing because the proposed connecting block would be 'occupied by patients as soon as the Home can obtain possession of Brookfield' with the aim of turning it into a nurses' home. In August 1935, the last tenant moved out, but as the Home could not then afford to undertake the major alterations required before Brookfield could be used as a nurses' residence, the house was leased to Dr C.H. Whittle, physician and pathologist at Addenbrooke's Hospital. So closely was the new tenant to be associated with the property that the name 'Brookfield' dropped out of current use; the house was always known as 'Dr Whittle's House', references to its actual name being met with incomprehension.

That Brookfield was not adapted for the nurses' use in the 1930s was a source of regret to those members of the inside staff on night duty. In fact,

The Evelyn Nursing Home, with Brookfield to the right, 1934.

they were soon anything but happy with their new accommodation, situated as it now was in close proximity to the new main entrance, main staircase and main thoroughfare. On 7 August 1936 the Committee of Management was empowered to erect a second storey over the Airspace Wing, and by October of the same year the work was progressing well. On 25 February 1937 the Finance sub-committee reported that 'the night nurses have been moved into the new ... flat', which was to be known, even after its abandonment by daytime sleepers, as the 'night floor'.

Although the cessation of fifteen years of virtually non-stop building work must have come as a relief to the staff and patients of the Home, one further scheme remains to be described. This scheme, the only one not to be directly influenced by considerations of accommodation for the users of the Home, nevertheless came about as a consequence of the increase in staff and patient numbers.

The first intimations appeared in the Annual Report of 31 March 1934, which noted that 'a large sum will have to be spent in 12 months' time on the Operating Theatre'. A year later, the report, reiterating the imminent expenditure 'of a large sum', continued the story: 'The Committee of Management ... found it was also absolutely necessary to increase the size of the kitchen which is too small for the enlarged Home, and, seeing that the kitchen is immediately below the Theatre ... the work must be done simultaneously. Plans have now been prepared by Mr C.W. Long.'

In March 1935 plans for the proposed extension were drawn up 'after consultations with the Medical Men using the Home'. It was envisaged that the work would be completed by September. Given the magnitude of the scheme, completion only six months after the planning stage seems optimistic, but the Home was anxious to have the work carried out. In fact, it was not until March and April 1936 that the kitchen and theatre respectively were back in action. For the nine months that the theatre was out of commission, two patients' rooms were adapted for anaesthetic and operating use, with some 'financial damage' caused as a result.

Surprisingly little comment appears in the minutes of the sub-committees concerning the work on the theatre, and nothing at all concerning that on the kitchen – other than that the latter required redecoration after the work was complete and that Cook was given a bonus (and an electric mixer for the preparation of the Christmas puddings!) because of the inconvenience she had to suffer with the builders in her domain and overhead. This lack of comment is unusual considering the magnitude of the scheme, involving as it did the pushing back of the entire north frontage of both kitchen and theatre by some four feet, and the concomitant strengthening of the walls of the foundations to take the additional weight of the storeys above. Furthermore, because no plans exist of what was a very major rearrangement of the areas involved, much of what took place is a matter of conjecture.

Although, in January 1936, the Finance sub-committee reported that 'it is impossible to say when the Theatre will be ready for use', it was, as we have seen, completed not long after. On 23 April 'The Dean of King's conducted a short service in the new Operating Theatre in the presence of several Medical Men and members of the staff', following which the first operation in the 'new' theatre was performed by the ENT surgeon, Alfred Walford. On 22 May it was agreed to have an 'At Home' early in the summer to which 'the Medical Men in the town and surrounding country

should be invited with a view to showing them the enlarged Theatre and Kitchen'; the At Home duly took place on 16 July. The subsequent increase in the Home's profits was held to be directly attributable to the improved operating facilities.

The story of the early days of X-ray at The Evelyn is so amusing that it is best transcribed verbatim from the minutes of the Finance and General Purposes sub-committee of the time:

Feb. 7th 1922: The question of the purchase of an X-ray apparatus was considered and an estimate of £303–6–3d taken from the catalogue of the Cox Cavendish Electrical Co. Ltd was put before the committee.

April 7th 1922: Mr Cooke … had not yet concluded his search for the best X-ray apparatus.

June 2nd 1922: It was agreed to purchase a Watson's portable X-ray apparatus for £250.

Sept. 30th 1922: The following resolution was passed with regard to the X-ray apparatus: 'The X-ray Apparatus belonging to The Evelyn Nursing Home is placed at the disposal of the Medical Man in charge of the case on condition that all responsibility connected with its use must be taken by him, and that he is liable for any damage to the Apparatus or injury to the Patient. The Charge for use of the Apparatus will be 1 guinea.'

Dec. 1st 1922: Mr Cooke reported that he hoped that the services of a suitable person to work the X-ray apparatus would be soon be obtained.

Jan. 12th 1923: Mr Cooke reported that nothing definite had been settled about the X-ray Apparatus as no-one had yet been found to work it. He was asked to consult Prof. Rutherford.[5]

Feb. 9th 1923: Mr Cooke had been unable to get anyone from the Cavendish Laboratory to work the X-ray apparatus.

March 9th 1923: The porter at the Home is taking lessons in the use of the X-ray Apparatus.

April 9th 1923: It was quite safe for Gislingham to work the machine and … he was making satisfactory progress in learning to use it. For the present … he is to be paid nothing extra for this work.

May 7th 1923: The use of the X-ray apparatus was discussed and it was decided to add the following to the minute of 30th Sept. 1922: 'The Home will be responsible for any damage done to the Apparatus if it is worked by one of their servants acting under the authority of the Committee.' The Secretary was instructed to have this minute typed and framed, and hung up by the apparatus.

Nov. 15th 1924: It was agreed that Gislingham's wages be raised by 3/- to 45/-.

Feb. 20th 1925: The House Committee had considered the question of the use of the X-ray apparatus and recommended that … after the words 'injury to the patient' [2 September 1922] there be added 'it being understood that no-one but a qualified Radiologist or his assistant is allowed to make use of the Apparatus'.

5. Ernest Rutherford devoted his life to establishing the science of radioactivity, himself making many of the major discoveries in his field – he was the first person to split the atom. During his career, physics became one of the most exciting areas of study, with X-rays discovered in 1885 and radium (and other radioactive elements) by the Curies in 1896. He was appointed Professor of Physics at Cambridge in 1919. As head of the Cavendish Laboratory, The Evelyn decided he was the obvious person to approach!

The Medical Man in Charge of the Case

THE EARLY YEARS of the 1930s saw The Evelyn deprived of the four people most closely involved with its foundation, and the Committee of Management bereft of all three of its original life members.

The first to die, in 1930, was 'Mr Agnew's Architect', Sir Aston Webb. Morland Agnew was unable to attend Sir Aston's funeral, writing sadly in his diary that 'I should like to have gone but could not well manage it.' In fact, by the time of Sir Aston's demise, Morland Agnew's own health was failing. On 30 May 1931, a local paper noted, 'The death of Mr C. Morland Agnew on May 23rd … removes a benefactor to whom all Cambridge must be grateful. His memory here will remain as the generous donor of one of the most beautiful Nursing Homes in England.'

Less than a year after the death of The Evelyn's 'Donor and First Chairman', the Committee of Management announced the death of one who had been, in a sense, the Home's first patient. Although Evelyn Agnew's convalescence, following her sojourn in the Thompson's Lane Hostel, had been a lengthy one, her subsequent health had been good, inspiring her husband to write in his diary on Christmas Day 1922: 'Mother very fit (trying her digestive organs a bit, I feel!!).' By early 1930, however, she was suffering from palpitations and 'too much blood pressure'. Her death from angina in early 1932 was noted in the Annual Report, with the addition that her and her husband's names would never be forgotten in Cambridge and at The Evelyn: 'the existence of the Home we owe to

Mr Agnew's pious benefaction, the name of the Home to Mrs Agnew'. The Agnews' ashes were buried in the grounds of The Evelyn.

On a happier note, the Annual Report then announced that Mr Charles Gerald Agnew, the eldest son of Morland and Evelyn, was elected Chairman of the Home. Gerald Agnew was, as his son Geoffrey put it, 'proud of The Evelyn since he was devoted to his father'. Also described by Geoffrey Agnew as a 'man of sudden tremendous enthusiasms, each sustained for only a limited period', Gerald Agnew turned up faithfully to Annual General Meetings until 1938, but arrived on only two further such occasions thereafter. He did, however, keep in touch with what was happening at The Evelyn, the building schemes of the 1930s being carried out under his chairmanship.

The Annual Report of 31 March 1933 had yet another 'mournful duty' to perform when it recorded 'the death of the surviving Life Member, Mr Arthur Cooke'. The report then went on to state that, in losing Arthur Cooke, 'the Home had lost a devoted friend, whose services were always at the disposal of the Matron and Staff. They carried all their troubles to him, and, whether the problems submitted

Gerald Agnew, Chairman 1931–55.

to him were great or small, he gave to their solution the same careful attention. The loss to the Home is incalculable.'

As chairman of the House sub-committee, Arthur Cooke was effectively in charge of the day-to-day running of the Home. In view of this, and of the important role he played in the founding and early years of The Evelyn, it seems appropriate to make more detailed mention here of the surgeon who, in operating on Evelyn Agnew, was subsequently to be so closely associated with her husband's gift to Cambridge.

Arthur Cooke was born in 1868. He came to Cambridge in 1893 as the surgical partner in a three-man general practice in Bridge Street. Initially he lived at 69 Bridge Street, but later moved to Grove Lodge opposite Addenbrooke's Hospital, then situated in Trumpington Street. In 1903, he joined the staff of Addenbrooke's, subsequently becoming senior surgeon with ophthalmology as his main interest. At both the hospital and The Evelyn he was respected and loved, the then matron of the former recalling that 'those who were privileged to work for him in his wards will remember him as a surgeon who laboured ceaselessly for the benefit of his patients', and the Annual Report of the latter that 'Arthur Cooke's fame in Cambridge will not rest merely on his skill as a surgeon, pre-eminent as that skill was. He will be remembered as the most unselfish and least self-seeking of men … of whom it may be said with perfect truth that he never made an enemy and never lost a friend.' His marriage to the first cousin of Gerald Agnew's wife Olive brought him into the orbit of the Agnew family, with whom he shared many sporting and artistic interests. It is not surprising that when Evelyn Agnew's 'dyspepsia' required surgical intervention, a close friend with the necessary skills should be asked to operate on her. Fortunately Lieutenant-Colonel Cooke's return from service in various military hospitals in France coincided with her referral to Thomas Horder. The nursing home that later bore her name therefore had for Arthur Cooke 'a special romance and a special significance'.

A description of the 'medical man' who inspired the founding of The Evelyn and his connection with the patient who gave her name to that institution leads naturally to a discussion of those for whose benefit The Evelyn was founded: the local doctors and the 'cases' admitted under their care. As Arthur Cooke was primarily a surgeon by the time The Evelyn came into being, it seems appropriate to begin by considering surgeons first:

> The surgeon comes, alert and
> bright,
> And says he thinks perhaps he
> might
> Remove your heart or enlarge your
> brain,
> And put you quite on your legs
> again.[1]

The first operation at The Evelyn took place a short time after it opened. By 1925, a full range of major surgery

---

1. The poem, quoted earlier, continues in a vein with which later generations of surgeons might sympathise:

> How do the surgeons keep so fit?
> Does anyone know how they manage it?
> Do they never wake up glum and say
> 'I won't cut anyone up today'?

was undertaken. Surgeons working at The Evelyn employed their general practitioner colleagues as their anaesthetists, with GPs themselves operating on minor cases such as hernias, varicose veins, wisdom teeth and tonsils. Indeed, it is quite usual to find on the theatre lists of the time a GP shown as 'anaesthetist' one day and 'surgeon' the next. The later 1920s and the 1930s saw the arrival at The Evelyn of specialisation in the shape of ENT surgery, dentistry and orthopaedics, and of an increasing number of general practitioners concentrating on the giving of anaesthetics.

The results of the close collaboration at The Evelyn of surgeons and general practitioners were twofold. First, an enormous amount of medical expertise was available to the patients admitted there; second, the patients were likely to be very well known indeed to the surgical and anaesthetic teams – it was perfectly possible for a patient to be operated on by their former GP and anaesthetised by their present one. This state of affairs gave rise to a mutually fulfilling relationship between patients and doctors, which, combined with the high standard of nursing care, contributed in no small measure to the

former's recovery, the latter's job satisfaction, and the good name rapidly gained by Mr Agnew's benefaction.[2]

Although by the early 1930s specialist physicians were in evidence, in general local GPs acted as physicians when patients with problems of a non-surgical nature were admitted to the Home. This meant that their admission was under the direct care of someone already familiar with their medical and family history, who made daily visits to supervise their treatment. Then, as now, doctors tended to turn up at inconvenient times – on 20 March 1936, Mrs Spittle of the House sub-committee 'appealed to the medical men to as far as possible postpone their visits till after the patients had been washed' because she had received a complaint from a patient 'that her nurse had been called off to interview a doctor while she was engaged in washing her'.

Local doctors not only admitted patients to The Evelyn, but on at least one occasion used it as a place of refuge. Charles Sharp, former newspaper reporter, tells an amusing story of a court case which took place in the Cambridge of this time, gaining national notoriety. It began, he said, with a civil action for enticement

2. As co-opted members of The Evelyn, local medical men of all persuasions were well represented on that institution's governing bodies, from the Committee of Management to the smallest sub-committee, and they played an active role in the running of the Home.

brought by a well-known local butcher against an equally well-known local doctor. The person said to have been enticed was the butcher's wife, a very attractive lady; she was immediately dubbed by one of the barristers acting in the case a veritable Helen of Troy, for whom two men were prepared to do legal battle. The unfortunate doctor was subjected to very close attention by the local media – nothing to compare with the kind of door-stepping he would encounter today, but sufficient to make him seek greater privacy than his own home afforded. But where could he find a place where he could be certain of not being discovered, where his presence would seem natural, where he would be with friends, and where he could enjoy good food and a comfortable bed? Where else but The Evelyn! And there he remained until the hue and cry died down …

Opportunities for 'surgical and medical treatment … under the direction of their own surgeons and physicians' (as the *Memorandum* put it) brought patients flocking to The Evelyn, the Admissions Registers of the time providing a fascinating record of middle- and upper-class ailments in children and adults from the local area, with occasional incursions from

East Anglia, the Home Counties and London – and sometimes even further afield, as witness a member of the West Indies cricket team.[3] Pressure on the Home's rooms meant that it was sensible to book one's preferred room well in advance. No more than three rooms could be booked in this way unless the room requested cost less than 7 guineas a week, and even then a booking was no guarantee that the room would be available when the patient arrived for admission. In the event of the chosen room not being free, the patient was accommodated in whichever room was vacant, or even in one of the 'emergency rooms',[4] until such time as the preferred room became free.

Surgery undergone by patients at The Evelyn involved very much the same specialties as the present day, albeit with one very important difference: the enormous amount of surgery performed for infections which today would be treated primarily with antibiotics, with surgical intervention as a last resort only. Both elective and emergency surgery took place, the large number of emergency admissions being accounted for by the fact that patients of the class for whom The Evelyn existed would be unlikely to go to Addenbrooke's Hospital even in an

---

3. Internationally well-known patients included J. M. Synge, the playwright, and the scientist J. B. S. Haldane. The poet A. E. Housman died at The Evelyn on 30 April 1936 with a diagnosis of 'cardiac'.

4. Two or three such 'emergency rooms' were reserved for unexpected admissions, which more often than not arrived late in the evening.

emergency.[5] Virtually all surgical interventions involved 'open' surgery, with only a small number of endoscopic events. With the exception of patients admitted with very severe infections or as emergencies, perioperative mortality rates were low, though a few unexpected deaths occurred after minor surgery.

Surgery was categorised as 'major', 'minor' or 'intermediate'. Anomalies occasionally appear in the assignment of operations to one or other category, with emergency airway surgery being labelled 'minor' and tonsillectomy 'major'. (Operations described as 'minor', namely 'excision of eye' and 'excision of penis', probably demonstrate the recording secretary's lack of knowledge of what actually took place rather than the operations' true magnitude.) A charge for the use of the operating theatre was made, varying from 10s 6d 'in the case of trivial operations' to 1 or 2 guineas for major cases. In March 1932, the Finance sub-committee noted that some surgeons were pressing for a reduction in what it believed to be very moderate fees, with charges for 'prolongued major operations' not to exceed 2 guineas. A compromise was made that if a surgeon appealed to Matron for a reduction of the theatre fee in a particular case, discretion would be exercised in granting it.

Patients admitted for medical treatment were fewer in number and fell into three categories:

a) those with circulatory, renal and chest conditions who were admitted with acute exacerbations or terminal manifestations of these – such as myocardial infarct, stroke, emphysema or uraemia;
b) those with conditions that would nowadays be unlikely to warrant admission to hospital – epilepsy, diabetics for 'standardisation' on insulin, pernicious anaemia, and Bell's palsy;
c) those with acute conditions whose prognosis in pre antibiotic days was grave – rheumatic fever, nephritis, nasal diphtheria and pneumonia.

Out-patient treatment, although more usually carried out in the surgeries or consulting rooms of the medical men concerned, began to be carried out at The Evelyn in the early 1930s, particularly when its nature required nursing rather than medical intervention – for example, post-operative dressings or colonic lavage for the seemingly omnipresent

5. By the early 1930s Addenbrooke's had its own private wing. It never appears to have posed a threat to The Evelyn, which was in any case careful to keep the prices for its cheapest rooms only marginally above those charged by Addenbrooke's.

constipation. Although there seem to have been few permanent residents in The Evelyn during the 1920s and 1930s, elderly patients with diagnoses of 'senile', 'debility' and 'chronic invalid' were admitted for periods ranging from two to three weeks up to six months, presumably in an effort to rehabilitate them or to cover holidays taken by their families or domestic staff.

Patients with infectious conditions posed particular problems, for Trinity had imposed restrictions regarding the nursing of such cases at The Evelyn when conveying The Orchard to Morland Agnew. In March 1930, an influenza epidemic hit Cambridge, and the Home officially requested Trinity to waive the restrictions; in practice, and in spite of the presence in Cambridge of an isolation hospital, The Evelyn had been admitting infectious cases for some time. As early as January 1927, the House sub-committee had issued a report giving a list of diseases which, in their opinion should 'i) be admitted, ii) be admitted with special nurse, iii) not be admitted'. In February 1927, a 'List of Diseases to be treated at the Home' was issued, though not until it had been vetted by the then Professor of Medicine, Sir Humphrey Rolleston. It

included 'for admission': tuberculosis (though not the pulmonary variety), malaria, dysentery, pneumonia and 'post-influenzal conditions', rheumatic fever and trench fever. (Against the last-named, someone wrote in red ink '? is it now necessary, as extinct'. Trench fever was more prevalent on the Somme in 1914–18 than in Trumpington Road in the 1920s!) 'For admission with special nurse' included acute poliomyelitis and encephalitis 'after fever has gone', ophthalmia neonatorum, acute eczema, the typhoid group, puerperal fever, tetanus and anthrax. 'Not to be admitted' were primary and secondary syphilis, influenza (*sic*), scabies and parasitic skin diseases, impetigo (of which cases certainly *were* admitted, as they were of glandular fever, also on the 'not to be admitted' list), childhood diseases (scarlet fever, measles, whooping cough, chicken pox and mumps), pemphigus, 'drug addicts and mental cases', 'acute alcoholism and delirium tremens', and diseases whose presence in Cambridge was unlikely but for which The Evelyn felt it ought to be prepared: plague and cholera.

The Evelyn also treated a large number of what were broadly termed 'nerve cases'. Patients with nervous illnesses fell into two groups. The first consisted largely but not exclusively of members of the University. Those in this group were admitted suffering from insomnia, or from nervous strain, debility, exhaustion, prostration or breakdown brought on by 'overwork' or 'overstrain'. Patients in this category were often admitted during the evening or at night (hence the need to keep emergency rooms readily available) and usually spent a comparatively short time in hospital. Patients in the second group tended to stay longer as they suffered from conditions which took rather longer to cure: hypochondria, depression, 'anxiety condition', neurasthenia, hysteria and mania. Cases of alcoholism (without, one hopes, delirium tremens) and anorexia nervosa, though less common, also appear in the Admission Registers of the time.

Admission of accident cases to The Evelyn was a small but important aspect of the work carried out there before the Second World War. Undergraduates formed the largest number of such admissions, although visitors to Cambridge also used the service. At the Finance sub-committee meeting of 15 January 1932, Arthur Cooke raised the question 'of the Police taking ... all accident cases ... to the Hospital, and suggested that certainly in the case of members of the University, they should be taken direct to The Evelyn'.

Accident cases dealt with by The Evelyn fell mainly into the following categories:

injuries of all kinds;
attempted suicides;
road traffic accidents;
gunshot wounds (a surprisingly large number);
and miscellaneous – epileptic fits, nosebleeds, burns, swallowed foreign bodies, and even sunstroke and frostbite.

Children – often accompanied by a parent, nanny or governess – were regular patients at The Evelyn. Some were from local families, while others were boarders at local schools. Most children were admitted for tonsillectomy and adenoidectomy, squint repairs, or minor urological surgery; others arrived as emergencies with appendicitis, acute mastoiditis, convulsions, or gastroenteritis, of which a number did not survive. Some very young babies were admitted with croup or for surgery for pyloric stenosis and these certainly survived. The Home also admitted a small number of maternity cases.

Although the actual, as opposed to the implied, importance of the University in the running of The Evelyn in the 1920s and 1930s is often exaggerated, the part played by the Home in the medical care of the undergraduates of the time cannot be lightly dismissed. The average proportion of 'gown' to 'town' patients in the early 1920s averaged 1:4, with monthly fluctuations according to the timing of University terms; as the 1930s progressed, the proportion dropped to 1:5. Regarding admission to The Evelyn of those *in statu pupillari*, it is significant that a special column in the Admission Registers allowed, where relevant, the 'college tutor' of the patient admitted to be entered. Although some undergraduates were admitted with serious physical illnesses from which they did not always recover, a one-night stay for 'encephalitis and dementia praecox' (i.e. schizophrenia) suggests either misdiagnosis or a remarkably speedy recovery. And as undergraduates will, the students of the 1920s and 1930s sometimes overindulged, witness to which are a two-day stay due to 'alcoholic unconsciousness' and an even shorter admission (1.15 a.m. to noon) to recover from the 'effects of dining not wisely but too well', as the Admission Register put it! The bills of undergraduates admitted to The Evelyn were paid either by themselves, if family circumstances permitted, or by the previously mentioned Crane's Charity.[6]

That The Evelyn was adversely affected by undergraduate admissions is indubitable, chiefly because it insisted that all undergraduates, wealthy or not, be charged a flat rate of 5 guineas a week for their room. It is also obvious that undergraduate admissions were regarded as 'loss leaders' which generated collegiate and University good will without in any way generating income proportionate to their numbers. With up to a quarter of all admissions paying less than the lowest room rate charged to non-undergraduate patients, it is noticeable that when with the onset of the financial depression of the 1930s The Evelyn began to feel the pinch, undergraduate admissions contributed in no small measure to its increasing distress.

6. As Arthur Cooke expounded in a letter to the *Cambridge Review* of 3 February 1933, 'Crane's Charity ... helps many men whose parents' income is very small, usually from £200 to £400 a year.' Undergraduates whose annual parental income exceeded, even marginally, the £500 limit set by the charity received no help at all.

What on Earth is to be Done?

THE MAIN AIM of the Finance sub-committee was to control expenditure, and this it did with reasonable success during the first ten years of the Home's existence. It was not, however, so successful in its execution of the necessary corollary to the control of expenditure, namely the generation of income. The causes of this were various. Some, like the Great Depression, were beyond The Evelyn's control; others arose in part because of the Home's desire to appear philanthropic, and in part because the Finance sub-committee's tendency to be reactive rather than proactive in matters financial meant that it was constantly overtaken by events well within its remit, without having made provision for them in current or future budgets. It is therefore hardly surprising that the Annual Report of 31 March 1939 noted with regret 'that the Committee of Management have to report that for the first time in the history of the Home, a loss, amounting to £72 … had been incurred'. That the Finance sub-committee were 'going thoroughly into the matter' provided small consolation with regard to what was only the most recent manifestation of the Home's increasing financial insecurity.

What had happened in the period 1936–9 to cause such a rapid and largely unforeseen decline in The Evelyn's fortunes?

Probably the most important factor was the Home's ambitious building programme, accompanied as this was by consistent underestimation of the cost of building and equipping the extensions and of altering and updating The Orchard, and its concomitant purchase of a large house (Brookfield), requiring a substantial mortgage not fully reimbursed by rental moneys received.

A justificatory statement dated 3 November 1932 to the Tutorial Representatives (i.e. the nominated members) explained that the alterations and extensions had been necessary for two reasons:

a) to 'raise the number of beds to something like the figure Mr Agnew had in mind when he first planned the Home', a statement which begs the question that the Home might have been wiser to have waited more than two years before beginning to expand, anxious though it was to fulfil its founder's dream; b) to house the nursing and domestic staff on site 'for the efficient running of the Home'. Unfortunately, the statement went on, enlarging the Home primarily for the purpose of increasing staff accommodation 'only increased the earning capacity of the Home by a small amount' while 'adding considerably to the overhead charges'.

A second factor in the Home's financial problems was the rising costs of necessary services. Coke, gas, water and electricity charges all rose during the 1930s, closely followed by those for laundry (the Home's own laundry could no longer cope with the amount of clean linen required) and the telephone. The cost of provisions also went up, although this was offset by The Evelyn's self-sufficiency in garden produce – and even by donations.[1]

A third factor was an increase in the Home's wages and salaries bill, not only because of the greater numbers of staff employed in all areas, but also because of the increasing necessity to pay them at a level commensurate with local or national standards. There was also the matter of salaries and superannuation having to be paid to nurses during periods of sick leave or leave of absence granted to cope with bereavements or family matters, and of compensation paid for injuries incurred on duty.

Fourth, prices of rooms did not rise in proportion to costs. By January 1923, for example, the price of the cheapest room had actually dropped to 5 guineas; the most expensive cost 10 guineas. Rooms in current use brought in £274 a week – assuming, of course, that all the rooms were full all the time and there were no negotiated reductions

1. Hence the story of Aunt Nellie's dripping. Like most working-class children of the time, Charles Sharp was a 'connoisseur of dripping'. As he explained, 'one of the less well-known aspects of … University life was the vast amount of top class dripping produced in the busy kitchens of the colleges, the direct result of the privileged feasting then enjoyed at the high tables. Large amounts of it, carted out of college kitchens in tins that originally contained … exotic fruit, were destined to end up on proletarian tables in Chesterton or Romsey Town.' Aunt Nellie's dripping, however, was something special. It was only many years later that he discovered the reason – the consultant for whom she worked in Lensfield Road (Mr Bowen) 'shot regularly on land owned by someone connected with The Evelyn, and as a consequence several brace of prime pheasants ended as a matter of course in the ovens of the nursing home … on the express understanding that the ensuing dripping was returned to his own household. He was convinced that pheasant flesh endowed it with a special medicinal quality.'

in force. In October 1929, the twenty-seven rooms then available brought in £232 a week after a recent increase in charges. In May 1931, income was £283 a week (i.e. an increase of only £9 a week in ten years), again after a rise in room rates. Three years later, in October 1934, the Finance sub-committee 'decided to alter the rents' of twelve rooms, the rents of nine being raised by 10s 6d or 1 guinea a week, but three actually being decreased by the same amounts. As a result, The Evelyn's only form of income, other than that brought in by the dwindling numbers of outside nurses, barely kept pace with costs and certainly did not always cover the service charges which still had to be paid even when the Home was slack. At the time of Miss Puckle's appointment as Matron in the autumn of 1938, the Home's existence was hand-to-mouth, with only £52 in the current account and bills of £400 due to be paid. A letter confirming her appointment noted the 'great anxiety' suffered by the Finance sub-committee over the Home's current financial affairs.

In April 1939, a special sub-committee was set up 'to consider the finances of the Home and all possible means of improving them'; sadly, it was unable to suggest any 'large scale economies' that could be made. It looked instead at ways of increasing the Home's revenue. The first suggestion was that every patient (undergraduates excepted) be charged an extra guinea a week; this would not only generate an extra £1,000–£1,200 a year income, but would also raise the fees of the ten cheapest rooms to a level at which the Home did not make an automatic loss on any patient housed there. Having put forward the suggestion, the sub-committee was immediately assailed by doubts: should the fees of *all* rooms be raised; and, if so, by how much: 1 guinea or 10s 6d? Should room fees be raised during University terms only, to compensate for a drop in patient numbers during the Long Vacation? Other nursing homes in Cambridge provided rooms at only four guineas a week – would The Evelyn suffer by continuing to charge more, and sometimes considerably more?

The Home's problem of being caught between the Scylla of charging (or appearing to charge) too much and the Charybdis of actually charging too little was not a new one – indeed, it was one which had bedevilled the institution since its inception. As early as November 1921, the Finance sub-committee had to send out a 'circular setting out all the maximum and minimum fees … to the Heads of Houses and Tutors and to local doctors' because of the 'widespread misunderstanding' which had arisen concerning the Home's current fee structure. At this time the maximum and minimum fees were 10 guineas and 6 guineas respectively, the decision not to alter these 'until it was clear that the Home was making a profit' obviously having been made in response to criticisms that the fees were too high. However, because fees were open to negotiation on a doctor's or the Treasurer's recommendation, and because the price differentials which resulted could easily give rise to resentment if patients in ostensibly similarly priced rooms compared notes, it is easy to see how such misunderstandings arose.

Unfortunately, agreed variations on the maximum and minimum fees never worked in the Home's favour. A Miss Stubbert, for example, had her room rate reduced to £25 a month in 1933 in spite of her cantankerous behaviour; while in 1937, with £15,000 owing to Trinity and Barclay's Bank, two rooms had their rate reduced by 3 guineas, and a 'fellow of a College who had been some time in the Home as a chronic patient' (and who therefore presumably required a good deal of nursing care) applied for and received a 1 guinea a week reduction on his 8 guinea room fee 'during the Vacation' – that is, at a time when efforts needed to be made to *increase* revenue. In 1939, during the period when the Finance sub-committee was desperately seeking ways and means of keeping the Home financially afloat, eight patients had their fees reduced by 1–6 guineas a week for a period of nearly two months, again during term, when it had been suggested that fees be raised. Added to this, various members of the public were admitted to the Home at favourable rates because of the services they or members of their families rendered to The Evelyn. While under certain circumstances this was fair (i.e. in the case of members of the committees, whose services to the Home were on a voluntary basis), in others it was rather less so, that of a sister of a former secretary to one of the committee members being a case in point. Philanthropic gestures of this nature, though no doubt much appreciated by their recipients, were not at this time, and financially speaking, astute – especially as they continued to be made when the Home's income was dropping by £1,000 a year.

As if things were not bad enough, with the Home having trouble both in paying off its bank loan and in keeping within its overdraft limit, 'false statements' (*sic*) began to circulate in Cambridge with regard to The Evelyn's financial probity. To counteract these, the Finance sub-committee felt it necessary in November 1937 to write to the *Cambridge Review* and the *Cambridge Daily News* letters which began defensively and ended as pleas:

Sir,

So many rumours have recently reached our ears of the fortunes apparently made out of The Evelyn Nursing Home by individuals – names unspecified – that we hope you will allow us to place some of the facts before your readers. These rumours are absurd. The Home is constituted under the Companies Act 1908–17, and it is clearly laid down in the *Memorandum of Association* that no portion of the income of the Home 'shall be paid or transferred directly or indirectly by way of dividend, bonus or otherwise howsoever by way of profit to the members of the Home'. This clause has never been transgressed. [Then followed details of the Home's management structure and details of 'schemes carried through' since its foundation.] The Home has no endowment [and] as no benefactor has come forward to supplement Mr Agnew's munificent gift – since 1921 the Home has been given less than £1,000 – the above schemes have had to be financed out of borrowed money … Can you, sir, find us a benefactor who will do for The Evelyn Nursing Home what Lord Nuffield has done for The Acland Home in Oxford?

Correspondence ensued in which various writers pointed out in The Evelyn's defence that the absence of student nurses meant a higher salary bill and that, while The Evelyn had only a limited number of rooms – not all of which were full at any one time – adequate levels of trained staff had to be maintained in case of a sudden influx of patients. Furthermore, fees charged by The Evelyn were for room and nursing care only; when to these was added the cost of medical care, dressings, theatre fees and so on, costs might seem high in proportion to those of, say Addenbrooke's or Papworth Hospitals but were not in fact exorbitantly so. By contrast, Addenbrooke's charges for private rooms were cheaper only because they formed part of a public institution built by public subscription and able to contract for supplies at a favourable rate because of its size.

To make matters worse – if, indeed they could be any worse – internecine warfare broke out at this point within the Finance sub-committee itself. This had obviously been brewing for some time but was precipitated by the House sub-committee's appointment of a home sister (Sister Bell) in defiance of the Finance sub-committee's attempts to control expenditure. Matters came to a head at a meeting of the latter sub-committee on 20 December 1938. Mr Mellish Clark, already sensitive to criticisms of the sub-committee's financial sagacity, suggested that it was the duty of that body to 'examine in detail any proposal, the adoption of which would involve increased expenditure', and that 'if the Home wished to make a reasonable profit expenditure should be cut down rather than increased'. To this a member replied ('If I heard him correctly') that he was not interested in making profits. The unfortunate member was then anathematised by Mr Mellish Clark to the effect that 'If the Finance Committee does not try to put the Home back onto its old profit-making basis ... and at the same time refuses to make an appeal for funds', what on earth was to be done?

The Exceptional War Conditions

THE OUTBREAK OF the Second World War provided respite for the beleaguered Finance sub-committee. The vicissitudes of the next decade notwithstanding, The Evelyn was saved from financial collapse by the very circumstances which in September 1939 appeared to presage nothing but disaster for the town, county and country in which it stood.

Intimations of the coming storm appeared as early as October 1938 in the shape of The Evelyn's response to the Munich crisis, the said sub-committee reporting that 'the Fire Brigade gave a lecture to the nurses … Fire extinguishers, Buckets of Sand and Stretchers were purchased.' With the outbreak of war in September 1939, the Home stepped up its preparations dramatically, continuing to maintain the high state of readiness imposed by the 'exceptional war conditions' well into 1943, at which point it was able to settle into a more established routine 'for the duration'.

Preparations were of three kinds: those pertaining to the fabric of the Home, those pertaining to the inmates of the Home, and those pertaining to stocking and supplying the Home.

As far as the fabric of the Home was concerned, The Evelyn's first move was to make the windows safe. The staff, 'assisted by voluntary effort', began the laborious task of covering each pane of glass with fabric netting. It was also necessary to 'black out' the windows lest a stray gleam of light from the so-profligately-used electricity attract the attentions of the Luftwaffe. Further advice on Air Raid Precautions (ARP) was obtained from a doctor living nearby, who arranged for the nurses' dining room to be turned into an air-raid shelter. In the absence of a suitable subterranean shelter, the dining room was probably the best-protected place, situated as it was on the north side of the Home behind the Airspace Wing, now called the Link Building. With the erection of a blast-proof wall outside the windows it could be rendered safe for the entire population of the Home – some fifty people – to take cover there during a raid.

The arrival of the 'new incendiary bomb' in 1942 occasioned the House sub-committee further worry and expense. Although the Home had already made arrangements for what to do in the event of a fire starting as a result of enemy action, in January 1941 it was informed by the Police that, because it employed over thirty staff, a 'firewatcher during alerts' was compulsory – that is, someone who would patrol the building at night and raise the alarm in the event of a fire breaking out. Eventually the Home recruited a team of thirty-five firewatchers and firefighters, including nurses and medical students, who duly paraded round the Home during night alerts.

But what would happen if an incendiary bomb landed on the flat roof of the Aston Webb Wing with its asphalt covering? Ever resourceful, Viva Cooke suggested painting the roof with 'fire-resisting' paint to 'delay the action' of this kind of missile. Though this seems a little optimistic given that incendiary bombs were capable of penetrating even a roof constructed by Sir Aston Webb, Coulsons were asked to provide an estimate. The Finance sub-committee, rejecting both the estimate and the idea, decided instead to install an extending horizontal ladder from which a firefighter armed with a long rake could 'dislodge' the offending missile. In order to prevent an overzealous firewatcher from stepping off the edge of the roof on a moonless night, a white line was painted round its perimeter; in 1943 the roof was also edged with 'protective hurdling'. Although the firewatchers attended a course on dealing with incendiary bombs in October 1942, it was not until April 1943 that the House sub-committee began 'looking into' different kinds of incendiary bomb 'extinguishers'. By the middle of the following month, however, they were able to report the imminent acquisition of 'more extinguishers', 'one tank or two big bins for extra water at the far end of the Home', 'stirrup pumps and buckets', and the reservation of certain cold-water taps 'for A.R.P. use only'.

Communication with the outside world in case of emergency was also a source of concern. Although the Home by now possessed several external telephone lines – an extension of the line in the front office had been run through to the nurses' blast-proof dining room in case the former was 'put out of action' – December 1942 saw the issuing of a new Fire Order forbidding the Home to use its telephone during an alert. In the event of a fire breaking out, a messenger was to be sent first to the ARP post in Newton Road, thence to the nearest fire station. As well she might, 'Matron felt this very unsatisfactory', and Viva Cooke was deputed to see if a better arrangement could be made. On 21 January 1943, the House sub-committee reported that a 'compromise' had been reached with the 'fire people', whereby 'we were to send our messenger to the Latham Road Assembly Point who in turn would send a messenger to the nearest fire station, and our messenger might return to the Home'. With the possibility of the Home being by this time engulfed in flames, the arrangement seems to modern eyes as unsatisfactory as the first, but the

Home seems to have accepted it without demur – probably they had no choice. Fortunately for all concerned, the Home never received a direct hit.

Not only did the House and Finance sub-committees have the responsibility of ensuring the safety of the fabric of the Home, they were also required to make provision for the rehousing of the Home's inhabitants in the event of enemy action rendering it uninhabitable. But where was the Home to go? Viva Cooke suggested Addenbrooke's, but a letter from the local office of the Ministry of Health stated the impossibility of this – the hospital would itself be clearing beds in order to receive casualties.

In May 1942, however, the Ministry of Health promised to allocate the Home to a suitable building 'provided the latter transferred to it only such patients as could not be moved home or to friends'; the Home's staff and 'necessary equipment' would also be transferred. 'In case of invasion the Home might get in touch with Homerton College' in Hills Road, as that college had been nominated as the Home's Reserve Hospital 'to be used in extreme emergency to provide accommodation for a short time'. It was also stated that 'the equipment of the … Home, so far as it is practicable to move it, should be transferred to Homerton … either for use in the reserve hospital … or to be stored at the college provided storage space is available there'. Fortunately no such extreme emergency ever occurred.

Stocking and supplying the Home were also important, stocks of all kinds being kept at a higher level than usual. Food, of course, was rationed; by March 1943, scarcities had resulted in the patients' breakfasts being 'a little scanty' and their lunch and supper menus 'monotonous'. Luckily matters were in hand to effect an improvement. The decision having already been taken to appoint 'someone to do the buying and take over the housekeeping', the first Catering Manager, Mrs Harvey, arrived in February 1943. She was initially engaged to work six mornings and two afternoons a week but, as she soon pointed out, she was having to stay till 4, 5 or 6 p.m. *every* day in her efforts to keep the Home adequately fed. Her pay, originally £3 a week, was then raised to £4, with the addition of 10s 6d a week to cover the cost of collection of daily provisions in her own car. But this, the Home reckoned, was money well spent; although food costs rose regardless, her arrival rapidly resulted in 'the provision of better and more food for all'.

Mrs Harvey was a resourceful lady. Soon after her arrival she was busy 'laying in a good anti-invasion stock of food', this including 'enough tinned meat … to last 14 days and enough other supplies for one month' in case of 'cessation of transport, supplies etc.'.

In October 1943 the House sub-committee was 'much impressed' with the amount of jam-making and bottling of fruit and tomatoes which Mrs Harvey had achieved; indeed so much was there that there was insufficient room in the kitchen to store it, and a cupboard was erected in the wider of the two lobbies leading to the garden. During Mrs Harvey's summer holiday, Sister Coleman (college nurse at Trinity) boosted the former's efforts by bottling 144 lb (65 kg) of gooseberries and 170 lb (77 kg) of rhubarb, an excellent demonstration of the prolific nature of The Evelyn's garden; the following year she bottled 230 lb (104 kg) of gooseberries and 105 lb (48 kg) of rhubarb – and this in a year when Mrs Harvey feared that 'we shall not be able to obtain much fruit'! On her return from holiday, Mrs Harvey was 'doing cherries' – the Home also grew raspberries, although they did not do as well as the other soft fruit, owing to their overshadowed position.

It was about this time that the Home began to keep chickens. Housed in the stables of 'Dr Whittle's house', they were reported as 'laying well' and in excellent condition; the eggs they produced allowed the dried eggs stocked 'in case of emergency' to be kept for that purpose. Their feed was supplemented by scraps from the kitchen; their manure went to improve the asparagus bed and to encourage the rhubarb, celery and onions. To supplement the Home's supply of protein, Mrs Harvey also located 'a source of young rabbits'; this meant that the patients could enjoy 'a rabbit meal' once a week. A report presented by her to the House sub-committee in June 1944 is worth quoting in full as it shows, first, the magnitude of her efforts on behalf of the Home and, second, the difficulty of obtaining foodstuffs and the expedients to which a food manager had to resort in order to resolve it:

> The committee may like to know the position of food reserves. Up to the present time, I have been able to keep intact the original amount of reserves in case of emergency. I have from time to time used and replaced all foods in order to keep them in good condition. I am not carrying quite so large a stock of cereals as these do not keep well, and there appears to be a plentiful supply on the market. I propose to purchase largely, as last year, whilst still decontrolled, packets of dried egg. The stock last year was of the greatest help when eggs were scarce and establishments not then allowed to buy. The tinned chicken has proved invaluable as live birds have been very scarce. I have bought six young cockrells [*sic*], $3\frac{1}{2}$ to 4 months old to fatten on scraps. The price I paid was 6/- each, I think the committee will agree the cost is a very reasonable one for the present time. A supply of young rabbits has been maintained which has provided one meal per week to give a little variety which is difficult to obtain nowadays … I have made an arrangement with an ex-policeman who is a rabbit breeder. He has agreed to buy tame young rabbits in the market and keep them until we need them, when he will kill and deliver. I am now sure of two meals for everyone, when and as we need one should the food position become acute.

The 'excellent quality' of the food of the time is demonstrated by an extant menu which lists, for a sample week, the patients' breakfast, lunch, tea and dinner choices. Following the cook's suggestion that patients could have, if they wished, a cooked breakfast, three days of the week offered a 'meat dish' (bacon or sausages), two offered fish, and one scrambled eggs; on Mondays only porridge or cereal appeared. Lunch provided both a light and a more substantial main course (steamed chicken, minced beef or a soufflé versus roast beef, toad-in-the hole or steak and kidney pie), and a similar choice of dessert (jelly and junket, semolina or stewed apple versus damson and apple tart, steamed pudding or bread-and-butter pudding); the dinner menu offered soup, followed by a main course preponderantly of fish and a light dessert – fresh fruit, chocolate mould or cheese. To sustain them in the gap between lunch and dinner, the patients' afternoon tea included cake, scones, oatcakes, potted meat and honey – though not all on the same day! At Christmas there were Christmas cakes 'most beautifully made and iced by cook'. It is, therefore, rather surprising to discover that soon after the end of the war (November 1945) the House sub-committee noted that Matron had been asked by one of the doctors 'whether she thought the patients really had enough food'. Her terse reply was to the effect that she enquired 'very frequently' if the patients' food both 'satisfied and pleased' them, and that it was, if anything, the nurses who went short!

To say that The Evelyn had a 'good' war may seem ironic, and in view of what has just been said concerning its problems of protection and provisioning, improbable; it is nevertheless true. First, the Home was blessed with a pair of Matrons who, together with a stalwart team of ladies, held the place together at a time when it would have been all too easy to succumb to the pressures of wartime conditions. Second, from 1940 to 1945 the Home was financially buoyant. On the one hand, it was almost continually full. On the other hand, because it was forced by the material stringencies of the time to put into abeyance all building schemes, other than routine maintenance and repairs and the repayment of the mortgage on Brookfield, it had no major outgoings. The Home therefore found itself for the first time in years in the position of having assured income without any major drain on its finances.

Although Miss Puckle's stay at The Evelyn was brief, she certainly ran it

Miss Margaret Quenilda Fynes-Clinton, Matron 1942–67.

with the required 'zeal and energy', for her resignation in January 1942 was accepted with 'great regret'. Her successor, the euphoniously named Margaret Quenilda Fynes-Clinton, came with glowing references from eminent surgeons. Her application to The Evelyn hardly does her justice: 'I am 36 years of age and in excellent health. I am a member of the Church of England. I am a State Registered Nurse and Certified Midwife, and hold a Housekeeping Certificate'; it was the references that said it all. Nor was she a stranger to the private sector; as she said, 'I have always been interested in nursing Private Patients and if appointed to the

Nursing Home would do my best to maintain its high standard of efficiency.' This she duly did.

How was it, we must now ask, that the onset of war brought patients flooding to The Evelyn with a concomitant improvement in its financial affairs? Possible reasons are as follows:

a) The return of modest prosperity to people's lives after the depression meant that more could afford to patronise it.

b) Regular patrons continued to arrive for medical and surgical care in a nursing home renowned for its high standards.

c) The cessation of the Home's ambitious building programme meant that it became a haven of peace and quiet in a noisy and uncertain world.

d) The closure of rival establishments before or during the war meant reduced competition for medical and residential patients.

e) Conscription meant that many of those who either did not wish or were unable to look after themselves were deprived of their usual help; they therefore moved into The Evelyn for longer or shorter periods, ensuring it an income independent of any rise or fall in medical or surgical admissions.

A study of the Admissions Registers for 1939–45 shows very much the same mixture of medical and surgical admissions as before,[1] with two important exceptions. The first was the marked decline in the number of 'nerve cases' as people rose to the challenges posed by the 'exceptional war conditions'; the second, the very obvious drop in undergraduate admissions – even allowing for the fact that some undergraduates continued their studies and that others were evacuated to Cambridge, the diminution in numbers is dramatic. That the marked decline in undergraduate numbers did not materially affect The Evelyn demonstrates just how busy it was; it must have also helped financially as far fewer rooms had to be let at completely uneconomic rates.[2]

Admission of patients for 'massage' heralded the arrival at The Evelyn of physiotherapy and the first three physiotherapists: Mr Pope, Miss Piggott and Miss Narborough ('Narby'). As masseur and masseuses, they brought to the Home the new technique of Swedish massage developed in that country chiefly for the treatment of rheumatoid arthritis. Swedish massage consisted of active and passive exercises applied to affected joints and muscles, accompanied – and this was thought to be very important – by massage of a light (*effleurage*) or deep (*pétrissage*) stroking nature. Treatments were enhanced by the application of heat by means of fomentations, hot baths, warm paraffin wax, hot-water bottles, electric pads and heat lamps; or by short-wave diathermy, which heated deeper tissues by passing a high-frequency current through a resistance, in this instance a rheumatic joint. This latter treatment explains Mesdemoiselles Piggott and Narborough's title of 'electric' or 'electrical' masseuses.

As noted earlier, patients also entered the wartime Home on a 'permanent' basis, some for the duration of the war, others for the duration of their lives. Interestingly, people in the position to know exactly how many permanent patients the Home housed at any one time always tended to underestimate (the number is not difficult to ascertain from patient records of the time); indeed, in September 1941, the Home itself seemed unsure how many 'chronic

1. In the early years of the war, surgery at The Evelyn was curtailed by the calling-up of some surgeons and GP anaesthetists. Operations continued in spite of this, with older surgeons and general practitioners holding the fort in the temporary absence of their younger confrères. One or two theatre cases were carried out each weekday to a maximum of four. Both major and minor surgery was carried out, one patient receiving The Evelyn's first recorded blood transfusion (donor: 'Mr Brown').

2. The Home continued to admit its share of celebrities during the war (Margot Fonteyn, the ballerina, for example, and Donald Wolfit, the famous Shakespearian actor); on the other hand, Eleanor Roosevelt, wife of the President of the United States, merely 'broke her schedule to make a brief call at The Evelyn' when opening a US servicemens' hostel in Brooklands Avenue.

Peggy Leonard and Brenda Bott, kitchen workers at the Home during the Second World War.

cases' it housed, recording only three rooms as 'let permanently' when it is obvious from research that at least five such patients existed. In April 1944, the Committee of Management asked the House sub-committee 'for the exact number of chronic cases permanently in the Home', stressing the importance of not admitting any more because of the pressure on beds. The House sub-committee's reply that there were only three such patients may have been true at that point, but its statement that 'no more had been taken for several years' was patently untrue. It did, however, state its 'present policy', which was 'to take no more ... until after the war and to keep all new cases in for as short a

time as possible'. Possibly the Home wished to play down the existence of permanent patients, both because this projected the wrong image to the general public, and because it might affect college sponsorship, notwithstanding that a high proportion of such patients were retired members of the University.

The presence of so many patients of all kinds required adequate numbers of staff to care for them; this, during the war years, was not always easy to achieve. Catering presented the smallest problem, with three cooks, a kitchen maid, and a 'woman to do the dishes'. The large garden, though a boon to the Home, was more of a problem; although the head gardener's post was recognised as essential, the undergardener's was not, successive occupants being called up in 1940 and 1941. Domestic help created a bigger headache. In 1941, the Home was five maids short out of a possible twenty, and because the majority of domestics now lived out and were daily and/or part-time rather than resident and full-time, fewer maids were available to work during what would now be termed unsocial hours. By January 1943, 'the domestic situation was causing Matron grave anxiety', the local Ministry of Labour adding to her problems by refusing to fill vacancies for 'cooks, general maids and cleaners' unless The Evelyn adhered to new nationally agreed wage scales.

Fluctuating numbers of domestics were paralleled by intermittent shortages of nurses. The Home's continual veering between short periods of being 'well off for nurses' and extending its thanks to Matron 'for having done so well with an inadequate nursing … staff' must have made life very difficult for Matron and staff alike. To add to the problem, there was a nurse-rationing system in operation, the Ministry of Health's quota for The Evelyn being thirteen trained nurses (including

administrative sisters) and fifteen assistant nurses. That nurse numbers at The Evelyn dropped during the war is shown by a comparison of the 1946 figures with those of October 1942, when the Finance sub-committee had counted five 'assistant nurses' and twenty-seven nurses, the latter including six sisters; there were also five outside nurses, now exclusively college nurses.

The Evelyn's own nurses, overworked and short-handed though they were, were cheered by the results of the Royal College of Nursing's 1930s campaign for improvements in the recruitment, training, pay and working conditions of the nursing profession. Discussions between the House and Finance sub-committees resulted in the announcement of a 'New Scale of Nurses' Pay' whereby salaries rose by £10 to £35 a year, depending on grade. Estimates of what this would cost the Home ranged from the House sub-committee's £585 'approx' to the Finance sub-committee's £700 'at least', with both agreeing that to cover this the cost of the cheapest rooms should be raised to 6 guineas a week.

A further shock to the sub-committees occurred in 1943 with the publication of the Rushcliffe Report on nurses' salaries. The Evelyn, although initially dismissive of its recommendations, describing them as 'especially formulated for hospitals', nevertheless adopted a modified version of them on 1 October after a quick check with other nursing homes to see if they were doing likewise. The Annual Report of 1 March 1944 noted the inevitable: the salary bill had gone up by £1,500 p.a. and would continue to increase on 1 April each year, the Rushcliffe Report having recommended a uniform annual incremental date. In 1945, the report continued, the salary bill would amount to just over £6,000 p.a., with further rises set for 1946 and 1947.

Although fees earned by the Home in 1944/5 amounted to £18,224, it began once again to feel financially pressured, with nurses' pay a continuing cause for concern.

To cheer everyone up and with the end of 'the difficult war years' in sight, Miss Fynes-Clinton asked the House sub-committee for permission to hold a Victory Dance 'possibly at the Dorothy', a popular social centre in Cambridge at that time. The sub-committee paid £30 towards the cost, the Sickness and Benefit Fund the remaining £20; the dance was held 'in the big ballroom of the Dorothy Cafe' on 10 October from 9 p.m. till 1 a.m. and was voted by all 'a great success'.

A Return to Normal Working

THE END OF THE WAR brought about a literal as well as a metaphorical lightening of the spirits to the weary Home. Beginning as early as March 1945, 'blackout' was stripped from the windows, the blast walls protecting the air-raid shelter in the nurses' dining room were taken down, and a programme of complete internal and external renovation and redecoration begun. The programme began in 1945 and ended in 1949, during which time every corner of the building was revitalised.

'Post War Reconstruction of the Home' was planned as early as 1943. In September 1944, a Reconstruction sub-committee was set up with a view to making 'investigations and recommendations for the post-war Home'; the doctors were invited to present any 'suggestions and requirements' they too might have. Matron herself was noted to be very keen on 'formulating post-war plans', some of which came to rapid fruition; others took rather longer to achieve. But with renaissance in the air, it is pleasant to note a visit which occurred on 13 February 1948: Viva Cooke, widow of the man without whom 'it would never have been started', brought 'young Mr Agnew' (he was actually 37) to view the Home founded by his grandfather. Geoffrey Agnew, the erstwhile schoolboy who so vividly remembered visiting his post-operative grandmother in the 'black hole' of Thompson's Lane, was reported as being 'much interested' in what he saw.

The war may have been over, but The Evelyn soon had another battle to fight. Intimations first appear on 13 March 1947, when Mrs Mellish Clark received a letter from Dr French, County Medical Officer of Health. This was in reply to one sent by her to him a few days previously following the House sub-committee's decision 'to try to learn the future of Homes like The Evelyn under the new bill'.[1] Dr French's letter ran as follows:

Dear Mrs Clark,

In reply to your letter of March 9th I have now discussed the position of The Evelyn Nursing Home when the National Health Service Act comes into operation … It appears that the Ministry has not definitely made up its mind as to what it will do with regard to nursing homes of this type. They started by assuming that they would not be touched under the Act, and then changed their minds with the idea that they would be included under the buildings to be appropriated as hospitals by the Minister. Now they have gone back to the original position but no official decision has been taken … With regard to your second question … even if the Ministry does not decide to take over The Evelyn Nursing Home at the outset it would be open to the Nursing Home Committee to apply for the Home to be taken over at any date subsequent to the coming into force of the Act. It does not of course automatically follow that the Minister would agree to take it over … but it can safely be assumed that he would not allow a place like The Evelyn Nursing Home to go out of use in view of the existing shortage of hospital beds …

A letter from the Ministry of Health dated 24 September 1947 proved more alarming: 'On the information at present before him the Minister is of the opinion that The Evelyn Nursing Home, Cambridge is transferable to him and he has so advised the Regional Hospital Board.' The Evelyn, believing that conscription to the National Health Service (NHS) was imminent and unavoidable, called two Special Meetings of the Committee of Management, attended by Gerald Agnew. It subsequently transpired that had the Home read the Minister's original letter more attentively, it would have realised that 'under Section 6 (3) of the Act the Minister has the power to disclaim any hospital, the transfer of which would not be required', and that were it to apply for exemption it would be likely to achieve it. This meant that The Evelyn had the

---

1. The National Health Services Act 1946 inaugurated a state-run health service free to everyone in the country at the point of service.

choice of being taken over subject to the Minister making 'certain concessions' or, if it preferred, not being taken over 'in any circumstances'. The Home made the decision to remain independent.

The coming of the NHS was a blow from which The Evelyn took the best part of three decades to recover. Unprepared for its arrival – there is no mention of it in the Home's records previous to the correspondence just quoted – the Home had given no thought to the consequences of this event for private medicine. In fact, full realisation of the consequences only came about two years later in October 1949, when the Finance sub-committee, concerned about rising prices and a drop in income, counted up the number of operations performed at The Evelyn in the years immediately following the arrival of the NHS. To its dismay it discovered that whereas in 1947/8 1,046 operations had been carried out, in 1948/9 only 802 had been performed, a drop of 25 per cent.

Another destabilising occurrence was the post-war departure of stalwarts who had supported the Home in various capacities for longer or shorter periods. While this brought about an infusion of new blood, it also meant that The Evelyn was deprived of people experienced in its running.

The kitchen, supported so efficiently by Mrs Harvey, saw her departure in 1945. This coincided with a sharp rise in catering costs, owing to the loss of her provisioning expertise, to an increase in the number of resident nurses and domestics, and to a post-war growth in the cost of commodities. Although this last-named cost was still offset by the Home's own garden produce, the cost of staff and patients' food per head per day rose from 2s 3d in 1947 to 3s 0d in 1949. To make matters worse, by July 1948 the 'kitchen situation' was 'very grave', especially at breakfast and supper, following the resident Cook's departure. The situation was saved by a member of Miss Fynes-Clinton's own family – as the House sub-committee reported, 'Matron's sister is kindly cooking for us and doing so very satisfactorily.' As late as June 1949, however, the Home still lacked a 'Head Cook', the sub-committee's advertisements in England and Scotland not having produced a suitable candidate; could the Home, it begged, look abroad to find a 'well-educated German' to fill the post?

In 1946, the Finance sub-committee noted with dismay that

Matron was 'putting in' for other posts; that she was persuaded to stay is obvious – and fortunate. She was even invited to attend meetings of the House sub-committee for more than just the reading of her report. The post-war period also saw the departure of long-serving members of the nursing staff, some with over twenty years' service, and of members of the Home's committees and sub-committees, some of whom – like the Mellish Clarks – had supported The Evelyn since its inception. A typical retiree was Gislingham, the Home's porter and radiographer manqué. Born in 1881, Gislingham started work at the infant Evelyn in 1922. Throughout the war, though in failing health, 'Gizzy' (as he was called) carried out the work of two men. Apart from portering and looking after the Home's coke boilers, his duties included emptying slop buckets and dirty-dressing pails, cleaning patients' boots, bathing and shaving male patients, and attending the surgeons in theatre. For this he was rewarded with every other weekend off duty from 12 noon on Saturday to 8 a.m. on Monday and 50s 0d a week 'on condition [he] was helpful and agreeable to the staff' – which was not always the case!

The third post-war problem faced by The Evelyn was the conversion of Brookfield into a nurses' home. The decision to proceed was influenced by the following factors:

a) the Home still felt bound by the promise made in the *Memorandum of Association* to provide 'houses or accommodation' for its nurses, swollen though their number was since the *Memorandum* was drafted;
b) it was still very much the fashion for nurses to be resident at their place of work;
c) it was believed that the lure of cheap and pleasant accommodation would encourage nurses to apply for posts;
d) it was thought that nurses attracted to The Evelyn by its provision of accommodation would be full-time staff amenable to shifts involving the working of unsocial hours, which – it was becoming evident – married part-timers who lived out were not.

A bigger nurses' home would have two further benefits: first, departure of the nurses from The Orchard meant that house could be wholly given over to domestic staff, more of whom could then be housed on site to the Home's advantage; and, second, relocation of nurses would clear rooms in the Link Building for conversion to patients' use.

Why, we may ask, was the Home so anxious to open more patients' rooms, when it was, virtually at the same time, touting for custom? The answer is threefold: first, to answer the colleges' criticism that undergraduate rooms were frequently unavailable (the Link Building rooms were very small but would serve admirably for emergency beds); second, to increase the Home's income overall at a time when the advent of the NHS and the addition of Brookfield to its properties were having a dramatically deleterious effect on its finances; and, third, because in spite of a drop in surgical patients occasioned by the arrival of the NHS, the Home was in the strange situation of needing to open more rooms to reduce its (medical) waiting list and to enable it to admit even more non-surgical patients. The reason for this was that, although the bed-occupancy figures remained high (in March 1946, for instance, the average number of patients per day stood at 37 out of a possible 43, and this figure did not greatly diminish in the later 1940s), the medical and long-stay patients who occupied the beds did not generate anything like the same income as surgical patients. This was because, on the one hand, loss of fees for dressings and time spent in theatre; and, on the other, because long-stay patients often had a proportion of their room fees remitted. This meant that even more non-surgical patients had to be admitted in order for the Home to keep itself financially afloat.

There were, of course, certain disadvantages in taking over Brookfield, as the minutes of the House sub-committee of 21 March 1947 foretold. These took the form of additional expenditure on services, insurance, maintenance and rates, and on the wages of a caretaker and cleaners. There would also be loss of rental income and, because of the greater number of both nurses and domestics resident in the Home, an 'extra strain on the kitchen'.

In July 1947, the plans for the Brookfield conversion were put out to tender. Work started in October 1947 and was completed by the middle of February 1948, four nurses being installed in Brookfield as early as September 1947 and five more joining them in November with further conversion ongoing. In July 1948 the Annual General Meeting reported that twenty nurses were now living in the fully converted and redecorated house.

Percy and Dorothy Willis, caretakers of Brookfield Nurses' Home, on their wedding day in August 1947. Their reception was held at The Evelyn.

Unfortunately for The Evelyn, the 'reasonable cost' of conversion originally envisaged was soon exceeded. The cost of labour and building material went up and conversion of an older property brought to light unforeseen problems: 'essential repairs to the slate roof', the fitting of a new mains cable because the existing cable was inadequate for the increased load, and the replacement of the forty-year-old electrical wiring of the first and second floors. To add to the problems, the architect's suggestion that Brookfield's central heating and domestic hot-water system could be run from the Home itself with no loss of efficiency to either establishment was found to be impractical: although a new and larger boiler had been installed, there was insufficient space in the boiler room for the extra pumping equipment needed to service two buildings some distance apart. As a result, Brookfield had not only to retain its independent hot-water system, but in 1948 to have the ageing complex replaced by a completely new one. As if this were not enough, the Ministry of Works refused to allow subdivision of the larger rooms by timber partitions, and more expensive hollow clay blocks had to be used instead. It also seems that

the Finance sub-committee had insisted on 'rather extensive modifications of the original plan'. These, and misunderstandings and lack of control on the part of the architect and building contractor, meant that a conversion initially costed at £1,250 actually cost a fraction over £3,000.

A means of generating income, admittedly on a small scale, was the Pig Club. In February 1949, Matron asked the House sub-committee for permission to keep pigs – accommodation would not be a problem as a 'pig sty had been offered' which could be sited well away from the Home in Brookfield's garden. The sub-committee agreed: 'The formation of a Pig Club with the Matron as ... Chairman. All expenses will be paid by the Club, which will have the use of the sty and the swill from the Home without payment and the Home will get the manure. Profits will be used to provide extra amenities for the Home, and particularly the garden.' Whole litters of piglets were acquired to be raised under the auspices of the Small Pigkeepers Council, with conditions for their welfare laid down in a booklet entitled *Rules for a Canteen Pig Club*.[2]

The Evelyn's Pig Club flourished from 1949 until the early 1960s, with

2. A Canteen Pig Club was defined as a club associated with a factory, school or licensed institution which bought and raised pigs with the twofold objective of using up waste from the organisation's own kitchen and of providing meat for its canteen. That the Home did not eat the pigs it raised is shown by Matron's report for June 1951, which noted that pigs sent to market raised £87 8s 1d.

'Profit on Pigs' appearing regularly in the annual Statement of Accounts. That the club was financially prosperous is shown by the fact that in May 1956 the Pig Fund Account contained £83 4s 5d 'cash in bank', while in March 1959 £149 was put towards the cost of resurfacing the nurses' tennis court. Matron took her duties as chairman seriously; one member of staff's abiding memory is of Miss Fynes-Clinton proceeding majestically towards the sty, Wellington boots on her feet, a swill bucket in one hand and a cigarette in the other …

Matron also appears to have made herself responsible for looking after the chickens, bought during the war, who roamed freely in the garden's orchard area during the day but inhabited a 'Night Ark' at night. It was the night nurses' duty to shut them up – indeed, it was their first task on coming on duty at 9 p.m. One particular evening, the nurse on whom the duty devolved was too busy to do this, and the hens roosted in the trees instead. Matron, discovering them there the following morning, was extremely cross and removed poultry-keeping from that nurse's sphere of responsibility forthwith!

Financial embarrassments notwithstanding, The Evelyn entered the next decade in a spirit of guarded optimism, preparing, after the battles of the 1940s, to settle down for the next two decades to do what it did best – to look after, and with luck deserve the encomiums of, its patients. It was helped in this by an influx of newly appointed consultants which brought fresh faces and medical and surgical innovations to the Home.[3] Surgeons specialising in ENT, general surgery, orthopaedics, ophthalmic surgery and gynaecology and physicians specialising in psychiatry, general medicine, radiology and radiotherapy all came to work in the Home in the years from 1947 to 1949. With them they brought new techniques: 'intravenous therapy', nerve blocks for pain, depot injections, penicillin therapy by injection or by instillation into antral cannulae for the treatment of sinusitis, and electroconvulsive therapy for the treatment of depression. In order that their specialty too might keep up to date, the anaesthetists began pressing the Home to buy its own and more modern anaesthetic machine. They were met, however, with continuing resistance; in December 1947, for example, the Finance sub-committee stated that, because 'the Home had never provided the Doctors with any

3. The new generation of consultants seem to have been rather rowdy. The minutes of the House sub-committee for 22 April 1949 record: 'the doctors … were the worst offenders and these were difficult to check. On the whole the noise was pleasant and good humoured and the Home might suffer if it was checked too rigorously.'

equipment', it was thought that to do so for the anaesthetists 'would set up a precedent and therefore the Doctors should arrange between themselves to buy the requisite apparatus'. (The sub-committee's decision not to buy equipment for the anaesthetists was probably influenced by the fact that other doctors were expected to provide their own instruments, setting out those needed for a particular operation so that the theatre staff could sterilise them.) In February 1949, and in spite of an increase in theatre fees (in which the cost of the anaesthetic was, of course, included) 'to provide a margin against any further expenditure' – as the House sub-committee put it – the anaesthetists were told that the problem was now 'almost entirely one of finance'. Because a new machine would cost nearly £200, the Finance sub-committee had arranged for the existing machine to be 'checked out'; it was found to be 'up-to-date and serviceable for the future'. Proof that this was so is shown by the increased number of patients surviving major surgery (especially bowel surgery), although the introduction of new drug therapies[4] and of surgical specialisation probably also contributed.

---

4. Penicillin, reserved for use in the Armed Forces during the war, was released for use on civilian patients in 1945. From then on, there was a dramatic drop in the number of 'sepsis' cases admitted to The Evelyn, with patients surviving conditions from which they would probably have died before the war. Also, surgery for tubercular glands disappeared with the advent of anti-tubercular medication.

Night Blaze at Nursing Home

16 PATIENTS MOVED TO SAFETY

Tribute by Chief Fire Officer

SIXTEEN patients were moved to safety when fire broke out in the nurses' quarters at the Evelyn Nursing Home, Trumpington Road, at about 9 o'clock last night.

One of them, Mrs. Lily Waring, of Queen Edith's Way, has her 102nd birthday in May this year.

The fire damaged two rooms and part of the roof of the nurses' quarters. Patients in rooms near the scene were moved by members of the nursing staff. No one was injured.

Cambs. Fire Brigade, tackling what was described as "the biggest job for a long time," brought the blaze under control.

The Chief Fire Officer (Mr. Tom Knowles) paid a tribute to the conduct of the nurses.

"They were cool, calm and collected, and completely unflurried," he told the "C.D.N." "They might just have been making a cup of tea."

The Matron of the Home, Miss Q. M. Fynes-Clinton, was at the Arts Theatre, watching "A Midsummer Night's Dream" when the blaze broke out. She was called from the theatre.

"The fire was confined to one and a half rooms in the nurses' quarters," she said to-day. "Sixteen of the patients—we have 50 in the Home—were moved. The fire only affected this 16 and they were taken to another part of the building as a precautionary measure.

"I think," she added, "they will be back in their own rooms later to-day."

Mrs. Waring, one of the patients moved, is the widow of Captain William Waring, of the Mercantile Marine. They were married in 1874. During the last war Mrs. Waring knitted woollens for Servicemen, and one of her knitted scarves was exhibited as an example of the way scarves should be knitted. She was born in Co. Wexford, Ireland.

Mrs. Waring's great-great-grandfather was also an centenarian. He died in 1814 at the age of 111.

Fire Brigade officials this morning visited the blackened burnt-out rooms.

"The damage is so great that it is impossible to say how the blaze started," the Fire Prevention Officer, Mr. W. P. Abbiss, said later.

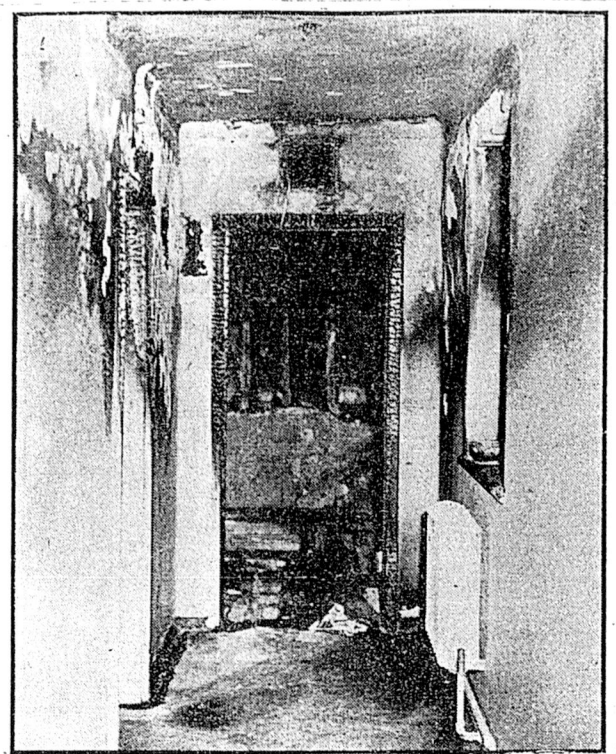

Photo   "Cambridge Daily News"
A picture of one of the gutted rooms, where the fire is presumed to have started.

Nurses and Police Rescue Patients

Fifteen patients in the Evelyn Nursing Home, Cambridge, were lifted on to stretchers and taken to safety by nurses and police when fire broke out on the second floor of the home last night.

NEW SECOND SEA LORD

F

SIR M

The funeral of
place yesterday a
church, Halstead,
Fasson officiated,
the lesson, and th
concluding prayer
mittal. Those pre
Mrs. R. M. Butler,
and Mrs. Middleton (s
Mrs. Richard Butler, M
S. Portal (grandchild
(brother), Mrs. Bernar
Mrs. A. Butler, Mr. a
Norman-Butler, Professo
Mr. Ian Macpherson, M
Leader and Mrs. Karr
Erle Richardson, Colon
Cicely Lady Courtaul
bridge, and Mrs. S. C
(Dean of Pembroke),
Mr. and Mrs. W. S.
Dr. G. D. S. Macl

It was all so Comfortable

The 1950s began with a conflagration. Headlines in the *Cambridge Daily News* told of a nocturnal drama:

> Night Blaze at Nursing Home
> 16 Patients moved to safety
> Tribute by Chief Fire Officer.

The patients, the report continued:

> were moved to safety when fire broke out in the nurses' quarters at The Evelyn Nursing Home, Trumpington Road, at about 9 o'clock last night. Patients in rooms near the scene were moved by members of the nursing staff. No-one was injured. Cambridge Fire Brigade, tackling what was described as 'the biggest job for a long time' brought the blaze under control. The Chief Fire Officer ...

Article in the Cambridge Daily News, *20 February, 1952, reporting the fire that caused serious damage to The Evelyn.*

paid a tribute to the conduct of the nurses. 'They were cool, calm, and collected, and completely unflurried. They might just have been making a cup of tea.'

The Home's Annual Report of 31 March 1952 went into more detail, but was similarly laudatory: 'A serious fire occurred on the top floor of the Home on the evening of 20th February 1952. The material damage was extensive, but although there were 50 patients in the Home at the time, no-one was injured. The behaviour of the Staff was exemplary and received commendation from the Chief of the Fire Brigade. The damage is estimated at nearly £4,000.'

The sixteen patients who were lifted onto stretchers and taken to safety were those housed in the recently converted rooms on the ground and first floors of the Link Building; although their rooms were directly below the seat of the fire, they seem to have been more at risk of drowning than incineration because of the volume of water needed to quench the flames. (In spite of Miss Fynes-Clinton's report to the *Cambridge Daily News* that they had merely been taken to another part of the building as a precautionary measure, her belief that 'they will be back in their own rooms later today' was over-optimistic.) That no-one was injured or killed was fortunate, given that the area was so badly damaged and contiguous parts of the Home were far from unscathed. That the nurses were in some personal danger is shown by claims for items of clothing ruined during the evacuation; for example, '1 pr nylon panties, cost 18/9d'. Exactly how the fire started was a mystery. The Fire Prevention Officer, visiting the scene the following day, noted that the damage was so extensive that it was impossible to say what happened. However, given that the nurse in whose room the fire started was a smoker and subsequently sacked, the probable cause is not too hard to find.

Luckily for the patients, life at The Evelyn was not always so exciting. Indeed for those admitted on a long-term basis it was like living in a cottage hospital, its rooms more often known by the names of their inhabitants ('Miss Finney's room', 'Mrs Usher's room') than their numbers. Although The Evelyn of the 1950s and 1960s always billed itself as an acute nursing home, in practice it was more of a place to recuperate, die, or be resident in, where the food was excellent and work virtually stopped at 5 o'clock.

The permanent and long-stay patients of the decades immediately after the war fell into two categories. The first consisted of those who could, in the words of Miss Fynes-Clinton's successor, afford the rapidly rising fees; the second of those with a University connection admitted at favourable rates in recognition of the now rather tenuous connection between the colleges and the Home. Yet, in spite of asseverations that The Evelyn of this time was filled by large numbers of University people, it was in fact during the 1950s and 1960s that undergraduate admissions fell to below twenty a year, with other University-connected admissions almost exclusively confined to elderly academics *in extremis*. Matron herself collected derelict (and usually unwilling) dons in her car in order to effect their admission on the grounds of physical and/or mental frailty amounting to self-neglect. The Evelyn, however, continued to assert the college connection for all it was worth. In fact, apart from those colleges which continued to underwrite the Home by means of small annual subscriptions (and even these were dwindling), the most active connection between the Home and the University was provided by the tendency of certain undergraduates, following the Bed Race on Rag Day, to dump their no-longer-wanted beds in The Evelyn's garden whence retrieval was arranged by the Proctors.

Well housed though they were, even the more able-bodied residents led rather sedentary lives. After breakfast they were helped to wash and dress by the enrolled nurses (SRNs were reserved for surgical and acute medical cases), following which, apart from visits to the toilet, they sat in their rooms – or in the patients' lounge (formerly the nurses' sitting room), if capable of walking that far. The tenor of their day was punctuated by visits from Matron, by meals, and by trips to the garden if the weather was fine and there were nurses free to take them. In summer they might be wheeled down to the orchard to pick an apple or pear and nurses would show off their party frocks before the summer dance, but it was not until the late 1960s that any effort was made to rehabilitate them. Even then it was acute medical admissions that were rehabilitated and stimulated rather than the permanent patients who created so much of the burden of care. By June 1962, however, with changes in the pattern of admissions and in the Home's use of its rooms imminent, the House sub-committee began to raise the question 'of the number of permanent patients in view of the demands they make on the staff and the blocking of beds for acute cases'. That the 'silting up' of beds by permanent patients was not regarded as much of a problem before the 1960s is obvious, except in so far as the presence of such patients in around 25 per cent of the available rooms meant that it was sometimes impossible to raise room fees to meet a further rise in the nurses' salary bill until a new permanent patient replaced a former one. By contrast, permanent patients were regarded as something of an asset to a nursing home threatened by desertion to the NHS of a large proportion of its surgical patients.

Medical admissions, conversely, covered a wide spectrum of acute and chronic conditions for which new treatments appeared and new diagnostic tools came into use. Psychiatric patients particularly increased in numbers for three reasons: first, the presence in Cambridge of a new generation of psychiatrists who, though they mainly practised at The Hope Nursing Home, also admitted patients to The Evelyn; second, the advent of new treatments, the nature of which ensured that they could be carried out in nursing homes like The Hope and The Evelyn; and, third, because Miss Fynes-Clinton felt that The Evelyn had much to offer psychiatric patients, encouraging doctors to admit them and training up her nurses in their care.

A rapid rise in the cost of rooms for all patients in the early 1960s was occasioned in part by the spiralling wages and salaries bill, and in part (although this may have been both cause and effect) by an equally rapid decline in patient numbers over that decade, August 1969 and March 1970 seeing the lowest number of patients admitted for over twenty years.

Although the early 1960s actually found The Evelyn advertising for patients in the national press and the House sub-committee noting in February 1961 that 'the general problem of the Home is to increase the number of patients rather than limit them', the same period, rather incongruously, witnessed local doctors complaining that they were unable to admit urgent cases because of the limited number of beds available. This curious state of affairs – low bed occupancy figures versus pressure on beds – had come about in part because of the 'silting up' of a percentage of the beds by long-stay and permanent patients; and in part because of a decrease in the number of patients' rooms from 48 in the immediate post-war period to 46 in 1955 and to fewer still in the 1960s. As a result – and in spite of a halving of the figures for surgical admissions from the 1,000-plus of the mid-1940s to 550 a year in the early 1960s – the anomalous situation developed in which there was not enough room in the Home to house all the acute cases requiring admission.

A further factor which complicated the admission of patients to The Evelyn in the 1950s and 1960s was the number of categories into which they fell: acute medical, surgical, psychiatric, respite/permanent, and – as we shall shortly see – maternity. That difficulties arose because of the range of patients admitted is demonstrated by the following factors all having to be taken into account:

1. Some rooms were too small to take a theatre trolley, so it was impossible to put surgical patients into them.
2. Orthopaedic patients needed large rooms.
3. Maternity patients used rooms specially reserved for them on the ground floor; if a maternity bed was empty, no 'dirty' (i.e. infectious or potentially infective) patient could use that room.
4. Patient preference had to be taken into account – patients often asked for a particular room on a particular floor, and even to be nursed by a particular nurse.
5. Psychiatric patients had to be nursed on the ground floor in case they were tempted to throw themselves out of the window.
6. Some short-stay patients had to be housed in one of the smaller rooms because their costs were based on this.

In other words, not just any patient could be put in any room.

Encouraged by the later 1960s' drift of potential private patients away from the NHS, The Evelyn came to the conclusion that one of its most important policies would be to encourage the admission of as many surgical cases as possible. That this would not be easy was soon apparent, chiefly because The Evelyn was not at that time equipped to carry out the increasingly specialised surgery which was becoming commonplace; it was nevertheless keen to emphasise both the high standard of care offered by the Home and that it would be a good idea to involve the surgeons in future considerations of surgery to be performed there.

The extreme specialisation of the 1980s and 1990s not yet having arrived, surgeons working at The Evelyn during the 1950s and 1960s (with some exceptions, particularly in ophthalmic, dental, ENT, gynaecological, and – increasingly – orthopaedic surgery) were still prepared to turn their hand to anything, although this became rarer as the latter decade progressed and surgical techniques became more and more the province of the specialist operator. Major surgery declined markedly but did not altogether cease; minor surgery, on the other hand, increased until the arrival of the 1970s reversed the trend. An increase in day surgery and in the numbers of patients staying for one night post-operatively necessitated the creation of a daily as well as a weekly scale of charges. Very few accident and emergency patients appeared, particularly now that few, if any, undergraduates patronised the Home.

The third largest group of patients admitted to The Evelyn at this time, after permanent patients and those receiving psychiatric care, were those for major and minor gynaecological surgery: more specifically still, termination of pregnancy. It is obvious from the Admission Registers that abortions were performed at The Evelyn well before the arrival of the Abortion Act in 1967 legitimised the carrying out of this operation 'in a hospital vested in the Ministry of Health or the Secretary of State under the National Health Service Acts, or in a place for the time being approved for the purposes'; indeed, the *Cambridge Evening News* description of the Home on 28 April 1970 as 'one of the country's top five private clinics' out of forty-six licensed under the Act was as accurate of its pre-Abortion Act activities as it was of its post-Abortion Act status.

Conditions imposed by the Abortion Act brought benefits to all patients at the Home. In order, for example, for the Home to be approved as a place 'within the independent health sector at which terminations of pregnancy may legitimately be performed', it had to comply with increasingly stringent conditions, some of which were quite expensive to implement. Proprietors of premises licensed to carry out abortions (the licence once granted was regularly reviewed) had to demonstrate that they were equipped to deal with any emergency situation that might develop by carrying out specified pre-operative investigations and by the provision of theatre and other equipment. They also had to ensure the provision of 'medical oversight' of all such patients at all times. The granting of the licence placed limits on the number of this type of operation that could be carried out per day, required that provision be made for an overnight stay if necessary, and demanded written evidence that patients undergoing termination had been examined and certified fit for discharge before leaving the Home. That all the above constitute good medical and nursing practice applicable to all or any patients admitted to the Home is obvious; equally obvious from the minutes of the sub-committees is that it also constituted one of the many instances in the 1950s and 1960s where external legislation forced The Evelyn to update its facilities and practices to comply with the law, something it might well not have done (chiefly on the grounds of expense) had it been left to its own devices.

A presence not formally established at The Evelyn prior to the period under discussion was that of outpatient clinic facilities. Up till then the few outpatients attending the Home were those undergoing treatments ordered by their doctors but carried out by the nurses in whichever room was available; outpatients requiring consultations with the Home's medical users saw them in the latters' private consulting rooms in town. Quite apart from its not then being the custom for doctors to carry out consultations at The Evelyn, there was, until the 1960s, no suitable space for them to use; indeed, it was not until Miss Fynes-Clinton's retirement in 1967 that an ideal one presented itself.

A small flat had been created for Miss Fynes-Clinton on the ground floor of The Orchard following the resident nurses' move to Brookfield in 1947/8. Although somewhat lacking privacy, Miss Fynes-Clinton did not appear to mind interruptions; indeed, she appears to have enjoyed being *in medias res*. Her successor, however, disliked the frequent and often unannounced intrusions (one consultant, entering without knocking, found her in her underwear) as much as she did the flat's small size and lack of amenities. A flat was therefore created for her in Brookfield (Miss McKay, the Assistant Matron, was already resident there) which provided her with a much more secluded and spacious establishment.

The problem then arose as to what to do with her previous quarters. In June 1968 it was suggested that the former flat be converted into 'a suite for an elderly couple not needing nursing but requiring service'. Although ideal for the purpose, given the flat's ground-floor situation and access to the garden, the notion was dismissed in favour of the recommendation that the rooms be rented out 'for consultation purposes'. The sum of £150 was therefore allocated for furniture and fittings, and an advertisement prepared.

In July 1969, the Home was happy to announce that the new suite was being 'quite regularly used' and hopes were expressed that this was the start of an increasing trend. This proved to be the case, Matron's report for March 1970 noting that over one hundred outpatients had been seen in the previous year. Although such numbers seem very small beer in comparison with the thousands of outpatients that passed through the much enlarged outpatient area of thirty years later, it nevertheless proved that the provision of consulting rooms at The Evelyn was worthwhile and might lead to greater things in the future.

Other changes which took place during the 1950s and 1960s involved the upgrading of patients' rooms and the operating theatre, the former because rising room rates were matched by the rising expectations of the rooms' occupants, and the latter because its structural condition constituted a health hazard.

As early as May 1951, the House sub-committee criticised the shabby appearance of the Home, adding that things were actually rather better than they had been because 'the backlog of delapidations caused by neglect during the war years had been dealt with'. Nothing more, however, was done because of the Finance sub-committee's refusal to countenance any decorative or constructional schemes 'until the bank overdraft has been considered'. As a result, neither redecoration nor the purchase of essential items such as electric fires (more of which were

needed as patients 'sat out of bed' earlier following surgery), crockery, furniture, an extra refrigerator, and even new bedpans was possible. In May 1954, the House sub-committee, anxious to improve the appearance and facilities of the Home but mindful that the annual income was down £1,000 on the previous year, suggested a selective increase in room rates to cover these; it was not, however, until a year later (July 1955) that the Finance sub-committee, following the implementation of the 'decision to raise the fees of various rooms', carried out a general survey of the condition and appearance of the patients' accommodation and was horrified by what it found. 'Many of the rooms', its report ran, 'were in a very shabby state … with cracked and crumbling linoleum, fading and shabby curtains and chair covers, thin and worn blankets … and poor quality chipped furniture.' The decision was immediately taken to 'bring at least eight of the rooms up to high standards comparable with the new scale of charges and to improve the general condition of rooms on a sliding scale'. That very little was carried out apart from some sporadic redecoration is evident from a doctor's report of June 1971 in which he criticised The

Evelyn's antiquated accommodation, furniture and equipment, and suggested a more vigorous policy with regard to the provision of up-to-date sanitary facilities, bedding and furniture.

The 1960s, however, saw fruition of a scheme dear to Miss Fynes-Clinton's heart, namely the installation of washbasins in the patients' rooms. Up to that point, the only intimation of activity in this area had been a hint from the Finance sub-committee in October 1950 that, though washbasins were needed in thirty rooms (it was not then intended to install them in all rooms), the Home would have to wait until the Brookfield overdraft was paid off before the project could be started. Eleven years later, the House sub-committee raised the matter of installing washbasins in the rooms on the south side of the Home and more toilets and bathrooms on the north side. Coulsons, asked about the feasibility of the scheme, replied that it was perfectly possible to bring water and waste-disposal systems to the south side of the Home but uneconomical to do it in stages; their estimate of the cost was £1,500. By early 1962, the decision had been taken to install washbasins in all rooms, and Coulsons were asked to

review their estimate; this came to between £4,000 and £5,000, later amended to £7,827 to include other plumbing work and the conversion of the boilers from coke to oil firing. Unfortunately for the patients, a sum of this magnitude was felt by the Finance sub-committee to be inconceivable 'in the present financial circumstances'; it also felt that, because the work would entail the temporary closure of many rooms, 'it might be more expedient if the Home … were closed completely … while the work was carried out', something it could ill afford to do, given the fragile state of its finances. For once, both sub-committees agreed; the decision was taken not to go ahead with the scheme, partly on the grounds of cost and partly because room closures for an extended period would be unavoidable and uneconomical.

Notwithstanding urgings to the contrary from individual members of the House sub-committee, it was not until February 1964 that the sub-committees' collective mind was wonderfully concentrated by the County Medical Officer of Health's criticism of the lack of washbasins, and by the fact that registration by the County Council (acting under the provisions of the Nursing Homes Act) would only be granted subject to certain conditions, one of which was the installation of washbasins in all rooms.

It was not, however, until March 1966 that the Annual Report was able to announce that a sub-committee had been appointed 'to consider the question of installing washbasins … and it is hoped that this work may be shortly undertaken'. It was. Matron's Report for July 1966 announced that Coulsons had quickly started on the 'Basin Programme' (there had been one '*very* noisy day'); luckily only four rooms at a time were out of commission, although there was naturally a drop in patient numbers while the work was in progress. All basins were in position by September and in use by 10 November, the Committee of Management extending its thanks to 'Matron and all Staff' on the occasion of the Annual Report of March 1967, adding that 'but for their devoted service there could well have been a complete breakdown of nursing facilities'.

The operating theatre, too, was in a bad state: by the early 1950s ominous cracks had appeared in the area of the window (later reports spoke of subsidence), and so bad had cracks in the walls and floor become by April 1970 that they constituted a bacteriological hazard, according to the Addenbrooke's bacteriologist called in to inspect them. Throughout the 1950s and 1960s repeated references are made to the dilapidated state of the theatre fabric – the glass skylight leaked, steam from the steriliser caused paint to peel off the walls, the window blinds ceased to function, the anaesthetic room sink was reported to be badly chipped, pipes snaking up the walls had to be boxed in the interests of hygiene and safety, and so on. The Theatre precincts too posed problems: the flooring immediately outside had become 'rotten', while in 1969 the lift gate was declared obsolete and was replaced at a cost of some £1,500 to comply with new legislation.

The siting of the theatre over the kitchen not only caused the area to become very hot – which it tended to do anyway, because of the sun shining in through the glass roof and because of the presence of the autoclave and steriliser virtually in the theatre itself – but also posed problems of infection. Opening the windows let out the heat but let in flies (fly-swats were provided!). It was not until early April 1970 that butter-muslin screens were applied to replacement window frames to ensure that some fresh and fly-free air could enter, but promises of a more effective and more modern system were forgotten when the advent of cooler weather in October made the matter less urgent. Opening the windows brought into view the flies' breeding and feeding grounds – the numerous small dustbins in the courtyard below (which the council refused to empty until they were replaced with larger commercial models) and the rubbish dump with its cargo of bottles and tins. There was, too, the not-far-distant presence of the pigs and chickens whose food was collected by Miss Fynes-Clinton from the back door of the kitchen immediately below the theatre windows.

Problems also arose because of ageing equipment, especially those vital items the steriliser and autoclave. Their frequent malfunctions were due in part to The Evelyn's policy of buying second-hand articles in a misguided attempt to save money, in part because no arrangements were made to have them serviced, in part because of a 'general carelessness and lack of efficiency' among the theatre staff, and in part because of circumstances beyond The Evelyn's control – for example, the Home's and Cambridge's original supply of soft water was supplemented at this time with hard water from artesian wells which caused scaling in the pipes, damage to heating elements, and holes to develop in the Home's 'George V plumbing'.

The autoclave, though not of Aston Webb vintage, resembled an enormous pressure cooker into which metal drums of material to be sterilised were placed. The lid was screwed down, and gas burners were lit underneath. Not surprisingly, it regularly blew up. There are several references in the House sub-committee's minutes of the time to sterilisation having to be done elsewhere. Peri Gwyther, appointed Theatre Sister in May 1963, managed during her short tenure of the post to have both autoclave and steriliser replaced; unfortunately the replacement autoclave soon proved both noisy and unreliable.

Finding sufficient nurses to staff the theatre was a perpetual problem during the 1950s and 1960s. The 'prehistoric' conditions may have been a causative factor, as also may have been the fact that, although a wide range of surgery was carried out, comparatively little work (i.e. between forty and fifty cases a month) actually took place. Additional factors may have been as follows: operations took place throughout the week, with surgeons operating on Saturdays and Sundays because they were not occupied at Addenbrooke's at those times and, as a result, the theatre staff found it difficult to take time off; the staff were permanently on call for emergencies, which made any form of social life difficult; and the theatre was run with a very small staff, which mattered more and more as the numbers of minor cases increased in the later 1960s and major and minor cases in the early 1970s, so that many hours' overtime became the norm. Two further factors increased the workload: first, all sterilising was carried out by the theatre nurses themselves; second, if the Home's sole porter was too busy to bring patients to theatre, the theatre nurses had to collect them themselves. It is nice to note that, in spite of this, more than once the Theatre Sister in post was 'congratulated on the running of the department'.

Requests made by some Medical Practitioners in Town

PATIENTS PATRONISING The Evelyn during the 1950s and 1960s expected and received much tender loving care; for a brief period too those two decades also made available to them more extensive radiological investigations than those hitherto provided by the Home's elderly fixed chest X-ray apparatus and the ageing, low-powered portable machine used exclusively for emergencies. In spite of the fact that, from 1944 onwards, there had been considerable pressure from physicians working at The Evelyn for the installation of more modern radiological equipment, prior to the installation of such equipment in 1956 patients requiring anything but the most basic radiological investigations went to Addenbrooke's, or to the private radiological clinic run by Dr Richard Berridge in the basement of the Parkside consulting rooms which he shared with a small group of surgeons and physicians.

In the early autumn of 1954, Dr Berridge expressed his willingness to move his private practice from Parkside to The Evelyn, conditional on suitable accommodation being provided and a reasonable rent agreed. Lengthy negotiations took place and rearrangement of rooms at the far end of the ground-floor corridor was required in order to accommodate Dr Berridge's requests for an X-ray room and contiguous darkroom before anything approaching an X-ray department transpired. It was not, indeed, until 15 March 1956 that the House sub-committee was able to inform the medical users that the unit was open. The Annual Report of 31 March announced that 'the X-ray is now fully working'. 'Fully' was unfortunately an exaggeration, for almost immediately operational and other problems arose which were to bring the unit to a premature close.

The first problem that beset the unit was underuse. On the one hand, the hoped-for attraction of patients to the Home by the new facility did not take place, the Finance sub-committee reporting that only eight patients a month were making use of it – adding that 'Matron thinks that none of them came because X-ray facilities were available'; indeed, it seems that only inpatients requiring radiological investigations during their stay in hospital were treated there. On the other hand, and as early as December 1956, suggestions were made that Dr Berridge himself was not making the fullest possible use of the Home's equipment, but was taking patients to Parkside instead. The House sub-committee, anxious that maximum use be made of equipment installed at considerable expense and after repeated requests 'by a number of consultants and doctors', asked that only in exceptional cases should a patient be removed from the Home's unit to Parkside.

The problems posed by Dr Berridge's difficulties in running private radiological practices on two separate sites and by a demonstrable lack of outpatient radiological referrals culminated in the Finance sub-committee's reporting that 'the apparatus was not being used as frequently as anticipated'. Cessation of all but the most rudimentary radiological investigations came about in January 1961, when an essential part broke on an item of equipment brought to The Evelyn by Dr Berridge himself. Dr Berridge stated that he was willing to provide radiological services to the Home only if the latter paid for a replacement item. The Home refused, and Dr Berridge was asked to remove equipment belonging to him, the Home defraying the expense. The Annual Report for 31 March subsequently noted that 'The X-ray room has been adapted as a small maternity ward.'

Although, as we know, obstetric cases had been admitted to The Evelyn for some time, most deliveries took place at home or in one of the several nursing homes in Cambridge that specialised in maternity care. It was not, therefore, until 1951 that The Evelyn first made formal provision for such cases, its reason being the impending closure of the Stella Maris Maternity Nursing Home nearby. The sudden closure of the maternity home in November 1951 meant that women whose babies were due in that and the following month had to be admitted to the Home as 'very special cases' – for whom no provision had been made other than Matron's emergency purchase of equipment from the Stella Maris itself.

Maternity admissions continued on a rather *ad hoc* basis until April 1955, when the House sub-committee, finally identifying 'a real need for maternity beds in Cambridge', decided to establish a proper unit on the ground floor. The unit, officially opened in September 1955, soon became the victim of its own success. A year later it was described as 'overfull', with thirty cases 'successfully nursed', twenty booked, and the demand for beds growing. By September 1959 the problem of space had become acute and the decision was taken to expand the unit further into the area shortly to be vacated by Dr Berridge. The unit was to be staffed independently of the rest of the Home by State Certified Midwives, two 'fully qualified' and four 'partly qualified' – that is, having completed only the first six months of their year's training. There was also to be a 'runner' of auxiliary grade. It was expressly stated that the Maternity

Unit staff were not to be supported by the Home staff because of the dangers of introducing sepsis to the unit.

By March 1961, the former X-ray room had been converted into a three-bed ward and 5.5 (*sic*) babies had been born to mothers housed there; in July the unit became fully operational. It consisted of the ward itself, a delivery room with contiguous sluice and sterilising area, a nursery converted from two smaller rooms knocked into one, and dedicated bathroom and toilet facilities created out of what had been the X-ray darkroom. In October 1961, the House sub-committee reported happily that the enlarged unit was in 'full swing', while the Annual Reports of March 1962 and 1963 were able to confirm that the number of babies born in the Home had increased 'by 50%' and 'considerably'. In March 1962 the unit gained its own phone; in 1963 a fridge was provided for pre-prepared bottles of feed, and in September 1964 a small milk kitchen was built at a cost of £176 as the then County Medical Officer of Health disapproved of feeds being made up in the nursery. Charges were linked to the current Maternity Benefit of £17 (later £25) a week. To this were added a 3 guineas charge for use of the delivery room and 2 guineas 'for the Drum' –

the container of autoclaved drapes, dressings, and instruments required for what the Home genteelly referred to as 'The Accouchement'. The Home's decision to publicise the unit widely among the 'Town and Country Doctors' ensured that bookings had to be made months ahead in order to ensure a bed – in May 1962, for example, the unit was fully booked till the end of December – and mothers often overflowed into other rooms, with extra beds put up as required. The 'baby boom' of the early 1960s also put pressure on the enlarged nursery, sixteen babies being born in June 1964 alone. Figures for the financial year 1967/8 showed only five nights when the nursery was unoccupied, the average number of babies accommodated being seven, and one exceptional night showing thirteen.

According to the Central Midwives Board Registers of Cases, preserved in The Evelyn's archives, 3,295 births took place there between 12 September 1955 and 14 December 1973, an average of 183 a year. The unit was immensely popular with mothers who gave birth there or who came there to convalesce after delivery at the Mill Road Maternity Hospital. Everyone spoke well of the care and kindness they received, remembering the unit as a happy and peaceful place with a pleasant nursery. A mother writing to Geoffrey Agnew on the occasion of the unit's closure in 1973 recalled how pleased she was with the care she had received: 'the food was excellent and the staff always cheerful and helpful'. She added that on the last night of her stay, 'Sister suggested that I ring for her when I had finished feeding the baby and I could not find the bell because I had not so far needed it!'

The unit's official status was that of general practitioner delivery unit. It was chiefly manned by a small group of local doctors to whom GPs in the surrounding area referred patients, although in reality any practitioner involved in obstetric work could deliver mothers there. Those most closely involved with the unit had worked as clinical assistants at Mill Road prior to the opening of The Evelyn's own unit – antenatal care was provided in the doctors' surgeries – and enjoyed working at the Home because they felt it was safer to deliver babies there than in the mothers' own homes. Obstetricians were nearby if complications occurred, and the Home was close enough to Mill Road to enable rapid and well-supported transfer of patients in an emergency by

Betty Prior, Maternity Sister 1956–68.

the Flying Squad, a dedicated ambulance service (with a medical element) for obstetric emergencies.

Popular though the unit was with mothers and general practitioners, midwives who staffed it found that there was not enough work to keep them fully occupied or their skills updated. As early as 1962, when the Home was otherwise attempting to offset pay awards and backdated rises by reducing numbers of general nurses, the shortage of staff on the 'Maternity Nursing' side was giving cause for concern. Things had not improved by November 1968, Matron's Report noting that the Home's 'main difficulty … on the nursing side' continued to be the shortage of midwives and the problems experienced in replacing those who left. Matters were complicated further by the Maternity Sister's post being hard to fill because it also involved the running of the Ground Floor Ward with its mixture of medical, surgical and resident patients who were of little interest to the practising midwives the Home hoped to attract.

Although Matron's Report also noted *à propos* the shortage of midwives that the Maternity Unit was 'a successful department which everyone enjoys, and it would be the

greatest pity if it could not continue', the writing was on the wall for other reasons also. By July 1969, for example, numbers of deliveries had halved in relation to those of the early and middle years of the decade, and the unit was rapidly becoming uneconomic. From being a speciality which – together with the permanent patients, psychiatry and certain types of surgery – had kept the Home financially afloat during the difficult years following the arrival of the NHS, the Maternity Unit (which never made large profits) became a financial liability. By February 1973, numbers of admissions had dwindled to fewer than nine a month and the unit's imminent demise was announced. The unit closed on 31 December 1973, the following year's Annual Report noting that 'it was with considerable regret that the Committee finally took the decision to cease to offer this service to the Community but took the view that sufficient advantage was not being taken of the facilities available'.

Closure of the unit had a poignant sequel. The birth of a baby at The Evelyn was an exciting event for the Home's permanent residents, and, following her admission in April 1967, new arrivals had to be taken to be ceremonially inspected by the

Miss Emma Heffer and Joey.

inhabitant of Room 11, Miss Emma Heffer, formerly owner and matron of the Priory Nursing Home in Newmarket Road.[1] With no more babies to inspect, Miss Heffer did not long survive the closure of the unit, dying in her hundredth year early in 1974 while enjoying her favourite food, ice cream; she was found by the nurses with the spoon still in her mouth.

1. Miss Heffer owned a parrot. The bird moved into The Evelyn with her, sitting on her shoulder as she did her morning round (old habits die hard!) of patients on the ground floor.

Unfailing Interest and Guidance

THE EVELYN OF THE 1950s and 1960s ran, as a committee member put it, 'frightfully well in an amateurish way', those concerned having 'enormous fun' and relinquishing their responsibilities only on retirement or because they felt they 'no longer had a useful function'. Management of the Home continued to devolve upon much the same people as before, drawn from the academic, lay and professional community – albeit with the difference that further gaps began to appear in the ranks of those who had served the Home for many years.

Perhaps the most significant departure was that of Mrs Mellish Clark. In June 1958, the Committee of Management announced her resignation ('owing to failing health') from the chair of the House sub-committee (a post she had filled for nineteen years), thanking her for all she had done for the Home and drawing attention 'to the many years during which she had given the Home her unfailing interest and guidance'. Although she continued to act as an ordinary member of the sub-committee for some months longer, the Annual Report of March 1960 had the sad task of making public the fact that:

> the Home has suffered a severe loss in the death of Mrs Mellish Clark O.B.E. She was one of the original signatories of the Home and had been intimately associated with it up to the time of her death. She always had time to spare for the concerns of the Home and her care for the welfare of the patients and staff, and her attention to detail

contributed in no small measure to its success.

She had had the interests of The Evelyn at heart for over forty years; her passing must have seemed like the end of an era.

The end of an era perhaps, but also – it is evident – the beginning of the end of the conservatism which had stifled so many efforts to move the Home forward. Changes did not happen overnight; indeed, it is obvious that tensions often arose between the forces of traditionalism and the newcomers who began to appear about this time to devote themselves to the service of The Evelyn in their turn. These newcomers – often, but not invariably – co-opted from the ranks of those who had already shown an interest in the workings of the Home, included booksellers, builders, engineers, solicitors, architects, teachers and accountants. Their wealth of experience was to contribute in more modern and more practical ways to the pool of experience from which the Home was to draw so much to sustain it in its struggles to escape the difficult years of dormancy in private healthcare and its own battles with rising prices and declining profits.

A further break with the past and the arrival of a force for change occurred in June 1954, following the sudden death of Gerald Agnew. He was succeeded by his son Geoffrey William Gerald (the 'young Mr Agnew' of an earlier chapter), born in 1908 and associated with the family business since leaving Trinity, apart from a spell as assistant history master at Eton, his old school, during the war. That Geoffrey Agnew recognised the importance of neither antagonising nor belittling the efforts of those who had run the Home for so long can be seen from the way in which he, in his own words, assumed his task rather tentatively. For some years, he said, 'though I attended meetings regularly, I sat on the sidelines learning the job'. A powerful man, Mr Agnew came to regard The Evelyn almost as a family enterprise with himself very firmly in charge.

The management structure of the Home continued as before, with *ex officio*, nominated, and co-opted members; an executive Committee of Management; and House, Garden, and Finance and General Purposes sub-committees for day-to-day business; numbers, however, showed either an upward or a downward trend, with *ex-officio* members reduced to four, nominated members increasing with

Miss Fynes-Clinton's retirement party, 18 October 1967. Geoffrey Agnew, Chairman 1954–81, on the left.

1. Although nominated members continued and, indeed, increased in numbers during the 1950s and 1960s, it was a sign of the times that by 1966/7 colleges were beginning to follow Trinity Hall's lead in ceasing to provide financial guarantees.

the post-war appearance of new colleges,[1] and life members dwindling from the thirty-eight of 1921 to the fifteen of the late 1960s. The number of co-opted members, which under the terms of the *Memorandum of Association* was to be eighteen ('of whom three shall always be of the Medical Profession'), alone remained constant.

The Committee of Management too made alterations to its numbers. By March 1965 it had increased from three to five members, for to the original Chairman, Hon. Secretary and Hon. Treasurer had been added a Deputy Chairman and Deputy Secretary. By 1970 the numbers had

further increased, the Committee having exercised its 'power to co-opt', appointing on a permanent basis people felt to be useful to the Home. Certain changes also took place with regard to the structure of the sub-committees, with the aim of increasing their efficiency. The first change took place in 1952/3 with the amalgamation of the House and Garden sub-committees. On 24 June 1964 the House and Finance sub-committees became one sub-committee, to be known as the General Purposes sub-committee.

The 1960s also ushered in changes in the post of Matron. The first intimations of these occurred in

October 1966 when Miss Fynes-Clinton informed the General Purposes sub-committee that she would be retiring the following year. In November 1967 her successor's Monthly Report noted her predecessor's departure on 18 October after twenty-five years as Matron: 'The staff gave a Sherry Party and a presentation was made'. Mr Agnew, on behalf of the Home, presented Miss Fynes-Clinton with a George III silver-gilt oval dish and a cheque for £52 10s 0d, and paid her a compliment worthy of those expressed in her references: 'she has brought an almost superhuman combination of virtues to her task but has managed to remain human as well. She has patience, intelligence, efficiency and a ready sense of humour.' What better tribute could any nurse receive!

The Monthly Report then continued, 'Miss Rendle-Short commenced duties as Matron on October 25th.'[2] She was fortunate in having as her deputy Helen McKay, long familiar with The Evelyn as staff nurse and sister, and Assistant Matron since December 1952; Miss McKay, unwilling to become Matron herself on Miss Fynes-Clinton's departure, nevertheless pledged her support to whoever was appointed her successor.

Miss Rendle-Short's main task, as she saw it, was to organise the booking and admission of patients, a difficult proceeding at any time because of the wide range of specialties and consultant preferences to be catered for and an increasing shortage of nurses. Although nurse shortages had occurred in the 1950s, the 1960s were to justify successive Matrons' complaints that staff were 'very hard to get', with shortcomings in care due to 'the difficulty of obtaining permanent staff' and to the consequent employment of 'temporary nurses from Agencies' whose 'characters and powers' were as unknown to the Matrons of the 1960s as they were to Miss Cracroft in the 1920s. Engaging agency nurses not only created gaps in the continuity of care; as successive Annual Reports noted, it also sent the salary bill soaring.[3] But while earlier shortages had been due to the exigencies of war or to the need to effect a temporary economy in order to offset a deficit, for the Home to be continually short of permanent staff was something new. High staff turnover compounded the problem.

With some exceptions, State Registered Nurses did not stay long – there was little opportunity for promotion or specialisation and no in-

2. Anne Morwenna Rendle-Short was of West Country origins and sister of a consultant gynaecologist. She graduated in history at Bristol University before training as a nurse at St Thomas' Hospital in London. She later became sister on the Private Wing at St Thomas', moving from there to Madrid where she ran a hospital whose standards were rather different from English ones and the work of nurses from leading London hospitals 'greatly admired' in consequence. Offering her the post of Matron at The Evelyn, the Committee hoped she would raise its profile in the private healthcare market.

3. A major contributor to The Evelyn's financial problems was the nationally agreed scale of nurses' and midwives' pay instituted by the Whitley Council. By March 1959, the Home was, as the Annual Report put it, experiencing a 'Working Deficit' due almost entirely to 'the large increase in Nurses' Salaries'.

service training of any kind. But while the nursing standards of the 1950s and early 1960s remained high – each nurse was allocated three or four patients and remained with them throughout their stay, and popular nurses were often asked for by name by patients who remembered them from previous visits – by the mid-1960s complaints from patients, relatives and doctors had become, if not commonplace, at least far more numerous than before. From the doctors' point of view, the standard of nursing had become, as an anaesthetist put it, 'rather more "tender loving care" than scientific skill', particular concern being expressed with regard to 'the aftercare of surgical cases' – as the General Purposes sub-committee put it in September 1968. A general practitioner was more concerned with the difficulty of finding 'any person who knows about the patients' and suggested that the floor sisters 'should not be involved in nursing … as well as the administration of the floor'. The General Purposes sub-committee, considering the matter in April 1967, noted that staff shortages, the shorter working week, and the tendency of doctors to visit very early in the morning or at meal times meant that

it was almost impossible for the floor sister to act in a purely administrative capacity or to be always available for interrogation. Patients' and relatives' complaints stemmed chiefly from the fact that bells were not answered promptly – or at all; to this the sub-committee could only respond that, although bells were clearly audible, the current shortage of nurses was bound to cause delays.

Another task which fell to Miss Rendle-Short was that of ordering patients' meals from lists provided daily by the floor sisters or their deputies. Miss Rendle-Short's orders were then given to the Cook Caterer, who was responsible for organising the food for staff and patients on a daily basis and for ordering provisions according to the current menus. Ordering meals, though time-consuming, did not present Matron with as many problems as did the staffing of the kitchens, in particular with regard to there always being sufficient cooks. Although there were supposed to be two cooks in post, there was sometimes only one – at which point the Cook Caterer was expected to assume the role of head cook. One left in November 1955 because 'she found it too much' to cook and cater at the same time.

The system finally broke down in the summer of 1969 when the coincidence of sick leave and holidays reduced the cooks to the Caterer alone (who was in any case leaving in November, no replacement having been found) and the Home was forced to use an expensive Chef Call Service whose 'temporary man cook' cost 25s 0d an hour. Because the staffing of the kitchen was such a 'difficult and vital issue', the General Purposes sub-committee decided to employ contract caterers, contacting a Leeds firm, Edward Barnett & Co. Ltd, already known to the Home from a visit made by one of their representatives in 1965. It was arranged that the firm should take over the catering on 1 December 1969.

In return for taking over the Home's catering, Edward Barnett & Co. promised close supervision by 'Area Managers, Supervisors, and Travelling Caterers' and managerial staff prepared to 'take a turn on the pastry board' if the need arose, collaboration with Matron and her staff, regular stocktaking, tight budgetary control and the monthly submission of cumulative statements of catering costs inclusive of staff salaries and management fees, negotiation of more favourable trading terms from local suppliers whose custom the Home wished to retain, and the meeting of special dietary requirements. Furthermore, in addition to this 'personal catering service' offering 'minimal costs, staff and catering problems' and 'maximised economy, popularity, and efficiency', Edward Barnett also offered 'the very highest standards of hygiene' and 'the complete release of senior staff from day to day catering problems'.

It all sounded too good to be true. It was. Although Matron's Report for January 1970 noted that the new caterers seemed 'to be progressing quite well', and the Annual Report for 31 March that the appointment of Edward Barnett & Co. Ltd (Caterers) to manage the catering of the Home had 'proved satisfactory both financially and in the standard of meals', problems soon made themselves manifest. In July 1970 Matron's Report noted that 'after a rather unsatisfactory interlude we now have a very good Cook-Caterer'; unfortunately he or she fell ill the following month and the district manager had to take over. A further series of unsuitable Cook Caterers ensued, one of whom left without warning at 8 a.m. on Christmas Eve without completing preparations for the following day. As Matron's Report and the General Purposes sub-committee's minutes for January 1971 recorded, 'Barnett's ... managed to get a replacement by 8pm ... but naturally he had no idea as to the Christmas running of our kitchen.' Miss Rendle-Short herself 'spent an anxious day obtaining cakes, mince pies etc.' (Adding insult to injury, Christmas Eve was her birthday.) Since then, 'there had been relief caterers for short spells but ... not a permanent Caterer'.

Worse still, catering standards were maintained only by the efforts of staff employed before the takeover, vigilance on the part of the Home's own staff was necessary to 'curb some of the greater excesses' perpetrated by the 'singularly unsuitable' Cook Caterers provided, general dissatisfaction was expressed with the quality of the food ('too many sausages' was one complaint) and with the amount of waste occurring, and the cost of catering appeared to have risen rather than fallen. In October 1971, therefore, the decision was taken to terminate the firm's contract, and to revert to 'the previous status quo'. Salvation finally appeared on 21 December in the shape of Doreen Hojsack. Already employed at The Evelyn at the time of Edward Barnett's arrival – the firm had been happy to take on suitable incumbents – Mrs Hojsack was appointed Head Cook in October 1969 on Miss McKay's recommendation, and it was largely thanks to her that kitchen management did not completely disintegrate during their reign. Her appointment as Cook Caterer in 1971 led to comments that 'we are very lucky in having this lady ... with so much energy and enthusiasm for the job'.

Overburdened with too much Land

AMONG THE MANY PROBLEMS which beset The Evelyn in the 1950s and 1960s were those concerning its real estate in the shape of its bricks and mortar and its extensive grounds.

Many improvements which took place in the 1960s had been suggested earlier in connection with The Evelyn's post-war policy of modernisation. Some, indeed, dated back to the 1950s or even 1940s, but had been postponed *sine die* for financial reasons; this was particularly likely to happen if they involved 'substantial construction work', as the Finance sub-committee minutes of 19 October 1950 put it. Two schemes which came to fruition in the 1950s and 1960s were the replanning of the main kitchen and the creation of a new dining room for the nurses. The schemes were, in fact, interdependent;

as the Annual Report for 31 March 1953 said: 'Since the Home was enlarged in 1930 and 1936 it has been realised that the size of the kitchen was inadequate to deal with the increased numbers', but because the siting of the new nurses' dining room next to the kitchen required certain structural alterations to be made to the latter, it was decided to reorganise the kitchen completely at the same time. The Annual Report of 31 March 1954, though happy to announce that 'during the year the new dining room for the Nursing Staff and the alterations to the kitchen premises' had been completed at a sum only marginally over that mentioned in the previous year's Annual Report, also noted that the alterations in particular had caused 'a considerable upheaval which lasted for many months'. Despite the difficulties, 'the … catering and kitchen staff carried on cheerfully, never failing to produce the normal service of meals during the whole period'.

In spite of the problems posed by the physical limitations of the kitchen or by insufficient or unsuitable catering staff, The Evelyn of the 1950s and 1960s was noted for the high standard of its food, incorporation of the Home's 'fresh garden produce from its own garden' being an important part of the menu. No mention was, however, made of garden produce in the Annual Reports after 31 March 1968, which suggests that something happened to affect the prodigious amount of fresh food produced by the Home's gardens prior to that date; indeed, as an Annual Report went on to say, 'the vegetable garden has been relinquished'.[1]

What, we must ask, had happened to a garden which in the early 1950s required the addition of no less than 4 tons of manure, and which continued to be actively planted, which produced excellent crops of apples and pears and such a glut of turnips that 'the Master of Selwyn offered to enquire about the possibility of selling these to the Colleges'? The answer is that in order to finance the post-war improvements to its fabric, the Home

had had to think of ways of raising money other than that of alarming Barclay's Bank by further increasing its overdraft. It therefore decided to capitalise on its real estate by selling some of its land.

Given the current value of freehold land, this seemed an excellent idea, and it was decided to consult the University Estate Management Office regarding the scheme. But before the matter could be taken further, the Finance sub-committee received notification that a land developer, Priory Hall Ltd of London, had expressed an interest in developing the whole of the Newton Road frontage for housing. In November 1956, it was informed that not only was Priory Hall interested but also that it had acquired outline planning permission for both the Newton Road frontage and for the 'back land' beyond it – that is, the Home's kitchen garden and orchard.

Disposal of the Newton Road frontage was problematical because of the restrictive covenant placed on it by Trinity at the time of that college's sale of The Orchard to Morland Agnew, so on 15 June 1957 the Committee of Management authorised only 'the sale of the garden land at the Eastern End of the Home', amounting to 1.423 acres (0.576 hectares), for £7,200. This

1. The gardener at this time was Valentine Brown, so-called because his birthday fell on 14 February. The General Purposes sub-committee, noting the current difficulty of obtaining help for him, decided to acquire more mechanical help in order that Brown would be able to manage the now much reduced garden on his own. Brown himself remained in post until he retired on 29 September 1984.

The gardens c.1960, tended by Val Brown the gardener.

resulted, according to the jubilant Annual Report of March 1958, 'in the current overdraft being repaid' and a certain amount 'becoming available to be spent on improvements to the Home and the Garden'. On 20 August 1958 the Committee resolved that 'the Seal of The Evelyn Nursing Home be affixed to all documents in connection with the sale of the garden land', and the new development was christened Applecourt in honour of its position on the Home's former orchard.

Continuing drains on its income, however, caused the Chairman to emphasise at the June 1957 meeting of the Committee of Management 'the urgent need of the Home for capital'.

In fact, The Evelyn had become locked into a cycle of surpluses and deficits, surpluses veering wildly from £208 to £4,728, and deficits from £421 to £3,395; indeed, the General Purposes sub-committee's statement of 20 May 1968 that 'in a year happily free from any large financial emergency the Home has only just paid its way' supports a committee member's description of The Evelyn of the 1950s and 1960s as 'just about viable'.

In September 1968 the Home's decision to call in an outside adviser indicated both realisation that the situation could not be allowed to continue and a desire to put matters right. The organisation approached was the Nuffield Nursing Home Trust (NNHT), chosen on the grounds that while it had great experience in running nursing homes of its own, it was in no way anxious to take over or become responsible for those to whom it was asked to extend help or advice.

In November 1968, therefore, the General Purposes sub-committee and other representatives of the Home discussed with the company secretary of the NNHT a report issued by that organisation which not only provided a synopsis of the Home's present position, but also pointed the way in which its future was largely to be determined. Noting that the Home's fabric was in a good state of repair and decoration, that the ratio of nurses to patients was 'about right', and that the food was good and the kitchen 'efficient', the secretary went on to suggest, *inter alia*, that:

(a) In order to generate income, theatre fees be increased and the 16-guinea differential between the largest and smallest rooms be reduced 'as the cost of treatment for patients is the same whether they occupy a large or small room'.

(b) An X-ray department be re-established.

(c) Consideration be given to competition arising from the New Addenbrooke's Hospital being built on Hills Road.

(d) The difficulty of obtaining nurses might be overcome by paying them above the Whitley Scale.

(e) Patient diversity be reduced and serious consideration given to the direction in which the Home was to proceed – should it become an 'Old People's Home' (which would be one way of dealing with its 'geriatric patients and geriatric nursing problem') or should it concentrate on acute medicine and surgery?

(f) The Home should take into consideration that 'there were either too many or too few rooms to make the Home an easily manageable or paying unit', and make the decision to either contract or expand in the near future.

g) Brookfield should be 'disposed of' with a view to reducing a major drain on the Home's finances; a corollary would be the re-establishment of the nurses' home on The Evelyn site.

It was, in fact, the last suggestion on which the Home acted first. Since its purchase in 1929, and more especially since its conversion to a nurses' home in 1947/8, Brookfield had either cost or lost the Home money. Frequent major and minor repairs had to be carried out and, although the house's freehold value stood at £7,824 in 1954, upkeep and depreciation remained high in proportion to the building's nominal worth. By January 1959, the Finance sub-committee had begun to ask if it was not 'in the interest of the Home to treat Brookfield as a liability and dispose of the property'. By 1966/7, the idea of selling the Brookfield site was becoming more and more attractive, the Finance sub-committee raising the possibility of selling, if not the whole site – there was the question of where to house the nurses if this were done – but a major part of it, on the grounds that the Home was 'possibly overburdened with too much land'. Opinions differed as to how much should be sold – as little as half an acre was suggested – and on which frontage, Trumpington Road or Brooklands Avenue; but gradually the consensus grew that the whole site should be disposed of and a new nurses' home built somewhere in the grounds of the Home itself.

In February 1969, the General Purposes sub-committee received a letter from January, the estate agents, which ran as follows:

> We have been retained by substantial clients to secure a site for redevelopment in a location such as that occupied by the Brookfield Nurses' Hostel. We appreciate that this property may be fully used but we would like to enquire as to the possibility of the building and land being purchased in the event of an attractive offer being submitted. Our clients appreciate that you will require a substantial inducement to sell plus the opportunity to provide

alternative accommodation in a convenient position …

The sub-committee's response was that it would like to be informed 'as soon as feasible who the prospective purchaser is and for what purpose the site is required'; it would also need to make provision for a new nurses' home at an estimated cost of £30,000. To this January replied that their client, whose name they were not at liberty to divulge, did not have residential plans in mind but would have a very good appreciation 'of the likely figure … involved'. In September 1969, The Evelyn learnt that January's client, shortly to be revealed to be Trust Houses, intended to build a hotel. In January 1970, Trust Houses offered £75,000 for the Brookfield site, subject to contract and the granting of planning permission, with a two-year option on the land; they also expressed a wish to start developing the site as soon as possible.

Later in the negotiations, January's clients indicated an interest in acquiring the *whole* of The Evelyn's 5 acre (2.02 hectares) site, though they understood 'the problems involved in a possible sale of The Evelyn Nursing Home itself' and that the sale might depend on the Home finding another suitable site. The Evelyn, after some rapid mental arithmetic, announced that it would only consider selling if the prospective purchaser were willing to pay £400,000 – £250,000 for a new nursing home, £30,000 for a new nurses' home, and £120,000 to cover expenses and provide some capital for the new venture. Not all members of the General Purposes sub-committee were, however, disposed towards the sale of the Home itself (there seems to have been no argument over the sale of Brookfield), the more businesslike urging that the benefits of a move to a smaller greenfield site (reduced running costs, standardisation of room size, creation of a new operating suite etc.) outweighed any 'sacrifice of the amenity grounds', and the traditionalists emphasising the convenient placing of the Home's present position. A third possibility, that the Home, be rebuilt on a small portion of its current site, was dismissed on the grounds that the £200,000 offered for the proportionately smaller amount of ground to be sold would not cover the cost of rebuilding the Home, even on its own land.

All in all, the early 1970s found The Evelyn in a state of considerable uncertainty as to the direction in which it ought to go with regard to its finances, its clientele and the management of its real estate. It was not then in a position to know that within ten years the situation would have changed completely, with the uncertainties which currently beset it transformed into a spirit of optimism for the future. Luckily, too, it was unconscious of the upheavals – practical, personal, and pecuniary – it would have to undergo as a result of its determination to escape the inertia of the preceding decades. Indeed, had it foreseen in 1970 just how much individual and collective effort would be required to effect that escape, it might have been discouraged from taking up the burdens it was to assume during the decade to come.

The Future of a Large Private Nursing Home Hangs in the Balance

THE FIRST ISSUE to be resolved was that on which many others were to hang, at least in so far as finance and the material development of The Evelyn were concerned: namely, the sale of Brookfield. The sale, unfortunately, took nearly five years to resolve as Trust Houses battled with planning permission, problems of access, and tree preservation orders, not knowing until November 1974 if the site was finally theirs. Further delays then took place while they decided whether or not to take up their option; this they finally decided not to do. The six-year saga came to an end with the Annual Report for March 1975 announcing that 'negotiations are now in hand for the sale to another buyer'. In May 1975, the Granta Housing Association expressed an interest in the site and its desire to

submit an offer. The offer, of £110,000, was accepted and the deal finalised on 22 December of the same year. On 21 January 1976, the Brookfield site was evacuated, apart from some outbuildings which remained in use by The Evelyn until provision was made for incorporation of the services they contained into the fabric of the Home itself. Shortly after its evacuation, the house was demolished, bringing to an end The Evelyn's association with a building which had never lived up to its promise as a 'really good nurses' home' but which had always acted as a drain on its parent institution's finances.

Another cause – and effect – of the Home's state of uncertainty was that in spite of the NNHT's urgings in November 1968 that decisions should be taken with regard to the direction in which the Home should go, the beginning of the 1970s saw it very little farther forward. The impossible situation in which it had been placed by Trust Houses with regard to Brookfield was undoubtedly a contributing factor, but the fact remained that four years later very few of the suggestions made at that time had been implemented.

A small Development Committee was therefore set up 'to consider the future requirements and usage of the Home', and to list 'alterations … or new buildings that would be required as a result of their conclusions'. In addition, visits were made to other East Anglian nursing homes to see how their facilities compared with those extant at or proposed by The Evelyn, and a review of the Home's own premises was commissioned in order that up-to-date advice could be taken with regard to the carrying out of proposed alterations and/or the creation of new buildings. As a result of the Development Committee's deliberations, the General Purposes sub-committee was able to announce on 22 November 1972 the decision that 'a long term plan for the modernisation of the Home, coupled with a financial policy for the redevelopment' would shortly be drawn up.

But before either modernisation or development could take place, the Home had to work out how to pay for them, for one of The Evelyn's current quandaries was that pertaining to its financial situation and the relationship of this to the prevailing national financial climate.

Some of the factors affecting the Home's finances during the early part of the 1970s have been mentioned already: the delayed sale of Brookfield and the closure of the uneconomic Maternity Unit, which, we must remember, did not take place until December 1973. Added to these was the marked decline in patient numbers for the period 1967 to 1971, in part because of a deliberate policy to reduce patient numbers in order to reduce the nurses' salary bill, in part because self-financing permanent patients left because they were no longer able to afford the fees, and in part because of the Home's tendency to run on rather gentlemanly lines (good for public relations but not for financial stability). This last led in 1974 to patients' unpaid accounts having mounted to £9,000 or, as its accountants pointed out, to the equivalent of some six hundred patient nights not having been paid for. As if this were not bad enough, 'inflationary tendencies', as the General Purposes sub-committee described them in April 1972, were increasing. The rapid inflation of the time was perhaps the Home's biggest financial bugbear, especially as it was about to embark on an ambitious building programme at a time when costs were rising annually 'by an enormous proportion'. The 'generally inflationary situation of rising costs of all the activities of the Home' also affected more than alterations and additions to its property – on 1 April 1973 the Home's rateable value rose overnight from £2,040 to £7,880, while a 30 per cent increase in wages and salaries in 1974 ('long overdue' the sub-committee noted, but happening nevertheless at an inconvenient time for the Home's budget) meant that this and general inflation of 15 per cent added an extra £40,000 to £50,000 to the Home's required income at a time when such a sum loomed large in proportion to its current income of £250,000 to £300,000.

But before the Home could move forward with its plans for the future, one further problem remained to be solved, namely under which Matron's leadership the move would take place.

The 1970s was to be the first decade in its history in which The Evelyn was administered by no fewer than three such senior nurses – Miss Rendle-Short, Miss McKay, and Miss Gwyther. Miss Rendle-Short began the decade by tendering her resignation on 20 July 1971 following a short period of ill-health. Her resignation was accepted and she left on 31 August, one of the sisters taking over the running of the Home pending Miss McKay's return from holiday on 13 September. Miss McKay, who on Miss Fynes-Clinton's departure had professed herself unwilling to become Matron, was prevailed upon to take up the reins this time, 'willingly', as the Annual Report for March 1972 put it – or, as she herself said, 'when I took over (without option) the post of Matron'.

Miss McKay, only a few years from retirement, and feeling the need of support from a younger and familiar colleague, asked Miss Gwyther, then working at St Bartholomew's Hospital in London, to join her as her deputy with a view to taking over as Matron when she herself retired on 31 January 1975. Miss Gwyther, who had been Theatre Sister at The Evelyn for a short time during the 1960s,[1] agreed and was appointed Matron on 1 February 1975, albeit not without

1. Ann Peregrine Gwyther (always known as Peri) trained at Addenbrooke's Hospital. On completing her midwifery training in Ipswich she returned to Addenbrooke's, where she worked in the operating theatre. After her short spell as theatre sister at The Evelyn, she worked in Australia as a theatre nurse, undergoing, as she said, some unusual 'theatrical' experiences there. Returning to England, she worked briefly at St Peter's Hospital before taking up the post of theatre sister at St Bartholomew's, which she left to rejoin The Evelyn.

Miss McKay's retirement party, 31 July 1975. Left to right: Miss McKay, Miss Fynes-Clinton, Miss Gwyther.

expressing a concern that she was both inexperienced in hospital administration and about to step into the shoes of two illustrious and long-serving predecessors. She promised, however, to 'endeavour to do my best for The Evelyn' as it embarked on what the Annual Report of March 1973 called 'a heavy programme of modernisation'.

Miss Gwyther, inexperienced at administration though she may have been, grew rapidly into her new role, standing no nonsense from the doctors and being particularly supportive to the nurses and theatre staff. (She also recommended that equipment be bought to make the running of the Home easier – bedpan washers, dishwashers, washing machines, and vacuum cleaners, the use of the latter having been abolished some years before in the interest of quietness!) Shortly after taking up her appointment, Miss Gwyther married – rather appropriately in view of the Home's University connections – Arthur Mundell, who was shortly to become Administrator of King's College Chapel, thereby gaining both a new surname and the distinction of being The Evelyn's first married

Matron. In 1977, so well was the Home running that she was able to become non-resident, leaving, as the General Purposes sub-committee put it, 'a very competent staff who can all cope in her absence'.

To assist the new Matron and 'in view of the increased activity of the Home', the Committee of Management decided 'to appoint an administrator to take full time responsibility for the administration of the Home under the direction of Matron'; on 1 October 1975 Wing-Commander Peter Finlayson was selected to fill the post. The future Administrator's job description was all-embracing. He was to be 'personally responsible' for the following: general administration; 'maintenance of all accounts'; maintenance of staff records and pay scales; contracts of employment; supervision of all building and maintenance work and contracts, including the grounds; ordering, safeguarding and issuing of stores; supervision of catering (he was not expected to take a turn on the pastry board!), 'servicing the Committees'; and dealing with any outside agencies connected with the Home. Wing-Commander Finlayson himself described the Administrator's role as that of 'Grand Housekeeper' in charge of everything which did not pertain directly to nursing matters (except in so far as these might touch on matters covered by his job description), which remained the responsibility of Matron. It was not an easy role to assume for, as he said, he was expected to 'take the administrative weight off Matron' while at the same time 'looking to her for everything' because she herself remained in overall charge. Luckily for him, Wing-Commander Finlayson was supported by a first-class committee that he could always apply to. The General Purposes sub-committee of the time, though unwieldy in size, contained 'a professional in every aspect' so that an Administrator more experienced in the management of squadrons than of sterilisers (he regarded The Evelyn, he said, as a very large aircraft with an equally numerous crew!) could easily make the necessary formal or informal contacts if need arose. Physicians and surgeons on the sub-committee helped with medical matters and a gossip in the kitchen provided useful inside information.

Agnew House, 1976.

In the Spirit of Hope rather than Certainty

UNCERTAINTIES OF ALL KINDS notwithstanding, the Home of the early 1970s had become imbued with a desire for progress and reform. The way forward, as it saw it, was to embark on a building programme which would prevent it from fading away as a geriatric home, to which end a Building Committee was formed with a view to preparing 'a 3, 4, or 5 year phased programme'. This, dependent as always on 'the financial situation', would, with luck, result in the carrying out of a 'masterplan of improvement' and the transformation of The Evelyn into an acute private hospital.

The Home's priority once the sale of Brookfield had been decided upon was to build a new nurses' hostel somewhere on The Evelyn site. A planning application submitted to the local planning committee in January 1972 was passed by that body in November, and the Home decided to go ahead with the construction of the new hostel, even if this meant borrowing the money with the hostel itself as collateral. It therefore asked for detailed plans to be prepared and formal planning permission applied for. In October 1973, the NNHT generously announced that it was prepared to lend the Home the sum of £35,000 'on very advantageous terms'. The loan enabled the Home both to work out a budget and to proceed with detailed plans in the knowledge that it could start work on the hostel regardless of the timing of Brookfield's disposal or to whom it was eventually sold.

But where in The Evelyn's grounds was the new hostel to be built? The site chosen was almost exactly that proposed in 1926–9 'to the south of the Old House' but later dismissed in favour of the Link Building. During the course of 1973/4 the Building Committee, as the Annual Report for 31 March 1974 recorded, 'met on a number of occasions with their architect, Mr David Thurlow … and completed plans for building the Nurses' Hostel'. In February 1975, in the spirit of hope rather than certainty which characterised so much of the Home's endeavour during the decade, the proposed Hostel was put out to tender and the suggestion made that it be called 'Agnew House'. The foundation stone was unveiled on 8 October of the same year and, although some minor works awaited completion, resident nurses were able to move in early the next year, the Annual Report for 31 March recording that 'the new Nurses' Hostel is now occupied and the greatly improved conditions are already benefiting the nursing staff'. Following the nurses' move to Agnew House, domestics currently resident on the first floor of The Orchard were relocated in order that their rooms could be converted into further consulting rooms.

Agnew House's design followed very closely that of the domestic architecture undertaken by David Thurlow in the late 1960s and early 1970s in and around Cambridge. This was especially apparent with regard to patterns of fenestration such as irregularly placed, or recessed dormer, windows; to roofs which sloped more steeply and more closely to the ground on one side than the other, this being as evident inside the building as out; to white-painted outer walls; and to the extensive internal use of exposed timber. In plan it pursued a diagonal course across an imaginary square, two rectangular blocks of rooms at opposite 'corners' joining at a square front porch (divided crossways by the glazing of the entry) facing Trumpington Road; a lobby led diagonally through the point at which the blocks approximated to open onto a square glass-enclosed stairwell overlooking the garden. The house contained within this dynamic design two flats and twelve bedsitting rooms, all of which faced south or south-east and overlooked either the lawn or the trees and shrubs bordering Newton Road. Most were well away from the comings and goings of traffic in the car park and along Trumpington Road, for the north side contained only bathrooms and kitchens, a service room, a utility room, and the separate

Designed by David Thurlow and built within a year, Agnew House was ready for occupation by 1976.

*Imaginative features of the exterior design
at Agnew House.*

entrances and bedroom windows of the two flats.

Agnew House's external appearance was striking. It is best gauged from a description which appeared in the *Cambridge Evening News* of 12 December 1976, quoting the judgement given by the Royal Institute of British Architects on the occasion of the building receiving the only full RIBA award in East Anglia: 'the white painted brickwork, stained timber trusses, and grey slate roof have been elegantly detailed and very well built; although these materials are frequently seen in combination they have rarely been used with such freshness'. The judges also noted the building's 'engagingly inventive interpretation of traditional forms' and the way in which the overall diagonal symmetry was modified 'by some minor asymmetric elements'. An earlier report, of 4 August, also echoed the judges' comments, describing the building as 'an excellent work … worthy of public recognition', which not only displayed 'a fresh approach to the use of traditional materials' but also showed that 'money had been spent in the right places'. The building, it was felt, would both weather well and 'survive a lot of knocks and changes'. The clerestory windows which lit the entrance hall and upper corridors were singled out for special praise, on the grounds that they gave the building a 'refreshing quality and clarity which made it … a cheerful place in which to live'. Sir Leslie Martin, Emeritus Professor of Architecture at Cambridge, presenting the award, stated that 'there was never any doubt' that Agnew House would be the winner; he also congratulated the Home, noting that 'imaginative architecture called for imaginative clients'. Criticisms which emerged later concerned lack of privacy (blinds concealing the long windows at the outer ends of the upper corridors had to be kept permanently drawn if residents were not to be seen *en déshabille*, and the glass-enclosed staircase and porch also posed problems in this respect), Agnew House being in essence a private house built on a site where residents were very much in the public eye; poor insulation (the building was too hot in summer and very cold in winter, and reverberated with noise at any time); uneven floors on the upper storey; and, following the well-known Evelyn tradition, a leaking roof.[1]

With Agnew House completed, The Evelyn was free to concentrate on other aspects of its programme of

---

1. Sad to relate, Agnew House was not used as a nurses' home for very long, modern nurses preferring to live out. During the 1980s and 1990s the building was adapted for administrative and storage purposes and for medical use. See Chapter 19.

Sir Leslie Martin presenting the RIBA award for Agnew House, 30 September 1976. The architect David Thurlow is second from left.

modernisation. In June 1973, Mr Thurlow had been asked by the General Purposes sub-committee to 'establish a brief in relation to the future changes in the Home'. On 1 August Mr Thurlow's plans were 'enthusiastically approved' by the Building Committee and he was asked to proceed with a master plan to be implemented over the following five years. It was estimated that the project in its entirety would cost around £85,000. With this in mind, Geoffrey Agnew, aware that the Home's current financial state would not permit its raising such a large sum entirely on its own, proposed 'a wide appeal for outside finance'. The Annual Report

for March 1975 therefore announced the Home's decision 'to launch an Appeal, and an Appeals Committee was set up'.

It was probably the very concrete nature of the Appeal which was primarily responsible for the measure of its success. No longer would the Home emphasise the precarious nature of its finances by canvassing in a limited and, one must say, rather genteel fashion for financial support of a rather general nature. This time it actively blew its own trumpet by emphasising the value it represented to Cambridge and the vicinity, what it hoped to achieve, and how far it had already progressed in fulfilling those achievements. It had, an Appeal Brochure stated, completed the plans of the new nurses' hostel and was about to start on those for the modernisation of the Home's own buildings, including in this accommodation for a resident doctor, provision of X-ray facilities, and the upgrading of the existing operating theatre by, *inter alia*, the addition of a recovery room. A brochure of 1976 went even further: the nurses' hostel (Agnew House) and X-ray department were completed, 'modernisation and general improvement' of specific areas of the Home were in hand, and forecasts (with approximate costs) were made of benefits yet to come: improved car parking arrangements, and the building and equipping of a 'completely new' operating theatre complex.

By the time the Appeal was a year old, more than sixty private and public companies and organisations had contributed to it (Trinity College donated £5,000), as well as numerous local firms, general practitioners' surgeries, and trusts such as that belonging to the Gibson family of Exning – described by Geoffrey Agnew as 'the largest single donors over many years'.[2] In addition, the 'thirty two consultants who regularly use the

facilities of the Home' provided support in the form of a surcharge, contributing amounts related to their use of the said facilities. The staff of the Home too raised money through bring and buy sales and raffles. The Appeal's initial target was modest – £50,000 – but even before it was officially launched, the Gibson Trust had donated £10,000, at which point the General Purposes sub-committee announced (on 12 February 1975) that the Appeal 'could be considered to have started'! By October 1975, the intended amount had been exceeded by £25,000, while between January and December of the following year the fund increased from £92,000 to £136,000. Besides the sources already noted, moneys were also obtained from seven-year covenants (on which the Home could, of course, reclaim tax paid), and from bankers' orders. The provident associations too were generous with contributions, mainly in the form of interest-free loans amounting to over £130,000. By March 1978, over £200,000 had been raised. By February 1979, even larger amounts had been received or promised – and this in spite of the Appeal's having become rather inactive the previous year and having had to be revitalised. In October 1979, earlier

---

2. It is also possible that the overwhelming response on the part of the general public, 354 of whom had contributed in the first twelve months, was due to the Home's emphasis on the fact that the Labour Government of the day was bent, as the Appeal Brochure put it, on 'an early phasing out of private medicine in N.H.S. hospitals', with the result that 'people who wish to have private treatment … will soon only be able to obtain it in a Private Clinic or Nursing Home'. It was therefore evident, the brochure continued, that there was 'an urgent need for Nursing Homes such as The Evelyn in order that adequate provision of private medical care in Cambridge could continue'.

All three houses: Agnew House (foreground), The Orchard and The Evelyn (to the right).

inactivity notwithstanding, the Appeal Fund stood at £255,000, while a year later it reached £364,000 – a magnificent effort on the part of an organisation which only ten years before had been in the doldrums financially speaking. This was fortunate, given that the Home had already expended or committed to capital projects the even greater sum of £653,000. Furthermore, loans so generously given would have to be repaid, and there was the ever-present menace of inflation to be taken into account when costing works still to be carried out. There was, therefore, no room for complacency, especially as increasingly ambitious plans for development would require the raising of at least another quarter of a million pounds.

To Modernise and Improve the Home's Buildings

IN SEPTEMBER 1975, the Building Committee decided that a necessary preliminary to development of the Home was provision of an ancillary services area. Unfortunately, the extension built to house the ancillary services (stores, dispensary and laundry) was something of a compromise and, like most compromises, was not wholly satisfactory. The Home's need to squeeze all services onto the site following the sale of Brookfield – combined with its desire not to encroach onto the remaining garden area – meant that the extension was restricted in area and doomed to be idiosyncratic in layout because of the need to incorporate into it structures belonging to the original Home which were still in use. The adding of the extension onto the north face of the Link Building meant that natural lighting and ventilation were somewhat restricted in both the extension and the area it abutted. Also, there was no space left for any further expansion.

An area particularly affected by the positioning of the new extension was the main kitchen, which lost three important north-facing windows. This, as the General Purposes sub-committee noted on 28 July 1976, not only rendered the kitchen dark, but also restricted 'the dispersion of cooking aromas' so materially that 'extraction and control of noxious odours' required urgent attention. Of benefit to the kitchen, however, was the enlargement of it effected by the addition of the new extension – though it was, ironically, erection of the kitchen area of the extension that caused the loss of one of its windows.

The noise and dust created by the building of the extension, conditions unfamiliar to most of those employed by the Home at that time, made it difficult 'for both staff and patients to work and be nursed', as the General Purposes sub-committee put it in September 1976. The upheaval was, however, but a foretaste of things to come. Although Mr Thurlow's 'brief' was not, fortunately, to be implemented all at once, much work went on simultaneously rather than sequentially, to add to the Home's discomfort. The 'brief' comprised five phases:

Phase 1. Agnew House and the 'provision of modern X-ray facilities'.
Phase 2. The northern extension as just described, and the provision of additional consulting suites on the first floor of The Orchard.
Phase 3. Extensive work on the Home itself, including improvements to patients' accommodation, creation of a flat for a resident doctor and of a suite of offices for Matron and the administrative staff, and provision of rest and changing rooms for non-resident nurses.
Phase 4. Enlargement of the car park.

Phase 5. Upgrading of the operating theatre. This phase, originally intended to encompass the existing theatre only, was later expanded to incorporate a whole new theatre suite.

As part of Phase 1, 'Modern X-ray facilities and ... necessary ancillary services' (i.e. a waiting room, darkroom, office, kitchenette and changing cubicles) were established in part of the ground floor of The Orchard. Work neared completion in March 1976, and commissioning started in May with acceptance trials of the equipment. The new department opened on 2 June, after which date 'Ex-Ray', as Mr Thurlow described it, would never again find itself exiled from the Home.

A stroke of luck for the new department was the presentation to it as a personal gift from Dr Duncan Gregg of the radiological equipment needed to set it up. This, though it did not provide for portable X-rays (for which the Home had its own apparatus) or for certain specialist procedures, nevertheless ensured that the radiological requirements of private practice in Cambridge would be met for the immediate future. With the equipment in place, as early as

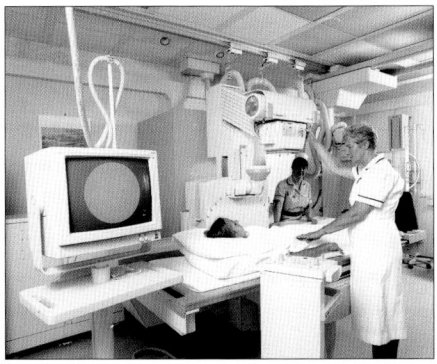

Diana Hawkins in the X-Ray Department, 1999 and, right, in 1976.

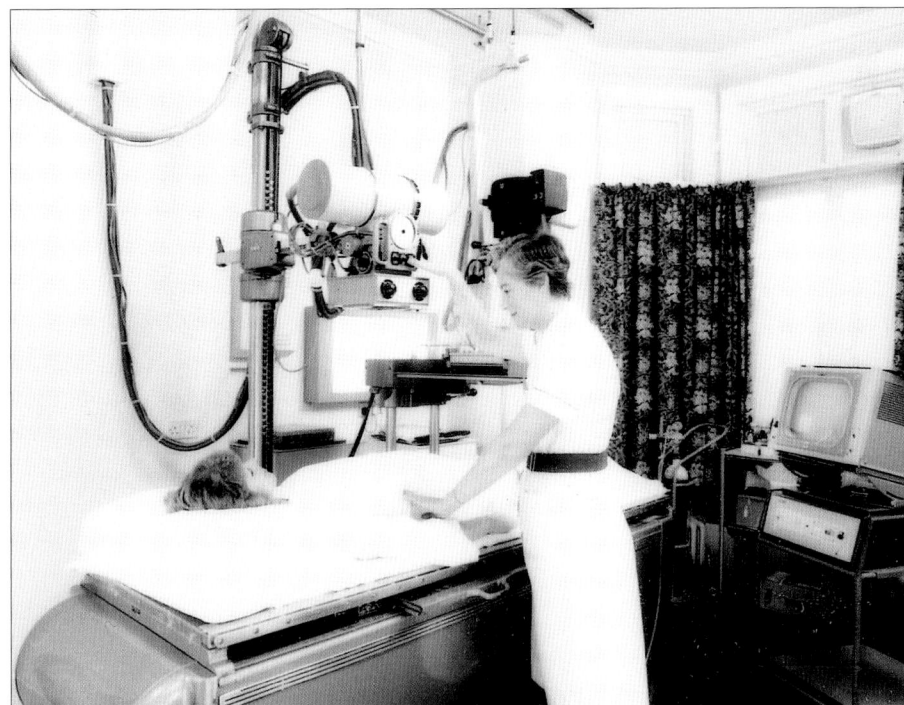

1. As early as December 1976 the workload of the new department had increased; by March 1977, with 1,487 examinations having been carried out in ten months, 'the prospects of further growth' were, as the Annual Report noted, 'looking encouraging'. Between March 1977 and March 1978 examinations undertaken exceeded 2,300, while those of the following year approached 3,000, a figure that was exceeded in 1979/80. With these figures in mind, the Annual Report of March 1978 noted that one of the principal areas of activity in the Home was its new 'Radiological Unit' (the other was the operating theatre).

16 June the department was operating, as the General Purposes sub-committee put it, 'very satisfactorily'. A year later, on 7 July 1977, it noted that 'there was an evident air of confidence and efficiency in the … department very much to the credit of those concerned'.[1]

In contrast to the statistics for its 1950s predecessor, outpatient referrals to the new unit far outnumbered those from inpatients. This meant, as Matron's Report for March 1979 noted, that not only were demands for X-rays already outstripping the

department's capacity, but also that outpatient activity affected 'the previous priority … given to examinations ensuing from consultants within the Home'. The increase in work also meant that the limited storage space within the department was already at a premium. A bid for *Lebensraum* being made by Dr Gregg earlier the same year, it was decided to extend the department onto the first floor of The Orchard immediately above.

The rooms taken over were used as rest and changing room for the

The Consultancy Suite, 1976.

radiographers, for storage, and for the housing of the Home's newest mobile X-ray machine, for which there was no room in the department itself. Housing the machine necessitated the construction of a moveable ramp in order that the apparatus could navigate the upper flight of the main staircase, which otherwise obstructed its path from the lift to its new quarters. That the new arrangement was a compromise was recognised to be indicative 'of a far larger requirement' by the radiologists. It was also appreciated that, although limitations imposed by the structure of the present unit were sufficient to deny its immediate expansion, thought should be given to the department's future needs in order that the Committee of Management could take note of how much extra space was needed and what other equipment required – the general feeling being that The Evelyn should add mammographic and ultrasonographic services to its radiological armamentarium as soon as practicably possible.

The completion of Phase 1 and of that aspect of Phase 2 that encompassed the northern extension

2. The new consulting suite was soon discovered to have one very real disadvantage: difficulty of access. The position of the suite on the first floor posed problems for those termed 'old and infirm' in the minutes of the General Purposes sub-committee meeting held on 28 July 1976. True, there was a lift, but this was a considerable distance from both the front door on the ground floor and the new suite on the first. Having successfully negotiated the distances, the aged and infirm were confronted by the short but steep flight of stairs which also created an obstacle for the mobile X-ray apparatus. Various suggestions were made as to how the problem could be solved, but eventually it was realised that the ramp provided for the X-ray apparatus could serve a dual purpose.

enabled the Home to move on to the provision of a further consulting suite on the first floor of The Orchard. The idea of creating more consulting rooms had been put forward almost as soon as the first suite proved popular; indeed, the revival in The Evelyn's fortunes was due in no small part to the outpatient facilities now offered. It was not, however, until its inclusion in Mr Thurlow's plans of 1975 that the decision was taken to add an 'extensive suite' of three consulting rooms, two examination rooms, and 'cloakroom facilities' in that 'self-contained and well-located' position. The new 'consultancy suite', as the Annual Report of March 1976 described it, opened in late October of the same year. Not only did it prove, as the report for the following year put it, 'excellent in all respects',[2] but it also served to attract 'a number of consultants who had not previously seen their patients in the Home'. By June 1977, the new suite was operating at almost full capacity.

Phase 3 involved a mixed bag of modernisations extending the entire length of the Home. It was also the most disruptive phase in so far as 'the considerable nature of the … upheaval' affected, as the Annual Report of March 1977 noted, 'over two thirds of

the Home's accommodation' – indeed, the General Purposes sub-committee's comment on 26 January 1977 when the phase was 60 per cent complete that credit was due to Matron and the staff for the way in which they managed to provide 'an excellent service throughout this period' was supported by its also noting that progress of this phase was necessarily slow, because of the need to ensure 'the availability of a minimum set of facilities to support a viable number of patients'.

There was, unfortunately, no escape from the 'disturbance caused by the building work' even in the garden, for the peace there was invaded when work on Phase 4 began. This phase involved, as the Annual Report for March 1976 put it, 'provision of a more adequate car park area' along the Trumpington Road frontage, which, when completed, would, make a 'vast difference to ease of parking'. The opportunity was also taken of improving traffic flow within the grounds by negotiating a joint access road with the Queensway flats built by the Granta Housing Association on the former Brookfield site.

By the time Phase 4 was completed, the modernisation and improvement project originally costed at around

£85,000, but with revised costings thought to amount to £240,000, had required the expenditure of £401,950 – chiefly because of the continuing effect of inflation on the capital cost of the building programme. Though the increased cost was counterbalanced by the profusion of funds flooding in as a result of the Appeal and raised within the Home through the efforts of its users and employees, it was decided to postpone the start of Phase 5 pending the raising of the further funding required for its completion. This gave the Home a brief but much needed breathing space, Matron noting at a staff meeting held on 1 October 1978 that 'as we have weathered the past two years it is to be hoped we may weather the next two ... and remain sane'. Correctly prophesying that after its brief respite the Home and its denizens would once more 'be inundated with dust and dirt', she optimistically, and in the main correctly, believed that all would 'smile through it'.

The Considerable Nature of the Day-to-Day Upheaval

IT WAS NOT ONLY the fabric of the Home that underwent radical changes in the 1970s. As Geoffrey Agnew – the prime mover of the scheme – recognised, the Home's attitude to change and to the adoption of new ideas also required modernisation if The Evelyn was to transform itself from a nursing home that, as Wing-Commander Finlayson put it, 'carried on ticking over despite itself' into an institution committed to going into the future. That the Home now had an enthusiastic new Matron whose stature and the Home's would grow together was one thing, but that The Evelyn did not wind down to become merely one of the several residential homes in Cambridge – or even, as Mr Agnew warned, fade away to a standstill and closure – was another, and changes would have to be made in a more than notional manner.

An indication of the ways in which the changes recently undergone by the Home began to affect its smooth running was the appearance of strains and stresses in its systems of administration and communication. These became even more prominent after the completion of Phases 1 to 4 and the addition or expansion of radiological and outpatient services, the problems inherent in running what was rapidly becoming an acute hospital along nursing-home lines becoming more and more apparent. In November 1976 the General Purposes sub-committee, recognising that the Home's channels of communication were not working as well as they ought and that it was becoming 'increasingly difficult to have the overall view needed to run the Home efficiently', suggested that the introduction of 'more formality into the methods which worked admirably when the Home was used less intensively' would be a good idea. One result of this was that staff meetings began to be held on a regular monthly basis. They were attended by the senior person from each department, and matters affecting the day-to-day management of the Home were discussed with the aim of ensuring that all wards and departments were kept up to date; to this end also minutes were recorded and published. In 1975, too, when medical input into the running of the Home had become a major factor in moving it forward, a Medical Users Committee was formed 'to represent the views of the medical staff and to advise the General Purposes Committee accordingly'.

Other changes were brought about by the Home's need to comply with the conditions of the Health and Safety at Work Act of 1974. Implementation of the Act's demands had already had considerable impact on the Home. It had, for example, to prepare and revise as necessary a written statement of general policy with regard to matters of health, safety and welfare at work affecting those it employed; and to inform them that the Act also placed a legal obligation on them to co-operate

in health, safety and welfare matters both in so far as they themselves were concerned and in so far as their acts and omissions might affect the health, safety and welfare of others. Furthermore, as pointed out at a staff meeting held on 11 November 1978, implementation of the Act's conditions was to be seen in the context of 'a natural progression of improvements within the Home'. Unfortunately, as Matron's report for the following month pointed out, implementation was 'causing stress', a surprising occurrence given that many of the 'improvements' had been in place since the passing of the Abortion Act of 1967 and that what now needed doing involved little more than an upgrading of existing facilities. Nor were the new practices required of an expensive or onerous nature, including as they did the institution of compulsory fire drills, the invoking of better hygiene measures and the establishment of a Control of Infection Committee.

Modernisations not included in the Act but inspired by the current desire for progress were wide ranging. Every employee was asked to produce a job description. The floor sisters expressed a desire for greater autonomy (they were of the opinion that 'as responsible State Registered Nurses

Nurses of the late 1970s modelling uniforms of the 1930s.

employed by Matron … they should assume complete responsibility for the floor's running and total care of their patients in conjunction with the medical staff; should problems arise, the Sisters to deal with them as they think fit'). Matron stressed at the staff meeting of 16 March 1980 the importance of there being written procedures in place ('everyone assumes that work is being done but there is no proof of this'), which would ensure that her ultimate responsibility 'for everything within the Home' was supported by evidence ('much more should be put in writing') and that everyone working there knew what they were supposed to do, did it

properly, and recorded that they had done it.

In May 1975 (i.e. the year preceding the start of the 'day by day upheaval and compromise engendered by the modernisation programme' as the Annual Report of March 1977 put it), the Home's administrative nursing complement consisted of Matron, the Assistant Matron, and two part-time administrative sisters. Each of the two wards was run by a sister, eight full-time and three part-time staff nurses, and three full-time and one part-time orderlies. The night staff, which covered both floors, consisted of two full-time sisters and four full-time and twelve part-time staff nurses. The theatre staff comprised a sister and a full-time staff nurse and orderly, shortly to be expanded into the two teams envisaged by Mrs Mundell. Ten nurses and orderlies were resident out of a total of nearly fifty; of the thirty-one ancillary and catering staff, eight were resident: one assistant cook, two kitchen maids, and five general domestics.

Three years earlier, it was noted that nurse numbers were 'well up to establishment' but that it was only just possible to meet 'the demand for care' with the numbers in post. This was due in part to the steady increase in surgical bookings and in part to the increasingly rapid turnover of patients. That standards of care were high in spite of this is shown by the General Purposes sub-committee's comment of 20 April 1972 that Matron and her staff had a 'down to earth personal interest in the care and welfare of the patients'; in April 1977 the same sub-committee described the nurses as a 'lovely lot'. The Annual Report of March 1977, noting that 'no difficulty had been experienced in maintaining a full complement of nurses and nursing auxiliaries', nevertheless sounded a warning note of another kind: staff turnover was high. It was not, however, until the autumn of 1978

that a third problem was noted by the sub-committee, at staff meetings and in Matron's Monthly Report: the nurses' salary bill was higher than ever, in part because of the increased volume of outpatient work, in part because there were now two complete theatre teams, and in part because of the large number of agency nurses employed on a regular basis. Although hopes were expressed that a reduction could be made in the number of expensive agency nurses (so firmly embedded in the Home's duty rotas that they appeared on lists of regular staff) by the recruitment of more nurses on a 'permanent' basis, in practice this was difficult to achieve. In fact, every indication was that 'the policy of phasing out agency nurses in favour of recruiting directly to the Home would not be quickly accomplished as it was proving difficult to match the calibre of the agency nurses' already in post.

In interesting contrast to the 'calibre' of the agency nurses were the concerns expressed by the General Purposes sub-committee in March 1978 concerning the deficient 'levels of professional knowledge among the nursing staff', their agency colleagues not excepted. The situation had, in fact, begun to be remedied the previous year when at a staff meeting held in June 1977 the nurses, through their representatives, requested the implementation of 'refresher courses' and doctors' lectures. In September 1977, it was noted that 'lectures on current topics' were about to start. Attendance at the lectures was strongly urged by Matron: 'I expect as many as nurses as possible to attend as the doctors are giving their time voluntarily and it will be in the interests of all to learn more about modern medicine and surgery'; to this end, lectures were held at 7 p.m., when most nurses had completed or not yet started their spell of duty. In-house training, too, was soon well advanced, and two clinic nurses were 'sent off to learn ECGs'. Instruction by a member of the St John Ambulance Brigade on resuscitation techniques was followed by a first aid lecture given in December 1978 by Mrs Holland of the same organisation[1] to, as Matron's Report put it, 'a great number of the staff'. By early 1979, so many nurses had attended external seminars and courses that the Finance sub-committee was forced to note, first, 'that should the requirement for training expand further, authorisation [by it] would be necessary' and, second, that a regular sum should be now be set aside for educational purposes.

A manifestation among the nurses of the corporate spirit now apparent was, as the General Purposes sub-committee noted in February 1979, 'the lively interest' expressed with regard to the establishment of a distinctive uniform; this, it was hoped, would also serve to enhance the newly dynamic corporate image. It was in fact only the staff nurses who wore what Matron's Report of the same month described as the 'pale blue of The Evelyn Nursing Home uniform', so reminiscent of the 'soft sky blue' of Miss Cracroft's day, for sisters continued to wear navy, and the newly named auxiliaries bright yellow.[2] The uniform 'which now identifies our own nurses' and which was to continue to do so for twenty years was bought by individual nurses using their £30 a year uniform allowance. A length of Petersham for a belt and black stockings and shoes completed the outfit.

Indicative, though in a different way, of the Home's changing outlook was its attitude towards its permanent patients. That these, a dwindling minority during the 1970s, took up a disproportionate amount of the General Purposes sub-committee's time demonstrates both the problems they posed to an institution desirous of leaving behind its nursing-home image and the heart-searching

1. Mrs Holland recalled being confronted by what seemed to be the entire nursing staff of the Home from Matron down, all in full panoply of starched caps and aprons. Her own St John Ambulance uniform, she felt, provided her with much needed moral support!

2. The soubriquet given to them by the patients was 'daffodil girls'; the colour was not popular with its wearers as it showed every mark and suited few complexions.

A 'daffodil girl'.

involved when such patients were no longer admitted as a matter of policy or had to leave because they could no longer afford the fees. That The Evelyn was torn between compassion and financial hardheadness is evident; although such patients provided only a comparatively small income for the Home, consideration had to be given to the fact that it had been their presence that had kept the Home financially afloat during the difficult war years and the period following the arrival of the NHS.

Between May 1976 and October 1978, numbers of residents fluctuated between five and nine, but never again reached double figures. In March 1978, it was noted that while 'present policy' limited the number of permanent patients to six, the number was in future to be reduced to five because of the reduction in the number of rooms occasioned by the modernisation programme. Although the Home did not actively seek to reduce the actual number of such patients 'unless our occupancy [is] adversely affected by their continuing presence', it is noticeable that between January and May 1979 numbers were maintained at five or below, though there were never none. The General Purposes sub-committee's view was that 'while there was much to be said for gradually phasing out all permanent patients and thus ensuring maximum flexibility for admissions', the time had not yet come when such a policy would be 'to The Evelyn's best advantage'. Furthermore, although the General Purposes sub-committee had noted as early as February 1975 that the room rates of permanent patients were 'falling behind and becoming uneconomical', it was nevertheless decided *not* to increase their charges, on the grounds that 'fees could not go up any more otherwise the Home would be priced out of the market'.[3]

Fortunately for The Evelyn, the problem solved itself, the Home's resolution that its future was 'as a Surgical rather than a Surgical/Geriatric Home' being assisted by the private health insurance companies' decision to cease funding geriatric care. This resulted in the number of permanent patients reducing by the early 1980s to one, and in 1987 to none.

Another 'upheaval' to which the Home of the 1970s had to adapt concerned its medical and surgical patients. Not only were greater numbers of acute (medical *and* surgical) cases admitted than had been seen since the 1930s (a factor which influenced both the style and intensity of nursing required), but it was noticeable that patient numbers were rising steeply from their post-NHS slump to over, and then well over, a thousand annually – and this with a concomitant increase in elective surgery.

The main driving forces behind the rapidly rising fees which the Home was unhappily forced to charge during the decade under discussion to all patients, acute or elective, medical or surgical – and this to an extent probably unparalleled in its history – were first, and as mentioned earlier, inflation, and second, Whitley Scale pay rises awarded annually to its nurses. As a result of 20 per cent and 10 per cent salary increases in 1970 and 1971 respectively, the Home had to increase its room charges in 1970 from £54 12s 0d, £60 18s 0d and £69 6s 0d a week to £61 15s 0d, £68 15s 0d, and £75 5s 0d for small, medium and large rooms respectively. In 1971, following decimalisation, they rose to

3. Recognising that rooms occupied by permanent patients always made a loss, the policy of allowing this to continue was adopted on the grounds that it would 'encourage extra patients'.

£66.50, £73.50 and £80.50. An overnight stay cost £15 and a day-case visit between £10 and £50 (with theatre fees added) which, though high in proportion to the daily room charge, reflected the amount of nursing care expended on even minor cases. By 1974/5, room rates had risen from between £140 and £189 a week to between £161 and £231 a week; a further rise in May 1976 brought them to between £189 and £224 a week with de-luxe rooms at £252. Only three years later, the standardised rate was £287, with outpatient surgery fees (inclusive of theatre charges) of £20 to £40 depending on length of stay. To inpatient charges were added theatre fees ranging from £15 to £40 'according to type of operation'; a charge for drugs and dressings; extras such as television hire, telephone calls and newspapers; and the cost of items given out by the nurses. Inpatient and outpatient charges alike contributed, in the continued absence of any other form of income, to the 'total remuneration' of the hundred staff (just over half of whom were nurses) employed by the Home at the time of the Annual Report of March 1979.

That the Home continued to provide high standards of care throughout the 1970s in spite of the many changes it underwent during that time can be seen not only from the various amenities it provided, but also from the numbers of patients who – in the words of the General Purposes sub-committee minutes of March 1979 – generally expressed themselves 'most contented with the nursing and the treatment they were receiving'. A year earlier, in June 1978, the same sub-committee noted 'a general impression of cheerfulness and kindness in all areas' to which patients responded with little gifts and profuse thanks. For patients whose stays were longer than average, much entertainment was provided by details of the nurses' daily lives, and it was usual for them to be extremely well informed about the affairs of the heart, holidays and family happenings of the nurses looking after them.

It was, however, unfortunate that the high standards of care were not matched by equally high standards of accommodation, for although minor piecemeal improvements were carried out over the years, the overall impression was that the patients' rooms continued to lack 'any sense of generosity at any level' because of their 'blank and uninteresting walls' of 'drab green', darned candlewick bedspreads and inadequate curtains. Various sub-committee members also pointed out that 'while thoughts of conservation and economy were admirable, too much could be counterproductive'; that because the Home was currently doing little more than maintain the status quo in its attempts at redecoration and replacement, it was not making a 'measurable improvement' in either; and that there was a great need to bring the rooms up to the standards set by other nursing homes charging comparable prices.

To see what could be achieved when funds permitted, comparisons were made under Mr Thurlow's guidance with the Wessex Nuffield Nursing Home. Following this, Mr Thurlow suggested that very small rooms be used only for 'clinic cases' and that new rooms be built to Nuffield standards. That the idea existed of increasing the number of rooms at a time when the Home already exceeded the Nuffield-recommended number of thirty-six is indicative of how strongly both it and its architect were committed to the notion of further expansion; indeed, by May 1979, the Building Committee was seriously considering Mr Thurlow's proposal that the Home build a whole new two-storey 'bedroom wing' of twenty-four

rooms, all Nuffield specified as to size and all with en-suite bathrooms.

Discussions between the General Purposes sub-committee and the Building Committee resulted in recognition that plans should be made for 'an overall scheme for the future' which would demonstrate 'the maximum potential development of the Home'; provide the basis 'for any future Appeal and of discussion with the Medical Users' Committee' (who were, for their part, 'continuing their deliberations' on the subject); and allow the decision to be made about where, in Mr Thurlow's words, 'it would be correct and feasible to expand The Evelyn's facilities'. But whatever plans were made, one thing was obvious: something had to be done, and done quickly. In spite of the extent of the building programme to date, the Home, it was noted in February 1979, was still 'trying to contain a quart of organisation in a pint pot of space' and was 'bursting at the seams, coping with a job which is growing and changing'. Furthermore, it was not only the Home's layout which was inadequate for its expanded and expanding purposes; thought would have to be given to 'the change in the nature of the Home as it becomes more and more like a hospital'.

Further Projects are being Actively Pursued

IN JANUARY 1977, a report was issued concerning the Home's need to modernise its operating theatre facilities. Indicating that the last few years had been a time of unprecedented change at The Evelyn, it went on to state that 'a decision has to be taken on the operating theatre, a decision … more far-reaching than any we have taken yet, since the theatre is increasingly the prime factor in the occupation of the Home as the trend moves away from long-stay patients to acute surgical cases; the theatre thus dictates the nature of the entire Home'. Assuming, however, that modernisation of the theatre was essential, what options were open to the Home? Should it, for example, spend a large sum on improving the existing theatre, or an even larger sum on the creation of a whole new theatre suite elsewhere on the site? If the latter, should the new theatre be built to the highest possible standards, or should it be built as cheaply as possible, given that large-scale borrowing was risky and expensive?

The form the new theatre was to take and where it was to be sited were the next decisions to be made. The idea of siting the 'new' Theatre near to the existing one seemed sensible, given that the latter could be rehabilitated for complementary use when money allowed. The Building Committee, meeting on 20 October 1976, therefore decided to examine 'provision of a new theatre to be positioned on the roof of the existing building'. The idea of siting the new operating theatre on the roof of the Aston Webb building had been put forward by Mr Thurlow as early as 1974, and studies had been carried out to ascertain the load-bearing capacity of the structure's roof and walls. Placing the new theatre on the roof, besides being the most obvious position because of the Home's desire to amalgamate the new with the existing theatre services, would also – the General Purposes sub-committee and Building Committee believed – prevent any further problems arising from Sir Aston's innovative but perpetually leaky 'flats … floated with cement for asphalte'.

Having decided on the position of the new theatre, the next question concerned the form it should take. Mr Thurlow having agreed that 'only a single theatre would be required … now and in the foreseeable future', the Building Committee then had to ask itself a number of questions. Should it be a theatre with 'simple' ancillary services used in conjunction with a rehabilitated existing theatre, the Home ending up – as the Building Committee put it – with 'one and a half' theatres 'built and equipped within the financial framework to 'a level of amenity … that would ensure long term facilities'? Or should the theatre also contain the patient reception and recovery areas deemed essential by the nursing and medical staff, in which case at least three bed-space equivalents would be required? Should it include one of the latest modular units, incorporating its own air-conditioning system but modifiable to suit local conditions, such as had been installed at the King Edward VII Hospital for Officers?[1]

In order that suitable answers could be given, advice was sought from surgeons and anaesthetists who already used the Home's facilities, and visits were made to other hospitals to see what facilities they possessed and which would be the most suitable for The Evelyn. The most important considerations – which, as the doctors and Mr Thurlow recognised, could prove crucial to the long-term viability of the Home – were to do with the 'level of amenity and resources' to be provided. These were not, they noted, solely to do with 'additional hardware'; they were also to do with physical provision of a suitable working environment. This was believed to be of particular importance because the surgeons on whom The Evelyn relied were used to the first-class facilities provided at the new Addenbrooke's Hospital on Hills Road, and unless they were forced by government legislation to give up private practice altogether they might opt for the establishment which offered

1. The Finance sub-committee meeting on 27 July 1977 noted that 'controlled ventilation standards … were of great interest to the medical staff', the orthopaedic surgeons in particular disliking the open windows and fly-swats of the existing theatre.

2. A major problem was occasioned by the new lift linking the theatre with the Home's ground and first floors. In an echo of Morland Agnew's anguished cry of sixty years before that the lift was 'much too narrow; will not take a bed and barely a stretcher', it became immediately apparent that, due to the space occupied inside the lift by its sliding door, there was insufficient depth in the car to take a standard theatre trolley. 'The lift', Matron's Report of February 1980 noted tersely, 'was not accepted.' A manually operated door was substituted for the automatic one, Mr Thurlow subsequently reporting that 'a bed trolley was wheeled into the car and the new gate closed'. The lift being restored to use, Matron was able to report that 'the first patient to use this unusual facility was a Committee member who was safely transported to the operating theatre and back'.

such facilities as a matter of course.

It having been decided that what was required was a single theatre incorporating all the features suggested by its future users, building work began early in 1979 and was completed – after protracted delays, a staggering rise in building costs which occasioned the Committee of Management much unease, and considerable disturbance to the Home[2] – in July 1980. The first operation in the new Theatre was carried out on 1 September 1980, and marked, as Geoffrey Agnew noted, 'a major step forward in the 59 year history of the Home'. Matron's Report for October 1980, the month following the theatre's opening for work, noted that it was 'working very efficiently and is enjoyed by … staff and surgeons alike'. It was officially opened on 27 October 1981 by HRH the Duke of Edinburgh, Chancellor of the University, at a function described in the Appeal Progress Report No. 2 (1981) as 'attended by many representatives of those who had so generously subscribed'. Although the Duke's visit was brief – he left after inspecting the theatre and performing the opening ceremony, during which he described the facility somewhat truistically as 'probably the most modern operating

theatre for miles around' – the Home used the occasion 'to look back at what we had achieved and to look forward to what still remains to be done'.

Once commissioned and open, the new theatre generated a greater demand for surgical services than The Evelyn had ever before experienced. On 4 April 1982, the General Purposes sub-committee reported that the Home's income for the previous financial year had exceeded £1 million for the first time, thanks largely to the increase in theatre fees, and that the surplus made as a result marked a welcome departure from the 'breakeven policy' of the previous ten years. The surplus itself (£76,825) was described in that year's Annual Report as 'far in excess of anything achieved in the present decade' – or, indeed, ever. In July 1987, the theatre was named the Geoffrey Agnew Theatre in recognition of the immense contribution made to The Evelyn over the years by the third member of the Agnew family to head the Home. That Phase 5 ended on such a triumphant note was in no small measure due to his vision and encouragement.

Financial and surgical vindication of the decision to go ahead with the major constructional project

The Aston Webb Wing, with the Geoffrey Agnew Theatre above.

culminating in the creation of the Geoffrey Agnew Theatre inspired the Home to go ahead, not only with the refurbishment of the old theatre to a standard much higher than originally envisaged, but also with the construction of the 'bedroom wing' mooted in 1979, both projects being regarded by the General Purposes sub-committee as 'vital to the future success of the Home'.[3]

The old theatre, described in May 1978 as 'usable but only just so', was more than ripe for refurbishment. The Home's original intentions had been to upgrade the theatre at minimum cost, but these were subsequently amended to include, at greater expense,

installation of air-conditioning and the addition of a recovery room positioned in such a way as to connect the theatre to the surgical floor of the new 'bedroom wing'.

In June 1983, as the scheme was put out to tender, the possibility was raised of cardiothoracic surgery being carried out at The Evelyn if the conversion could be sufficiently upgraded to cope with this. At a project meeting held in July 1983, it was decided to proceed with refurbishment of the theatre 'including Cardiac Unit', and to upgrade the recovery room to one suitable for the post-operative surveillance of the type of cases now envisaged.[4]

3. The 'bedroom wing' was, in fact, built before the old theatre was renovated, but because of the functional interdependence of the two theatres, a description of the latter project at this point better places it in the context of improvements in The Evelyn's surgical facilities than would a description of a more strictly chronological nature.

4. The suggestion was also adopted that the refurbished theatre be called the Gibson Theatre in recognition of the Gibson Trust's generous donations to the Appeal.

The official opening of the Geoffrey Agnew Theatre, 27 October 1981. The Duke of Edinburgh with surgeon Alastair Smellie and theatre superintendent Joyce Fraser.

The first operations in the renovated theatre were carried out on 27 April 1985, with interesting though unforeseen consequences arising as a result of there now being *two* up-to-date operating theatres at The Evelyn. The first concerned the surgeons' new ability to establish regular, formal operating sessions instead of being constrained – as formerly – by the first come, first served, booking system which made it so difficult for them to structure their working week. The second came about in part because of rising expectations among the surgeons using The Evelyn's state-of-the-art theatres, in part because of recent legislation, and in part because of rapid developments in surgery which took place during the 1980s and were both the impetus for, and result of, improvements in operator-assisting devices. This second consequence took rather longer to resolve than the first but, like it, brought about an improvement in The Evelyn's surgical services.

Legislation in general and the Abortion Act of 1967 in particular had already required The Evelyn to provide and maintain emergency sets of instruments to which all surgeons, not just the gynaecologists, had access. Unfortunately, by April 1978, of the three sets provided only one basic and rather antiquated one still existed, supplemented by instruments belonging to individual surgeons. The Evelyn also lacked sufficient suitable instruments to enable it to deal with emergencies occurring in specialties other than gynaecology and general surgery. Furthermore, with more and more intermediate and major surgery being carried out and with more and more surgical specialties appearing, surgeons patronising the Geoffrey Agnew and Gibson Theatres began to press for the purchase by The Evelyn of a range of instruments which would enable them to deal with a wider range of cases. They also urged the purchase of larger items which individual surgeons could hardly be expected to own (or transport) themselves. In January 1985, with the legally required complement of instruments restored, the Finance sub-committee decided that, although it had been traditional Evelyn policy that consultants provide all other instruments, the sub-committee was now prepared to consider specific requests for the purchase of instruments and equipment on their individual merits. By November 1986, the Medical Users Committee was able to report that specialist surgical instruments were now to be bought by The Evelyn and that instruments currently owned by individual surgeons would be replaced as necessary by the hospital, replacement instruments becoming the property of The Evelyn itself.

But what, we may ask, happened to the cardiothoracic surgery for which the Gibson Theatre was intended? The answer is that such surgery *was* carried out, but only twice and not in that theatre. In 1982 two patients underwent coronary artery bypass grafts in the Geoffrey Agnew Theatre, the General Purposes sub-committee later noting that such cases were more an 'interesting exception to the rule than a precedent for the … future', chiefly because of contemporaneous feeling among the nurses that The Evelyn was neither equipped nor staffed for the care of patients of this calibre. (The Medical Users Committee also expressed doubts concerning the suitability of The Evelyn as it then was for the care of such patients, even with back-up provided by the cardiac surgery team.) The project, which had been intended to start with thoracic surgery and with the care of convalescent cardiac surgery patients before progressing to open-heart surgery, was therefore abandoned without further operations of this type taking place. In spite of this, The Evelyn gained a theatre and recovery room of a much higher standard than it might have had if the notion of cardiothoracic surgery had never been entertained.

Vastly Improved Facilities for the Patients

AN UPDATE ON THE REPORT issued in January 1977 concerning the ways in which external factors affected the running and development of The Evelyn was issued shortly after the opening of the Gibson Theatre in April 1985. Its content, though pertaining to a later 'bedroom wing' than the one about to be discussed, is nevertheless extremely relevant in so far as it demonstrates how much had changed both nationally and domestically in the intervening period.

The opening of the Gibson Theatre, the later report began, had created an upsurge in the bed-occupancy figures, so much so that 'within a few months there will be pressure on the number of beds available and … a danger that The Evelyn … would be unable to satisfy the rising demand for private medical care in Cambridge and the surrounding area'. The reasons for this, the report continued, were fivefold:

First, the number of subscribers to private health care schemes continued to rise, albeit more slowly than the 25 per cent increase of 1980.

Second, the political climate now encouraged both personal and corporate private medical insurance schemes and co-operation between the private sector and the National Health Service.

Third, East Anglia was a growth area, having changed dramatically since the time of the previous report from a relatively undeveloped region to one characterised by much the same prosperity as the affluent south-east.

Fourth, Cambridge was expanding, and businesses were attracted to it by the creation of new road schemes linking it to the capital, to the north of England, and to Europe. Fifth, Addenbrooke's Hospital and its expanding medical school continued to attract high-quality medical staff to Cambridge and hence to The Evelyn.

For these reasons Cambridge would see an above-average demand for private healthcare facilities in the near future, and this The Evelyn was ideally placed to fill.

Long-term plans, the report concluded, should therefore incorporate the following:

a) a day surgery unit;
b) a third operating theatre;
c) a separate medical wing, because the increased volume of surgery had affected the admission of non-surgical cases by reducing the number of beds available for them;
d) a dedicated outpatients' wing;
e) a CT scanner for the soon-to-be extended X-ray department;
f) centralisation and modernisation of the administration;
g) last, but not least, 'computerisation'.

Most important of all was an immediate increase in the number of surgical beds, particularly as there were, as the General Purposes sub-committee had noted as early as February 1982, urgent intimations from the medical users that the number of rooms at The Evelyn should be increased, if only because 'against mounting pressure for rooms not every doctor's demands could be satisfied'. By May 1979, therefore, the Building Committee was seriously considering Mr Thurlow's ideas for the proposed new 'bedroom wing' of twenty-four rooms of Nuffield-specified dimensions equipped with en-suite bathrooms. Studies of the 1.1-hectare site proposed for the wing showed that just enough space could be provided for the required number of rooms and for the ancillary and circulation areas.

Details of the new wing were hammered out at meetings held throughout 1981 with a view to receiving tenders on 30 July 1982. The period of construction was estimated at eighteen months. Preliminary estimates of costs at first quarter of 1982 rates came to £633,000 if the wing were constructed in one session or £694,000 if construction were phased, the phases costing £370,000 and £324,000. The building contractor's figure came to £622,427, with equipping and fitting-out accounting for a further £100,000 and furniture another £30,000, giving the total arrived at by the Appeal Committee on 21 July 1982 of £730,000. The Evelyn was therefore committed to further large-scale expenditure which the contemporaneous decision to raise the room rates would not cover.

The Home therefore decided to continue and extend the Appeal. It had been originally intended that the Appeal would be wound down from November 1980, with a view to either closing it on 31 December of that year or maintaining it as a low-key form of fund-raising dealt with by the Home's clerical staff. By early 1981, however, the Appeal, far from running out of steam, continued to thrive, and it was anticipated that further substantial funds might accrue. As by this time the 'new wing of 24 rooms equipped … to modern standards' was virtually on the drawing board, the Home realised that during the next two years the Appeal would have to be 'very thoroughly persuaded' to help to pay for it. Fortunately for the 'new wing', the Appeal went from strength to strength. In October 1982 it reached £483,750 and in September 1983, after a full

year's intensive fund-raising, £676,137. The Appeal was finally closed on 31 December 1983, by which time it had raised close on £1,000,000.

The factor that most encouraged the Appeal Committee to consider on 14 November 1981 'the continuation, reactivation, and broadening of the field of the Appeal' had been the decision by the David Robinson Charitable Trust to donate £300,000 towards the cost of the new wing, the budget for which was then estimated at £500,000, exclusive of fees. David Robinson, founder of Robinson College, part of Cambridge University, had earlier been admitted to The Evelyn as a convalescent. One day he asked Matron to come and see him, enquiring what she felt The Evelyn required. Matron, somewhat taken aback, replied that what it really needed was more rooms. For these, Mr Robinson said, his trust would supply at least some of the funding. Matron, in a state of shock, telephoned Geoffrey Agnew, who was equally incredulous. After a rather tense interval – during which Mr Robinson apparently withdrew his offer, on the grounds that he had been insufficiently thanked by the Committee of Management (he continued throughout to promise Matron that she *would* get

David Robinson, founder of Robinson College.

The official opening of the Robinson Wing, 27 July 1983. Left to right: Peter Finlayson, Mrs Peri Mundell, Lady Butler, Mr and Mrs Julian Agnew, Geoffrey Agnew.

her rooms!), but was mollified after a personal letter of thanks from Geoffrey Agnew was rushed by express delivery from London to Cambridge and hand delivered to his home near Newmarket – the Appeal Progress Report No. 2 was able to announce that 'a magnificent gift from the David Robinson Charitable Trust has ... put us in a position to prepare for the building and equipping of a new patients' wing'. Mr Robinson, as was his wont, also imposed stringent conditions on the timing and financing of the wing, but was not at all interested in its appearance, saying that as long as Matron was happy, so was he.

With the new wing's completion occurring as scheduled on 20 May

1983, commissioning took place throughout the following month with the aim of opening it to patients on 1 July. As that particular day was a Friday, patients were not actually admitted to the wing until the following Monday, 4 July. The first two patients to arrive were presented with flowers and champagne to mark what Matron described as 'this auspicious occasion'. The wing was officially opened on 27 July 1983 by Lady Butler, David Robinson himself having declined to do the honours or even, in keeping with his reclusive nature, to attend the ceremony. The wing, known henceforth as the Robinson Wing, created – as the Annual Report of March 1984 put it – 'a new standard of comfort and medical care' for The Evelyn's patients.

The wing's external walls were of red brick compatible with that of the Link Building and the existing Home, and its slate roof pitched at an angle in keeping with that of The Orchard, while the clear-glazed link corridors had flat roofs to marry with the areas of flat roof still visible at the east end of the Aston Webb Wing. The double-glazed windows of the corridor which ran on both floors round the outer face of the wing were of clerestory design on the ground floor so as to protect the privacy of the flats erected on the Brookfield site; on the first floor they were of vertical design but positioned so that they overlooked only obliquely the living areas of the next-door development, their smaller number being compensated for by the insertion of skylights. The full-height windows of the inward-facing patients' rooms were supplemented by Mr Thurlow's trademark, the circular window. Other trademark features appeared in the courtyard round which the wing ran – red transom ends like those of Agnew House and vertical timber-slatted screens to give support for climbing shrubs. The inward-facing rooms gave views from the bed over the internal courtyard; this would, Mr Thurlow hoped, 'be suitably landscaped and planted'.

The ground plan of the wing was of necessity trapezoidal in order to allow its containment within the constricted area between the eastern end of the original Home and the fences dividing the Home from the Housing Association flats and the earlier Applecourt development. This meant that, although the patients' rooms were rectangular in arrangement and each contained an en-suite bathroom opening off a small entrance lobby leading into the room itself, ancillary offices had to be fitted into oddly shaped interstices which – together with right-angle bends in the perimeter corridor – did not always make for convenience or ease of access.

As in the case of Agnew House, much use was made in the wing's interior of exposed timber, to particular effect in the beamed ceiling of the sitting area on the first floor. In the rooms themselves, sycamore-veneered doors and built-in furniture contrasted cheerfully with pale walls and brown and white carpets. Each room contained – besides the necessary bed, locker, wardrobe and dressing table – an easy chair, a TV and telephone, and bench seating for visitors. Lighting could be controlled by the patient without leaving the bed, and nurses could be contacted via an intercom system, which obviated much running up and down on their part – until then, nurses had to walk the corridors to see which patient had rung as the only indicators were directly over the doors of the rooms.[1] As the new wing consisted of twenty-four rooms spread over two floors, installation of a nurse-call system throughout the Home was a major step forward.

The wing was popular with staff and patients alike, the former appreciating the easier nursing conditions of the modern rooms and the latter finding them 'quite excellent' and revelling in how nice it was 'to be … cared for so luxuriously'. Matron's comment in her Report of July 1983 was succinct: 'the whole effect is superb'.

The opening of the Robinson Wing increased the number of rooms in The Evelyn to sixty-one, expanding it overnight by nearly 50 per cent. This, together with the opening three years earlier of the Geoffrey Agnew Theatre, had the effect of more than doubling the workload of all departments, the 'continuing increase in activity' noted by the Annual Report of March 1982 becoming more and more of an imposition on services already stretched almost to their limit. That problems might occur following the opening of the Robinson Wing was noted by the House sub-committee in June 1982. Although it made no suggestions as to how services could be physically expanded in preparation for the event, it did at least suggest that more staff would be needed in nearly all departments.

Although by no means all the planned-for staff were appointed by the time the Robinson Wing opened, it

1. Some older patients who were used to nurses entering their room to discover what was wanted complained that the new system made them feel isolated, but most patients appreciated the speed with which their calls were answered and their wants attended to.

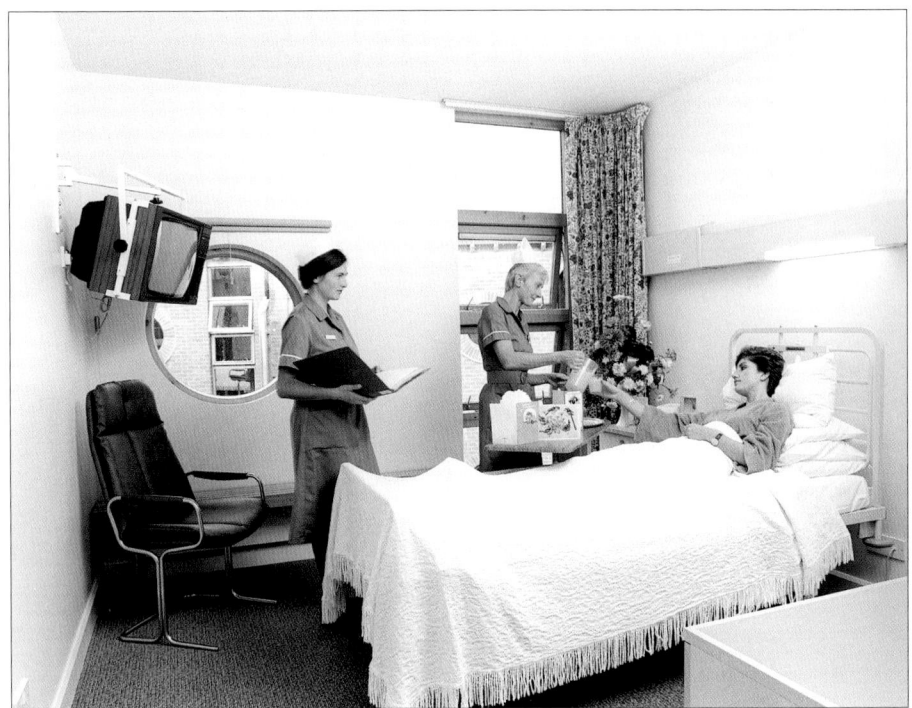

The Robinson Wing, 1983.

was not very long before staff numbers – already increased from what the General Purposes sub-committee meeting of 25 June 1980 described as the 'closely knit and experienced' hundred of the late 1970s to the 130 of 1982 – increased still further to help beleaguered colleagues already in post. Fortunately, as Matron remarked the year following the opening of the Robinson Wing, 'our patients think we are marvellous, and that the standards of nursing, food, and cleanliness are of the highest'.

More and More like a Hospital

WHILE PLANNING FOR the Robinson Wing was in progress, and just under a year after the opening of the theatre to be named after him, Geoffrey Agnew announced in the Chairman's Statement attached to the notification of the Annual General Meeting of 1981 that 'At the Annual General Meeting in July I propose to retire from the Chairmanship which I have held since I succeeded my father in 1955 … I have every confidence in the future of The Evelyn and hope that, through my son, Julian Agnew, my family's connection with the Home and with Cambridge will continue for the foreseeable future.' In his later memoir, he described how he had 'handed over the Chairmanship to my son Julian, the fourth generation of the family to serve The Evelyn'; his son, he added, had before his (Geoffrey's) retirement provided him with 'great assistance over the major decisions which had to be made during this growth period of The Evelyn's existence', with the result that he was well qualified to step into his father's shoes. In the Annual Report of March 1982, Julian Agnew both enlarged on his father's interest during his long chairmanship, noting that he had 'been responsible for masterminding the start of the process by which The Evelyn is being transformed from a nursing home into a modern … private hospital', and expressed a hope that under his own leadership the transformation would be complete. He also said that in spite of the changes it was undergoing, he trusted that The Evelyn would retain 'the friendly and personal atmosphere … so valued by our patients'.

Julian Agnew, Chairman, 1981–2003.

Following Geoffrey Agnew's retirement came the appointment in February 1984 of The Evelyn's second Administrator, Commander John Allen OBE, RN. As before, The Evelyn looked to the Officers' Association for its new Administrator, describing itself to the association as a 'busy and expanding private hospital'. In keeping with his naval training, Commander Allen ran The Evelyn like a shore establishment of the Senior Service, to the benefit of her buildings and all who sailed in her. His job description, in addition to listing his numerous duties and noting that qua Administrator he remained subordinate to Matron because 'the primary aim of the hospital is to provide excellent medical and nursing care', also supplied an interesting vignette of The Evelyn as it was in late 1983. It contained, besides sixty-one beds, a modern operating theatre ('the creation of a further operating theatre was envisaged'), consulting rooms, and an X-ray department; and its annual turnover in 1982/3 had been £1,112,255 – 'and this will rise'. Consultants in most medical fields, the description continued, practised at The Evelyn 'and nursing standards are of very high quality'. Employees, the numbers of which 'may well have to

increase', consisted of 80 nurses and 15 clerical, 24 domestic, 5 catering, and 7 maintenance and portering staff.

Although the number of employees did indeed increase, the number of people associated with The Evelyn in other capacities gradually began to fall. The process began in February 1981, with Julian Agnew's suggestion to the General Purposes sub-committee that – because of recent changes in the organisation and day-to-day management of the Home – the time had come for a new committee structure also. Reorganisation began in July 1981, following Geoffrey Agnew's retirement, with a rearrangement of the various committees' functions and times of meeting. The General Purposes sub-committee which, his son felt, spent a disproportionate amount of time on details, now met every three months to discuss matters of principle and to review reports submitted by the Finance, Building, Appeal, and House Committees which met in the intervening months (the House sub-committee) or were 'convened as required' (the other committees). The Medical Users Committee, it was agreed, would meet four times a year at times which tied in with the meetings of the General Purposes sub-committee.

Three years after the rearrangement of the General Purposes sub-committee's function, there took place an even more radical rearrangement of the other committee structures. Since 1981 the feeling had been steadily growing that the number of committees and the number of people in them could be reduced without detriment to The Evelyn's functioning, in order to promote – as the Annual Report of March 1984 put it – 'a more efficient and less onerous structure'. That this had to be accomplished slowly and tactfully was obvious, lest offence be given to those who, as Julian Agnew recorded, 'on an entirely voluntary basis gave so much time and effort to the running of the hospital'.

The process began with the publication in February 1983 of a report on the constitution of The Evelyn Nursing Home by the Home's solicitors, who had been asked to prepare a brief giving their recommendations relating to the Home's future constitution and management structure. Their recommendations were made on the basis that reorganisation was to be essentially a streamlining and updating of existing structures and the promotion of procedural clarity in terms of a revised constitution, rather than a radical change of direction which might have far-reaching consequences. They also proposed, first, that there was no further need for nominated collegiate membership, although colleges which individually supported it could subscribe for a share in the company if they wished; second, that life and subscribing membership also be abolished on the not-quite-correct grounds that no such members now existed; and, third, that The Evelyn retain both its status of a company limited by guarantee and its charitable status. The Evelyn's revised constitution was to be introduced on 27 July, the day on which the Robinson Wing was to be officially opened and the two theatres officially named. The final suggestion made by the Home's solicitors with regard to the revision of The Evelyn's constitution and management structure was that this should be reflected in a change to a name more representative of its new status and organisation, the new name, once decided upon, to be announced on the day of the official opening and naming of the Robinson Wing and of the commencement of the Home's new constitution.

The earliest intimations of a need to change The Evelyn's title to include the word 'hospital' appeared as early

The Evelyn in the late 1980s. The Robinson Wing lies below the Aston Webb Wing. The small building above it is all that remains of Brookfield, now used as a community centre for the Granta Housing Association flats nearby. The H-shaped blocks are the Applecourt flats.

as July 1966, when the General Purposes sub-committee realised that some American insurance companies were reluctant to pay for acute patients nursed in a 'nursing home'. It was not until July 1979 that the same sub-committee made formal representation that the name of the Home be changed 'with the intention of more accurately reflecting the nature of the facilities available to both in- and out-patients'. Although a body of opinion among the sub-committee's members felt strongly that the phrase 'nursing home' conjured up quite the wrong impression of the facilities which had developed at The Evelyn in recent years and that the inclusion of 'clinic' or 'private hospital' in the title would be a more accurate reflection of its activities, no further action was taken at that time. It was, however, noted to be essential that the word 'Evelyn' be retained in any title the Home might assume because of 'personal and historical ties'. Discussions recommenced in 1982, the General Purposes sub-committee of 28 April agreeing that 'the inauguration of a new constitution would be the correct opportunity to introduce a new name for the Home', but being unable to decide what the new name should be: 'The Evelyn Private Hospital' or 'The Evelyn Clinic'. It was not until the Annual General Meeting which took place on 27 July, immediately before the ceremony at which the name was to be announced, that it was formally proposed and seconded that 'the name of the Company be changed to 'The Evelyn Hospital''. The momentous event was announced at the opening of the Robinson Wing, the following day's *Cambridge Evening News* stating that 'A nursing home … has become Cambridge's newest hospital. From today the old Evelyn Nursing Home will be known as The Evelyn Hospital.' A retired consultant's comment that 'it is much more like a hospital than it was', was now reflected in The Evelyn's title.

A Continuing Increase of Activity in all Departments

EXPANSION OF THE EVELYN in the 1980s brought about the need to expand its support services also. Although pressure fell earliest on those services most immediately concerned with patient care – for example, the laundry – other services were affected sooner or later, with the result that throughout the latter half of the decade remedial measures had to be taken to bring them up to the standard required by The Evelyn in its new role of busy private Hospital.

By May 1978, the kitchen had run into serious trouble because a recent Public Health Authority inspection had been more than a little critical of the working conditions there. It was therefore recommended that the kitchen be completely refitted by a specialist firm, and that work be carried out as soon as possible after completion of what was to be the Geoffrey Agnew Theatre; the increase in patient turnover and staff numbers consequent on its coming into use would inevitably affect the catering department. Financing of the necessary work was not felt to be a problem, funds provided by the Appeal being enhanced from sources such as a nearly new sale. Work began in February 1982 and, after a temporary deterioration in catering standards while work progressed, the 'new' kitchen proved highly successful.

The need to expand the outpatient clinic area became apparent early in 1980, the General Purposes sub-committee noting on 27 February that the consulting rooms were to all intents and purposes fully booked. There was also, the sub-committee added on 25 August, an increasing demand for clinic rooms at weekends (Saturday *and* Sunday), although providing nursing service to 'weekday' levels at those times was difficult.

A 32 per cent increase in outpatient numbers over the next four years stimulated The Evelyn into asking itself where, on its present site, further clinics could be situated. In October 1984, the General Purposes sub-committee floated the idea of building a two-storey extension along the front of the Hospital between The Orchard and Agnew House, in which further consulting rooms could be housed. (It stated at the same time that this, the 'only acceptable plan', would cost around £337,899, a sum 'out of all proportion to the benefits to be gained'.) The suggestion was given serious consideration in November by the medical users, who suggested that the proposed eight consulting suites – together with a treatment room and secretarial and staff rooms, and possibly even a physiotherapy department – could be built in stages as finance allowed. By December 1985, the medical users' ideas had become more ambitious: the new block, they hoped, would be three rather than two storeys high and 6,400 square feet (180 square metres) in area (probably, they said, the last major building on

the site 'as it now exists'). It would incorporate eight consulting suites, 'some designated ... for individual specialities'; a treatment room and plaster room; a 'rest area containing six cubicles for patients to recover from minor surgery or other procedures'; a physiotherapy department; a 'secretarial facility' containing a Medical Records department, and further offices which could be rented by 'individual Consultants for the use of their secretaries and storage of records'.

In April 1986, a development plan for outpatients was put forward which was even more grandiose. A two-storey building, supported on columns tall enough to allow car parking underneath (with designated slots reserved for consultants) was to run parallel with Trumpington Road. It was to contain, on the first floor, eight consulting suites looking south-west over the garden with ancillary areas to the north-east, and on the second floor a day-surgery unit consisting of a theatre with adjacent services and ten small rooms for post-operative patients. The building would be entered via a ground floor reception area linking it with The Orchard.

Shortly afterwards, however, the medical users noted that the 'proposed building at the front of the hospital' would not be proceeded with, on the grounds that it had been found 'too expensive to justify its construction' (the estimated cost had now risen to £350,000), but that further clinic space would be provided by extending the first-floor clinic area along the top-floor corridor. (The loss to the ward of the five rooms in the Link Building into which the clinics were to expand was to be compensated for by the erection of another 'bedroom wing'.) Conversion of the Link Building rooms was carried out during the latter part of 1986, the Annual Report of March 1987 announcing the arrival of a fifth consulting suite, dedicated rooms for specialist treatments, ancillary services and office accommodation. The fifth suite soon proved useful in reducing pressure on the existing suites and in allowing more consultants to carry out regular clinics.

True to the Hospital's promise of early entry into the era of 'computerisation', the latter years of the decade saw the arrival of The Evelyn's first computer system. The first move had been made by Wing-Commander Finlayson in December 1983, his report noting the need to install computer terminals throughout the Hospital in order to provide a

service easily accessible by all, but with confidentiality maintained by the use of personal passwords. The new service, he continued, was to be used initially for patient registration, pay roll and accounts, the publication of operating and clinic lists, and the easier management of stores. He further noted, however, that neither of the computer systems looked at was entirely satisfactory; in fact, they were later removed from the majority of private hospitals in which they had been installed. It was possibly because of this rather negative first impression of 'computerisation' that nothing further was undertaken until 1989, at which point Commander Allen decided that a basic Medax computer system should be installed in some areas, with a view to a more sophisticated version of the same system being installed throughout the Hospital at a later date. Medax therefore went live on 1 November 1989.

A service which required urgent upgrading was that of pharmacy, together with the appointment of a qualified pharmacist. The absence of a pharmacist had mattered little to the 'quiet nursing home' which existed before the 1970s programme of modernisation and development, but the arrival of up-to-date operating theatres, the Robinson Wing and a new generation of consultants emphasised the deficiencies in the existing services. Although as late as 30 September 1986 the Finance sub-committee continued to state that there was no financial benefit to The Evelyn in recruiting its own pharmacist, Matron's statement in her Monthly Report for May 1986 that the 'District Pharmaceutical Officer recommends employing our own pharmacist', and her reiteration, after two 'rather serious incidents', that from the safety point of view if nothing else it was time to recruit one, eventually achieved the desired result. On 2 February 1987, The Evelyn's first pharmacist

The Evelyn's first pharmacist, 1987.

took up her post, a 'much improved' service being noted at the next inspection by the Chief Pharmacist from Addenbrooke's Hospital.

A department in which the 'continuing increase in activity' was particularly marked was X-ray, in which the need for expansion of both services and personnel had become pressing. The department now needed 'two general rooms and a separate special procedures room', a room for mammography and ultrasonography combined, and 'adequate' office space with a 'booking, sorting and records room for the secretaries and other bods'. Although staff manning the expanded department expressed trenchant criticisms of its layout and lack of space, doctors using the Hospital commented favourably on the improved service it offered and, as early as November 1986, noted that radiological activity at The Evelyn was 'even greater than estimated' following the appointment of three more radiologists.

In February 1988, The Evelyn decided to set up its own screening service to demonstrate an awareness on its part of the new national emphasis on primary and preventive healthcare. Clients were to be offered the facility of a health check without recourse to their general practitioner or having symptoms to declare, but with the assurance that screening carried out on 'well' men and women could detect unrealised disease and identify potentially significant problems.

The only space available to house the prospective department, generally agreed to be better sited away from inpatient areas of the Hospital, was a ground-floor area in Agnew House currently used for committee meetings and educational purposes. (In view of the general underuse of Agnew House by those for whom it was intended, the General Purposes sub-committee considered that converting a substantial part of it to medical usage would be unlikely to prejudice recruitment.) RIBA's 1976 promise that Agnew House was a building which would successfully survive a lot of 'knocks and changes' began to be tested during the early months of 1989, the House sub-committee noting that three rooms had been redecorated for use by shortly-to-be-appointed resident doctors;[1] two knocked into one to provide a 'conference room' with adjacent lavatory and kitchen; and a major part of the ground floor had been adapted for screening use, with an office, data storage, patient waiting and ancillary areas to the

1. The doctors' flat in The Orchard had been pre-empted for radiology and office use before any doctors took up residence there.

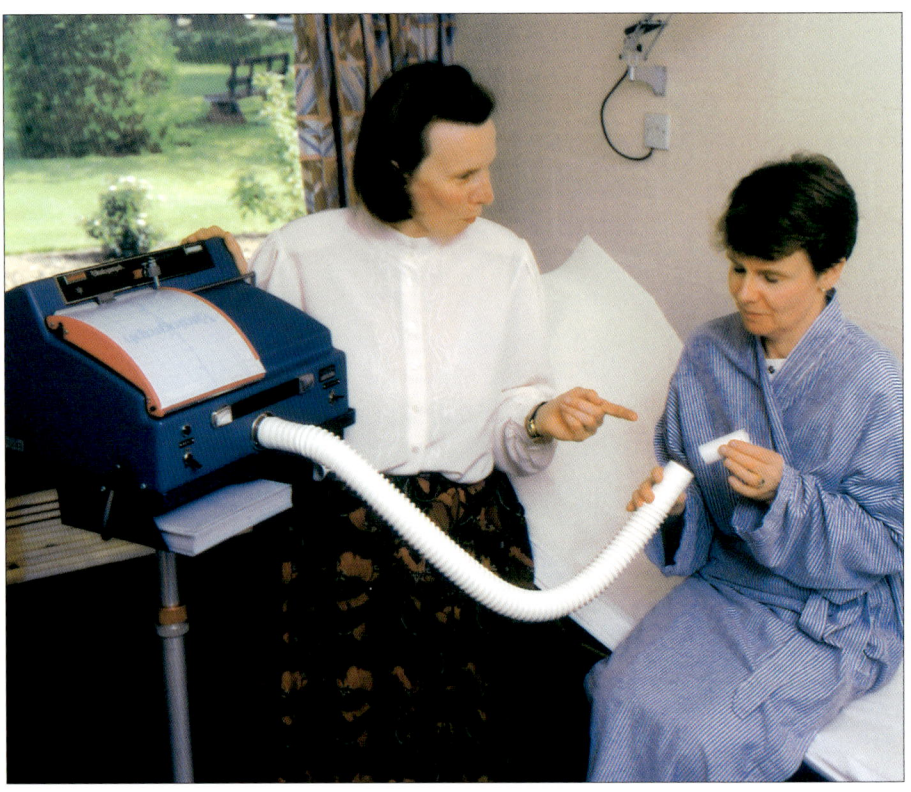

The Health Screening Department, 1988.

north and examination and consulting rooms overlooking the garden to the south. To the pleasant environment offered by the newly converted premises was added the convenience of having the main Hospital's services nearby. The department opened for client use on 2 November 1989. It offered a wide range of screening programmes besides the obvious ones of Well Man and Well Woman, with clients enjoying the opportunity of receiving personal attention from the service's Director with regard to all aspects of their health and lifestyle and to the maintenance or promotion of optimal fitness for their age and gender. Following a suggestion that the service be organised on the same lines as X-ray, the Director was remunerated by a proportion of the fees after deduction of expenses and was supported by administrative and nursing staff accountable to them and, where appropriate, to Matron.

A Particularly Competent and Kindly Group of People

MEDICAL COVER, especially at night or if a consultant was temporarily unavailable, had always been a problem at The Evelyn, but it became more acute with changes in the burden of care. Matron, noting in June 1982 that on two recent occasions there had been a delay in obtaining medical assistance, wrote to the medical users for guidance. They agreed that the presence of a resident medical 'practitioner' was essential 'for the public image of a modern private hospital' and that the trend towards more major surgery taking place at The Evelyn required the continuing presence of a doctor in case of haemorrhage or cardiac arrest, or to prescribe drugs the need for which had not been foreseen when the consultant last visited the Hospital. Twenty-four-hour cover, they also

noted, might soon become a legal requirement for hospitals in the private sector.

On 11 October 1985, it was announced that three doctors would be installed as The Evelyn's first resident medical officers on Monday 14 October 1985, those on duty being able to study for their primary FRCS when not actually employed on Hospital business, and those off duty serving as anatomy demonstrators in the medical school. The arrangement also saw the restoration of the University's links with The Evelyn for, in a neat reversal of roles, the latter's patients were now to be cared for by members of the very University for whose benefit the 'University's Hospital' had been founded.

Although the new medical officers' chief task was 'to provide on site

The staff of The Evelyn, 24 July 1986.

medical cover particularly in emergency situations', they were also expected to respond to 'requests for clinical advice and reassurance' from the nursing staff and patients, to visit the wards on commencing their spell of duty in order to 'receive reports on patients' progress' from the nurse in charge, to provide 'postoperative surveillance of all surgical cases and their medical requirements', to carry out specific investigations; and to prescribe, dispense, and administer drugs as necessary. They were to wear a white coat, name badge and smart dress 'whenever within the hospital' and to carry a pager at all times when on duty. By private arrangement with individual consultants, they could provide a full 'houseman' service to their particular patients and assist the consultant in theatre if not required on the wards. Medical users soon expressed satisfaction with the arrangement and with the high standard of the doctors appointed, agreeing that they had more than proved their worth. Indeed, so successful were they, and so much a part of the Hospital's supporting services, that those who worked at The Evelyn prior to 14 October 1985 were grateful when they remembered how

insecure they had felt without a doctor always on the premises.

The same year that saw the appointment of the resident medical officers also saw the issuing of guidelines on the eligibility of medical practitioners to use The Evelyn. The medical users' concern arose as a result of their discovery that the qualifications required of a medical user had never been formally established. They therefore decided that the time had come both to establish these and to identify areas in which problems of medical usership might arise, their aim being to uphold professional standards of care at The Evelyn and to protect its patients and reputation. At the same time, they noted that the establishment of effective guidelines should not prejudice the right of individual doctors to practise at The Evelyn, and that any guidelines should be flexible enough to avoid imputations of restrictive practices or of the medical users' intention of creating a 'clique or cartel'. The guidelines were issued on 15 July 1985. A practitioner would be deemed eligible if they met the following criteria:

a) They were of consultant or equivalent status, held an NHS contract, and lived or worked within twenty miles of Cambridge; if they lived or worked beyond the twenty-mile limit, 'acceptable arrangements for providing emergency cover' were to be clearly defined.

b) They did not hold an NHS appointment but were prepared to submit a curriculum vitae and the names of two referees to the Medical Users Committee; practitioners who had previously held substantive NHS appointments or the equivalent within twenty miles of Cambridge were exempt from this requirement, as were existing medical users.

c) They were under the age of 70.

Factors which might preclude a potential user from providing the required standard of service were as follows:

a) They did not live in or near Cambridge and so might not be available to provide effective cover in an emergency.

b) They worked entirely outside the NHS and so were not subject to its statutes.

c) They had passed the normal retiring age.

d) They had a problem that impaired their fitness to practise.

If there should be any doubt concerning the eligibility of a practitioner or of the fitness to practise of an existing one, the question was to be referred to the chairman of the Medical Users Council, with the right of appeal to the Committee of Management.

The Medical Users Council existed as a result of a Medical Advisory Structure document drawn up in November 1982. This followed agreement among The Evelyn's medical users that stronger united medical input into the running of the Hospital was required than that so far provided by the Medical Users Committee set up in 1976. The Medical Users Council met twice a year in May and November, with extraordinary meetings convened on request. The chairman and vice-chairman of the council were *ipso facto* medical users and were elected by written ballot at two-yearly intervals. The former, or in their absence the latter, was responsible for 'helping with the day to day problems arising in the administration of The Evelyn ... which require medical advice', with guidance, if appropriate, from other medical users. The Medical

Users Committee consisted of the chairman and vice-chairman of the Council and three other medical users elected every two years, no member being eligible for re-election until a stipulated length of time had elapsed; in this way imputations of 'clique or cartel' behaviour could be avoided. The committee met four times a year (or as required), its members being *ex-officio* members of the General Purposes sub-committee or, following the latter's demise, of the Committee of Management.

The arrival of the resident medical officers and the support they provided for medical users and nurses alike came at particularly crucial period in The Evelyn's existence. That the tempo of work increased enormously in all areas of the Hospital throughout the decade which saw its transformation from a nursing home with a single operating theatre into a busy private hospital with two can be deduced from Matron's monthly Reports, from the minutes of the General Purposes sub-committee, and from the Hospital's Annual Reports. The early 1980s, for example, saw such a sharp rise in the number of operations and admissions – following the cessation of the major building works involved in the creation of the Geoffrey Agnew

Theatre – that Matron's Reports included comments on 100 per cent bed occupancy for the first time in her eight-and-a-half years tenure, and on admissions having to be refused. Shortly after this, she was happy to announce that the figures were 'very encouraging' and 'the future as far as occupancy is concerned looks hopeful', adding confidently that 'the boom in private medicine [has] reached The Evelyn'. The upward trend continued, with occupancy running on average above 70 per cent, an ostensible decrease to mid-60 per cent which followed the arrival of the Robinson Wing in July 1983 merely concealing the contemporaneous increase in short-stay and day-case admissions. But although, as Matron put it, the Hospital was well on the way to achieving the 'near impossible' – it was about this time that she adopted the motto 'Grace under Pressure' – the patients themselves continued to praise the 'personable, pleasant and willing' team looking after them and 'the professional cohesion' that was so apparent in spite of the fragmentation which might have occurred in the presence of so many medical and surgical specialties.

Patients cared for at The Evelyn generally enjoyed their stay. This is evident both in the large number of contributions made by them to the Hospital's Staff Fund and in the many letters of thanks received by Matron. The content of the latter ranged from general praise for all concerned, describing them as 'a particularly kindly and competent group of people' whose 'cheerfulness and attention to detail' provided 'a sense of security … and a homely atmosphere' in 'clean calm surroundings' overlooking a garden which was 'a joy to behold'; to that lavished on particular groups of people: 'the smashing nurses and auxiliaries', 'the nurse in the Recovery room … and the porters', 'the cheerful Italian lady who cleaned my room', 'that nice lady ward clerk', and the night nurses who made consoling cups of tea in the small hours (but 'may I make a request to them to wear QUIET shoes please'). The letters included the humorous:

'I had my temperature taken 32 times!'
'Some of the things … nurses have to do for their patients make me feel glad I finished up as a secretary' (though, as the letter continued, 'everyone … undertook those tasks as if they were the nicest things they had to do all day').

There were the heartfelt too:

'I came home from hospital with the most lovely feeling of inner calm and well-being.'
'I miss you all very much and shall always remember you.'
'You have brought him back to us so many times in renewed health … but this time you performed the greatest service of all – sending him on his final road in peace and dignity in an atmosphere filled with love.'

It was to the nurturing atmosphere that patients chiefly attributed their recovery. Letters referring to the staff's ability to 'reassure, cajole, administer and listen', to the 'exceptional … courtesy' extended, and to the 'helpful, compassionate, supportive care' given meant that many patients found that what could have been a distressing experience was transformed into one on which they looked back with pleasure. 'I have saved up enough happiness and smiles for a lifetime' was one comment, and 'I never thought I'd hear my wife say "I *am* enjoying my stay in hospital!" ' another.

With tender loving care went efficiency; as another letter ran, 'the staff's capacity to make conversation, attend to detail unobtrusively, and pace the input of care according to the rate of recovery were much appreciated. I experienced a well thought out system, professionally and carefully implemented in a very congenial and relaxed setting'. Another letter said poetically 'I'm almost grievin' to be leavin' the Evelyn'. The one that announced 'I don't want to leave!' said it all.

Breakfast was served between 7 and 8 a.m., lunch between 12.15 and 1 p.m. and supper between 6.30 and 7 p.m., the traditional home cooking offered maintaining traditions instituted during the war. Visiting hours were from 10 a.m. to 8.30 p.m., although it was suggested that visitors should not arrive between 1 p.m. and 3 p.m. so as to allow patients to rest in the middle of the day. Changes in their post-operative and medical management meant that those once allowed, and even encouraged, to linger in bed to undergo the luxury of a 'blanket bath' were now so enthusiastically mobilised by legions of nurses and auxiliaries that they found themselves in the shower while still attached to drips, drains and catheters. The majority appreciated the freedom and the consequent reduction in complications arising from prolonged 'bed rest' but

realised at the same time that a post-prandial snooze was no longer a luxury but a necessity! Not only this, but the whole rhythm of the patients' day speeded up as shorter hospital stays meant that activities such as physiotherapy had to be carried out more intensively on the fewer days available. Operating lists, too, began earlier and went on later, with patients arriving for morning surgery as early as 8 a.m. (7 a.m. a few years later), and those undergoing minor surgery in the afternoon leaving the Hospital as late as 8 or 9 p.m. In April 1982, the General Purposes sub-committee, noting that the change in patterns of admission tended 'ever more towards the surgical field', realised that The Evelyn was now becoming almost wholly dependent 'upon the product of the theatre'.

In spite of the preponderance of surgery, medical patients continued to be admitted whenever and wherever beds were available. (There were also, of course, three permanent patients in residence at the start of the decade, the last of whom left only three years before its end.) Advances in treatment permitted a shorter stay, though health insurance companies' exclusion clauses allowed fewer to be admitted for investigations or treatments which could be carried out on an outpatient basis. Notably absent were conditions which no longer warranted admission because of the development of appropriate therapies. The beginnings of a growth area were demonstrated by the arrival of an oncology service in 1987, albeit on so small a scale that the House sub-committee, meeting on 22 December, decided that there was no need to provide special accommodation or equipment at a probable cost of £20,000 as 'present indications' suggested that their use 'would not justify such expenditure'. They were soon to be proved wrong.

One of the Best Hospitals of its Kind

ALTHOUGH, AS THE General Purposes sub-committee noted on 14 February 1982, The Evelyn had always been 'somewhat shy of publicity' and as a private (in both senses) institution had discouraged advertisement, in 1986 its attitude changed to one of promotion of itself and its works. With the invitation 'Come and see how your local independent hospital works', The Evelyn opened its doors to the public for the first time between 2 and 5 p.m. on Sunday 26 July 1987, with Matron and other senior nurses on hand to show people round. Areas to be visited included the Gibson Theatre, where a lifelike hip replacement was in progress (the Hospital's resuscitation dummy acted as patient); the newly decorated and furnished consulting, examination and waiting rooms on the first floor; the Robinson Wing; the kitchen and staff dining room; and the garden, where tea and scones were served in a marquee on completion of the tour. Those visiting expressed themselves 'most impressed' with what they saw (staff too took the opportunity of exploring parts of the Hospital to which they never normally penetrated), while Matron herself described the occasion as 'an enjoyable day [which] put over to the public what a superb hospital we are'.

Contemporary research by Scope Communications Management Ltd, however, showed that – although The Evelyn enjoyed a 'second to none reputation amongst older members of the local community', was a well-run establishment with excellent nursing care, and had a loyal consultant base and a new name – it retained a somewhat 'nursing home' image

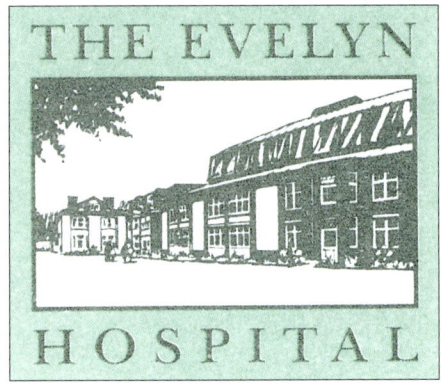

ABOVE: *As part of an initiative to promote its facilities, The Evelyn had a new logo devised.*

LEFT: *The refurbished reception area, 1987–8.*

because of the dowdy state of its reception and outpatient facilities and the lack of en-suite facilities in the Old Wing rooms. In order to improve its image, Scope suggested that the Hospital give priority to the refurbishment of its entrance hall and waiting areas and to the upgrading of its older rooms; this the Hospital duly did, though not all recommendations were completed during the 1980s. Also suggested was extension of the car park (which was done) and construction at the earliest opportunity of a further wing of patients' rooms with en-suite facilities,

plans for which were already in the pipeline.

Planning permission for the new wing had been sought as early as March 1986, though it was not until November 1987 that Mr Thurlow was able to outline his plans for it. The wing, three storeys tall, was to be built along the Hospital's eastern boundary with, he hoped, minimum impact on neighbouring properties because of the placing of only part of the building against the boundary fence, the other half leading diagonally away from the boundary in a south-westerly direction. Siting was further influenced by the position of the Hospital's existing buildings and services, and by the existence of mature trees – some of which bore preservation orders.

The design of the wing followed closely the Preliminary List of Requirements drawn up in October 1987, in which it was stated that the ground and first floors were each to contain seven or eight rooms (with en-suite shower rooms) similar in dimensions, design and fittings to those in the Robinson Wing. On each floor too there was to be a 'patient day area' and two bathrooms. Adjacent to the sluice was to be a dirty-linen room for the storage of linen skips and commodes, and, at the bend of the

The Arthur Cooke Wing.

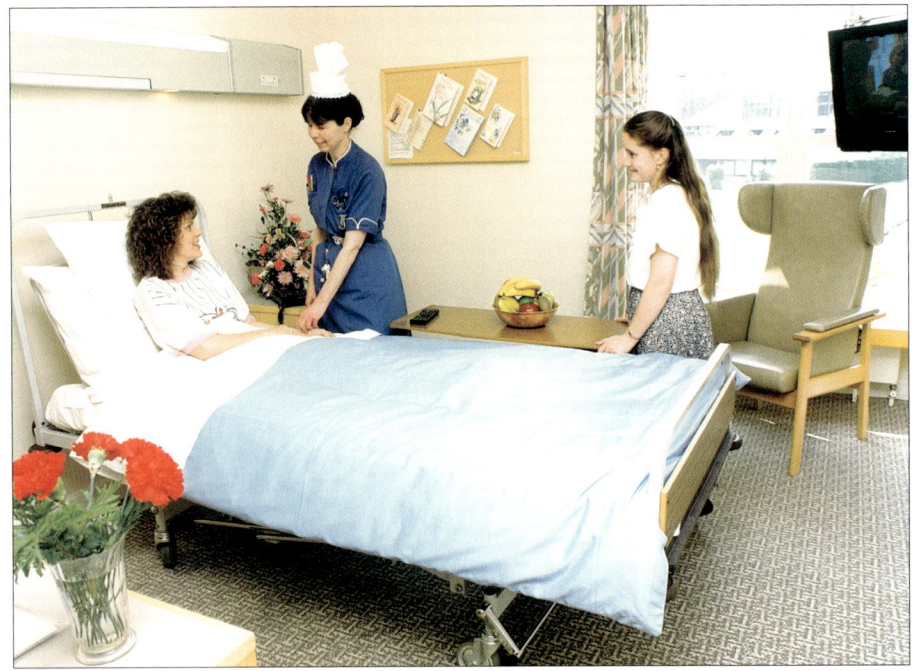

The Arthur Cooke Wing, 1989.

corridor, a staff toilet and changing area. (The exigencies of the site meant that the service rooms again had to be fitted into oddly shaped areas, which restricted their convenience and function.) A single-storey extension to the rear was to house a store accessible from outside and inside the building (in practice this became the plant room servicing the wing, as servicing it from existing plant rooms proved impossible) and an oncology room. The ward on the second floor, of seven or eight en-suite rooms, was to contain – besides a day area – bathroom, sluice, dirty-linen store, staff toilet and kitchen ('a rather larger room … is required, to serve meals, do washing up etc.'), a nurses' station, a treatment room, and an office for the sister 'if space available'. All floors were to have access to the Robinson Wing lift – the lower floors by corridors and the top floor by a ramped incline – and to an external fire escape; there were also to be stairs linking the first and second floors 'in the general vicinity of the lift', even though the position of the staircase would necessitate modification of the two nearest rooms in that wing. With some changes of use which occasioned modification of the original design, Mr Thurlow's plans of November 1987 incorporated all the requested features, giving twenty-three patients' rooms, eight on each of the ground and first floors and seven on the second, where the staff toilet, treatment room, and sister's office occupied an equivalent space.

The wing was formally opened on 4 October 1989 by Michael Bevan JP, Lord Lieutenant for Cambridgeshire. On one side of Mr Bevan stood Julian Agnew, great-grandson of the Hospital's founder; on the other, the Rev. Hereward Cooke, grandson of the doctor but for whom, as Morland Agnew put it, the Hospital 'would

never have been started'. The new wing itself was named the Arthur Cooke Wing in the doctor's honour.

The opening of the Arthur Cooke Wing on 4 October 1989, with Peter Pemberton and Hereward Cooke (above) and Julian Agnew and Michael Bevan (right).

Nearby stood Peter Pemberton, grandson of William Wingate Pemberton[1], the general practitioner colleague of Arthur Cooke who acted as his assistant during the operation on the lady whose name the Hospital bore. Equally appropriately, the Lord Lieutenant, describing The Evelyn as a 'wonderful thing for Cambridge and the people who live in and around it', unconsciously echoed Morland Agnew's earlier hope that his foundation would prove 'a boon to Cambridge and vicinity'.

Following the admission of patients to the first floor of the Arthur Cooke Wing on 25 September and to the ground floor on 5 October, the Hospital quickly realised that the addition of a third storey to the inpatient area made the wards' existing nomenclature (Ground Floor Ward / Top Floor Ward) confusing and inaccurate. On Matron's advice, therefore, the wards were named after local roads, the ground floor becoming Chaucer Ward, the first-floor Newton Ward, and the new ward Trumpington – invariably shortened to Trumps. At the same time, room numbers were rationalised so that they could be 'read' hotel style – rather than sequentially from and back to the front door – with rooms on Chaucer Ward prefixed 1 to demonstrate their position on the ground floor, Newton's rooms prefixed 2, and Trumpington's rooms 3.

Another problem was to decide on the use to which Trumpington Ward was to be put. The rooms on the ground and first floors of the new wing were to be run in conjunction with Chaucer and Newton Wards, but the second floor was by the nature of its position isolated from the rest of the Hospital and could not easily be run in conjunction with existing facilities. The House sub-committee, meeting on 29 September 1987, considered a number of possible solutions, but found them all inherently unsatisfactory. Although its final suggestion was that the space be left as a shell whose use could be decided at a later date – and in spite of the fact that the area's isolation from the rest of the Hospital would entail the presence of disproportionate numbers of nursing staff were it to become a ward – because the Hospital's overriding need was for more inpatient rooms, the decision was taken to establish it as a ward from the start. (This had the added advantage of increasing the Hospital's annual income by about £230,000.) Having agreed on its use as a ward, but noting

1. William Wingate Pemberton had assumed the surname on his marriage to Viola Pemberton of Trumpington Hall.

too that access to the theatres involved a ramp and one or two lift journeys, the House sub-committee and the medical users decided that the space, with its unparalleled tree-top views, would be eminently suitable as a 'specialist facility' of a specifically medical nature. The ward therefore began life as a gastroenterology unit with the appropriately named Nurse Nightingale as its first sister.

The 1980s, though adding immeasurably to the work load, were also the years which saw The Evelyn's greatest achievements since the 1920s. In real-estate terms these included building or refurbishing of its operating theatres, the addition of the Cooke and Robinson Wings, upgrading the reception and clinic areas and of certain service departments, enlargement and re-equipping of the X-ray department, and creation of the Health Screening Unit. (Raising close on £1,000,000 in order to fund the majority of these projects was a triumph in itself.) With a new constitution came new streamlined management structures and a new name. New communications systems, some electronic, improved the dissemination of information and imparted a more professional appearance to the Hospital's dealings with its customers and providers. The establishment of new or responsibility-enhanced managerial positions resulted in improvements in the Hospital's day-to-day running, even though its much extended ground plan gave rise to doubts that continuation on its present site was feasible. Greater medical input improved patient safety and placed the Hospital well to the forefront of advances in medicine and surgery, while the recruitment of highly qualified nurses allowed it to boast with justification of the standard of care it provided. Strong leadership emanated from a respected Matron and an able Administrator, and the vision and energy of Geoffrey and Julian Agnew inspired and oversaw everything. As the Chairman's Statement in the Annual Report of March 1984 presciently stated, 'the position of The Evelyn as the major centre for private health care in Cambridge and the surrounding area is now well established and ... we can look forward to a continuing development of the range and quality of the services which can be offered over the coming years.'

To Manage the Process of Corporate Change

AS IF EXHAUSTED by its efforts at modernisation and development, The Evelyn of the later 1980s seemed to have run out of steam once the Cooke Wing was completed; indeed – as the Administrator noted in his report issued on 9 November 1987 concerning the future development of The Evelyn – it was difficult for him to make financial forecasts in the absence of plans of any kind. Fortunately for all concerned, the pause was more of a *réculer pour mieux sauter* than a manifestation of the Hospital's being bereft of ideas for the future. Mr Agnew, for his part, noted on 24 November 1988 both the 'enormous changes' which had taken place over the past fifteen years and what he regarded as the necessity of there being an independent audit of the Hospital's organisation and resources to enable it

to move confidently into the new decade. In his speech at the opening ceremony of the Cooke Wing in October 1989, Mr Agnew therefore announced the appointment of a team of management consultants (John Randle Associates) to undertake a study of The Evelyn as it stood, in order to ascertain whether or not it was likely to be viable as an independent hospital in five to ten years' time and, if so, what form of management structure it should have.

Their report, published in January 1990, was compiled from studies of statistical and financial data, from information provided by senior employees of the Hospital, from discussions with most members of the Hospital's committees and with sixteen consultants, from questionnaires sent to all medical users, and from meetings with the Cambridge Health Authority and medical insurance companies. Its compendious contents were divided into chapters dealing with finance, development needs, workload trends, the role of the medical users, corporate identity and charitable objects, and committee and management structure. It covered everything from the way in which the dramatic increase in the use of cytotoxic drugs affected the cost of medical consumables to the need for a development master plan for the site. The Committee of Management having considered the report and decided its future strategy, the Administrator was able to release an interim budget and Mr Agnew to announce on 1 February that The Evelyn was well placed to retain its position as the area's leading independent Hospital, with strong medical support and a sound financial position. Because of this, he continued, the Committee of Management wished to confirm the Hospital's continuation as an autonomous charitable organisation whose future development would be 'actively pursued'. The Committee itself pledged 'personal commitment' from its members and the Hospital a 'universal commitment' on the part of its staff to the role it was to play in the future.

The Evelyn, as the report saw it, was a structure 'inevitably in need of some change after a period of sustained growth'. Priority should be given to developing a clear management structure, the present structure lacking definition and direction because of the Hospital's having outgrown the essentially 'nursing home' management structure which had evolved over the years. In future, therefore, the Committee of Management was to concentrate on matters of policy and strategy. It was to meet two or three times a year to review and approve the Hospital's financial affairs, development and business plans, and charitable status and objectives. Day-to-day management was to devolve on a Chief Executive Officer to whom substantial powers were to be delegated by the Committee of Management, to which they would be directly answerable. Their role would be to co-ordinate the Hospital's 'hotel', business, clinical, and nursing services and to draw up business plans, budgets, and detailed development plans within the limits of policies agreed by the Committee. The Chief Executive was to be supported by a small Executive Committee composed mainly of professional advisers in relevant disciplines, whose role was to evaluate and approve actions undertaken by the Chief Executive before they were passed to the Committee of Management for ratification. The Chairman's Statement appended to the Annual Report of March 1991 noted that the new slimmer management structure arrived at as a result of the report would be more effective and more suitable for a modern hospital, and that as a consequence of the Hospital's restructuring of its chain of command, proper management function would naturally follow. As a corollary to this, abolition of the erstwhile nursing home's simple management structure of a Matron in sole charge with clerical and ancillary support (now deemed unsuitable for a high-volume Hospital employing upwards of two hundred staff over a variety of disciplines) meant Matron's relinquishment of executive power in favour of concentration on 'ensuring the quality of nursing provision', and her ranking second in seniority to the new Chief Executive.[1]

Appointment of The Evelyn's first Chief Executive took place on 15 February 1990, Mr Agnew announcing to the staff and medical users that Commander Allen would assume the position on 22 March and that,

although some adjustments in the duties of administrative staff would follow, no further changes were envisaged for the time being. A year later the Annual Report noted that the Commander's 'long experience of the Hospital and enormous capacity for hard work' had made him an immediate success in his new role.

The Chief Executive was not, of course, expected to carry the burden of responsibility alone. Apart from support provided by the Executive Committee, day-to-day management of the Hospital's various departments was to be delegated to their respective heads, and public relations and marketing to a marketing manager, while developmental schemes were to be worked out after consultation with staff and medical users. The only notable omission from the Chief Executive's support system, and indeed from the new management structure, was that of a director of finance to whom he could look for help with the preparation of financial forecasts and budgets; in fact, so notable was the omission that the post was advertised even before the Chief Executive's job description was finalised.

The new chain of command having been established, the next consequence of the Hospital's desire to implement

---

1. The difficulties inherent in Mrs Mundell's becoming subordinate overnight to whoever assumed the mantle of Chief Executive were avoided by her having announced her impending retirement at the opening of the Cooke Wing in October 1989. Because of her fifteen-year tenure of the position, she then became one of the three Matrons who between them devoted nearly sixty years of their working lives to the service of The Evelyn; the others being Edith Cracroft (1921–37), who took charge of The Evelyn's formative years, and Margaret Fynes-Clinton (1942–67), who oversaw The Evelyn's progress from the darkest days of the Second World War to the first intimations of its need for modernisation and expansion. Mrs Mundell was succeeded by Jane Donald SRN, lately assistant director of nursing at the Princess Grace Hospital in London.

The Evelyn's first three administrators. From left to right: Mr Robert Swindlehurst, Commander John Allen and Wing-Commander Peter Finlayson.

as completely as possible the suggestions made by the management consultancy team was its decision to appoint a Chief Executive with formal training in hospital management. Mindful, however, that continuity and stability were important to an institution which had undergone so many changes in such a comparatively short time, the Committee of Management delayed their request that Commander Allen take early retirement in order that an appropriately trained candidate could take his place. It was not, therefore, until March 1992 that the Annual Report announced the departure from The Evelyn of one who had 'so ably served as Administrator ... and as Chief Executive', and the arrival of Robert Swindlehurst LHSM who had been hospital director of the Priory Hospital, Roehampton, since 1989, and deputy hospital director of the Lister Hospital, Chelsea, before that. Within a few months of his appointment, as Mr Agnew noted in the Chairman's Statement of May 1992, Mr Swindlehurst had made clear that professional skills garnered from seventeen years' experience of the healthcare market would 'make his tenure a success'.

Mr Swindlehurst's first task, as he saw it, was to create a strategy which would 'enable the Hospital to develop and grow over the next five to ten years in a cohesive manner'. The plan was to include consideration of the present and future position of The Evelyn relative to the NHS, to Addenbrooke's Hospital, and to its East Anglian rivals in the private sector, and an examination of the direction likely to be taken by the local and national economy. A study was also to be made of opportunities for further development on The Evelyn site and of the Hospital's resources relative to the funding of any such development.

Hospitals, as John Randle Associates noted, 'are dynamic organisations which cannot avoid being under constant pressure'. This was certainly true of The Evelyn of the early 1990s, as an institution within which changes in management style, structure, and personnel affected the motivation and behaviour of its staff and upon which potent forces of an essentially economic nature worked to disrupt its 1980s satisfaction. Although it was the former that more immediately affected the workings of the Hospital, it was actually the Hospital's need to respond to the latter that resulted both in management changes and in reconsideration of The Evelyn's position as a non-profit-

making organisation in an increasingly money-oriented market.

With turnover in 1989/90 standing at £3,934,790 and in 1990/1 at £4,559,071 (a fourfold increase in a decade), the Annual Report of March 1991 had cause to be complacent, noting that 'the Hospital ... is in a very strong position. The operating surplus ... is at a record level [£623,269] and [this has] ... put us in sight of the elimination from the balance sheet of ... borrowings taken out to fund the building of the Arthur Cooke Wing in less than two years from its opening. This provides a very solid base for further development and expansion.' The year 1991/2 continued the upward trend, with the Hospital on course, as the Annual Report of March 1992 put it, 'for the largest surplus yet produced' (£792,995); this allowed it to pay off remaining bank loans of £603,125, already down from just over £1 million the previous year.

That 1991 had been so successful was fortunate for, as the Annual Report just quoted also noted, the Hospital had already begun to experience the effects of the economic recession into which the country as a whole was rapidly sliding. The report continued that 1992 had started off reasonably successfully, but 'there can be no doubt that during the year we may face some problems' due to the country's 'economic uncertainties'; it was hoped, however, that The Evelyn's established reputation, together with support from 'an exceptional group of Medical Users' and from a 'young and vigorous management team', would allow it a reasonable measure of security 'even in a more difficult economic climate'.

The consequences to The Evelyn of a downturn in the fortunes of local and national economies had been noted by the Committee of Management as early as November 1990. Meeting on 29 November, the Committee agreed that, although the effect on The Evelyn of current recessive trends had been minimal so far, and the effect of a recession lasting between six months and a year would be 'hardly noticeable', a recession lasting two or more years might be 'more serious' – if only because of the effect it would have on health insurance schemes (e.g. fewer companies would start up or continue medical insurance packages for their staff) and on the ability of uninsured patients to afford private healthcare.

Although as late as March 1993 Mr Agnew felt justified in asking if the local healthcare market was recession-proof because of the continuing prosperity of the East Anglian area, he was to receive the pessimistic reply that there would be a time lapse before the local market too became depressed, but that this would inevitably happen. (This, of course, had also been the case in the 1930s when the financial depression of 1931 was not fully experienced by The Evelyn until later in the decade.) Predictions became fact sooner than expected, the Executive Committee noting on 25 November that the local healthcare market was already in decline 'as a result of recession' and that the effects of this (e.g. company closures and rising unemployment) were beginning to have a marked effect on numbers of admissions. The Evelyn, one might say, was in danger of becoming asset rich and cash poor – or at least poorer – even though still able to maintain its anticipated annual surpluses.

The difficulties faced by The Evelyn in 1992/3 resulted not only in a 'clear reduction', as the Annual Report of March 1993 put it, of progression on all fronts but also in its having what the same report described as a 'difficult' year for other, but related, reasons. For one thing, the Hospital's high fixed cost base relied on sustained levels of activity to fund it, but overnight occupancy continued to fall, with corresponding loss of revenue uncorrected by further increases in day surgery. For another, health insurance companies keen to drive down costs by controlling charges began to pursue restrictive practices in favour of local company-owned hospitals, and this had the effect of diverting patients away from The Evelyn. In addition, Addenbrooke's began its moves to acquire trust status, raising questions concerning the future relationship between public and private healthcare sectors in the Cambridge area, and there was a continuing lack of evidence of local economic recovery. All this occasioned The Evelyn in general and its new Chief Executive in particular a good deal of anxiety. Fortunately for the Hospital, its facility for regeneration even in the most difficult circumstances stood it in good stead. By June 1993, and in spite of the continuation of difficult and declining market conditions, revenue levels were noted to be holding up. This was due not only to the good name which it retained, but also to stringent cost control measures and to a 6 per cent increase in workload brought about by a wide-ranging case mix and by further increases in the numbers of orthopaedic, gastroenterology and oncology cases admitted. Thus although, as the Annual Report of March 1994 agreed, the past year had been one of 'comparative difficulty' because of the prevailing 'recessionary element' and because advances in medical practice (notably minimally invasive or 'keyhole' surgery) had still further reduced the average length of stay, the Hospital's finances showed a 5 per cent increase in turnover to £4,376,819.

It was, however, becoming increasingly apparent that for the Hospital to be able to fund both its charitable projects[2] and the site-development projects envisaged by John Randle Associates, it had to examine ways in which its high cost base could be reduced. The importance of its doing so as soon as possible was highlighted in a discussion paper submitted by Mr Swindlehurst to the Executive Committee on 24 July 1994. He stated, first, that the Hospital's only response so far to John Randle Associates' financial suggestions had been a review of its contracts and pricing policies, a slow but a steady reduction in staff costs due to natural wastage, and a shift in emphasis away from bed revenue to one on returns from theatre usage and consumables; and, second, that the Hospital's

2. Projects to which The Evelyn contributed included the Papworth Trust for the Severely Disabled, the Eastern Region Children's Hospice, Macmillan Cancer Care and the Red Cross, all 'bodies with objects similar to those of the Home', as the 1920 Memorandum put it.

seemingly satisfactory performance merely matched but did not improve upon that of years when higher levels of activity were enjoyed. The decision was therefore taken to erode costs as part of a long-term process by streamlining the existing workforce (the Committee agreed in principle to accept job losses) and by developing strategies which would enable the Hospital to respond more flexibly to market conditions and to seasonal fluctuations in workload.

Exposed as the Hospital increasingly was, even after implementation of the measures listed above, Mr Swindlehurst – keen that it should operate as far as possible from a position of strength vis-à-vis competitor activity in order to maintain its position and reputation in the local healthcare market-place, and to ensure the staff understood and implemented strategies enabling it to do so – asked for the advice of a further team of management consultants on how The Evelyn could best manage 'the process of corporate change'. Morton Hodgson Management Consultants, like their predecessors, began by assessing the current situation. Their initial examination, made in July 1992 and reinforced by further studies carried

out between that date and April 1993, concerned past and present styles of management and what they termed the staff's 'working attitudes'.

Management style and structure of the past (i.e. that pertaining until Mr Swindlehurst's arrival in April 1992) Morton Hodgson described as 'bureaucratic, benevolent, and leaning towards a command environment', with communications going 'all the way up and then back down again'. This, while no doubt helping to maintain The Evelyn's reputation as a first-class private Hospital, had a downside in that it contributed to stagnation (limited investment in management systems, limited staff contribution to business development etc.) and to people being expected to co-operate with instructions from above without being able to demonstrate individual or departmental initiative. To engender 'a new and competitive climate', it was necessary to move as quickly as possible from the former rigid command structure to one in which channels of communication were more 'open', individual contributions recognised, and departmental responsibilities fostered.

Three important consequences of Morton Hodgson's activities were, first, realisation by those working at The Evelyn (some of whom had been in post for over ten years and had become rather resistant to change) that change could be energising when used in the right way, especially when it concerned the future of an institution to which they were devoted; second, the development of what Mr Swindlehurst described as 'some newly formed skills in our workforce'; third, the institution of internal training programmes which resulted in staff becoming better educated with regard to practical and management issues; and, fourth, participation in formal quality-assurance schemes, epitomised by a mission statement promulgated in January 1993 which stated that The Evelyn was now to be 'the private hospital of choice in Cambridge and the surrounding area for patients and the medical community by providing the highest quality of care'.

It was about this time, too, that The Evelyn's first Philosophy of Nursing was promulgated and the manifesto pinned up for patients to see. Patients, it promised, would be treated as individuals and fully involved in the management of their own care, the said care to be assessed, planned, implemented and evaluated (as the current buzzword had it) holistically. The nurses, for their part, promised that patient care would be carried out to research-based standards and that they, as carers, would demonstrate sympathy and understanding, and endeavour to instil confidence.

That they very largely succeeded – and in doing so fulfilled the hope expressed in the management consultants' report that, while The Evelyn scored in location, reputation and motivation, it nevertheless needed to work hard at meeting patients' expectations if it wished to retain its pre-eminent position – is summarised by a letter received from a patient during the early 1990s which simply said 'how lucky we are to be in the orbit of such an excellent hospital'. A former Matron's discovery in April 1995 that 'nursing in all its forms' was alive and well at the Hospital over which she had once presided is illustrated by humorous letters describing 'the most efficient and friendly group of bottom-rubbing and suppository-shoving girls that I have ever had the good fortune to encounter'; the same girls, another letter noted, administered injections with 'firmness of purpose' and displayed an 'unwavering resoluteness ... when sitting patients up'. Yet everything, as another patient pointed out, was performed with the good humour characteristic of The Evelyn, to the extent that the 'super lot of girls' were 'candidates for sainthood'! What was more, behind those with whom the patients had most immediate contact there was also, as a thank-you letter of 1993 noted, an army of support staff of whom patients might well be less aware 'beavering away' in departments spread throughout buildings dating from the 1870s to the 1990s, all of whom contributed in different ways to their well-being.

To Enter into the Next Stage of the Hospital's Development

JOHN RANDLE ASSOCIATES' report of 1990 had dwelt not only on the running of the Hospital but also on what it termed 'imbalances' in facilities provided at The Evelyn in spite of the recently completed programme of modernisation and development; given that the Hospital had no intention of relocating, site constraints meant that redressing of these (and preparation for a possible 50 per cent increase in demand) would have to take place *in situ*. A site development plan formulated by Mr Swindlehurst subsequent to the Executive Committee Meeting of 28 May 1992 therefore resulted in prioritisation of the various areas requiring attention: refurbishment of the Aston Webb Wing rooms and corridors, creation of a third operating theatre, and further enlargement of the X-ray department.

The Evelyn's 1990s admission ratio of approximately 10 per cent medical to 90 per cent surgical patients broadly followed national patterns of private healthcare. John Randle Associates' research also showed that The Evelyn admitted around 65 per cent of all local private-sector medicine and surgery, the remaining 35 per cent going to other local private hospitals and to the small number of paybeds at Addenbrooke's. That The Evelyn maintained 60–70 per cent bed occupancy (described by John Randle Associates as 'good by … private hospital standards') was due to East Anglia's 'strong propensity' for private medical care. It contained 20 per cent more than the national average of the top three socio-economic groups, and the area's population continued to grow to include a 'significant influx' of people of working age with private company healthcare schemes. Additionally, the introduction in 1991 of tax relief on private healthcare premiums for the elderly would, it was hoped, attract this type of patient too to Cambridge's best-known and longest-established private Hospital.

Mr Swindlehurst's original time scale for the refurbishment of the Aston Webb Wing envisaged that work would be carried out floor by floor, beginning in September and December 1992. In practice, problems posed by working on one floor at a time resulted in simultaneous disruption of traffic along two trunk routes to and from the back of the Hospital, while the detailed planning required for the installation of new electrical, heating and plumbing systems, and the marrying of these to the Hospital's existing systems, meant that work was unable to start until the middle of June 1993. Although the Medical Users Council, meeting two months earlier on 28 April, hoped that 'patients would not be inconvenienced or operating lists curtailed' by 'a certain amount of disruption and noise', patients nursed at The Evelyn during the summer and early autumn of 1993 vividly recall being wheeled to theatre through and over heaps of rubble or

being deafened by the noise of drills attacking Sir Aston's 9-inch (23 cm) thick walls; and staff unfortunate enough to work in the kitchen, stores, pharmacy, and the Gibson and Geoffrey Agnew Theatres recalled the clouds of creamy Cambridge brick dust which percolated everywhere. As the Executive Committee noted on 22 July 1993, in words that echoed those of the victims of all previous Evelyn building programmes, 'a considerable amount of noise, dust and disruption has been caused'. The wing reopened for use in November 1993.

Provision of additional operating facilities was next to be considered, the Chairman's Statement appended to the Annual Report of March 1993 being pleased to announce that 'twin operating theatres will be added to the existing two, providing facilities for all our consultants, including some whom previously we were unable to accommodate', allowing them to operate 'in the most up to date surroundings'.

The decision to position the new theatres at the end of the Cooke Wing, rather than contiguous to the Geoffrey Agnew and Gibson Theatres, was taken to avoid the access problems of the former (the lift was too small to take the beds on which theatre

The Morland Theatre.

patients were increasingly transported) and the proximity to one of the Hospital's main thoroughfares of the latter; it meant, however, that strenuous efforts had to be made on the part of the planners lest it encroach too much on the Hospital's grounds. In fact so important was the maintenance of a 'peaceful and attractive environment' thought to be 'to the recovery of patients' that additional landscaping was provided once the building was completed, small trees and shrubs being planted around its base, trellises erected for the training of climbing plants up the walls, and an arbour placed on the lawn where patients and visitors could enjoy the play of light and pattern on its expanse of glass. The first turf was

Robert Swindlehurst and Julian Agnew cut the first turf of the Morland Theatre, 27 May 1993.

cut by Mr Agnew on 27 May 1993, and work started early in June. Completion in April 1994 allowed the first operations in the new theatres to be carried out on 9 May 1994. It was decided to call the new theatres the Morland Suite in honour of the C. Morland Agnew who had been too modest to give his own name to the institution he founded. Appropriately too, old friends were reunited by the placing of the Morland Suite at the end of the Arthur Cooke Wing. The suite was opened by the Duke of Edinburgh on 14 June 1995. As was the case with the Geoffrey Agnew Theatre, which he had opened in

October 1981 thirteen months after its coming into use, His Royal Highness's declaration in June 1995 that the Morland Suite was 'more open than usual' was apt, the new suite too having been brought into use thirteen months earlier. Following a guided tour during which he watched a demonstration of minimally invasive surgical techniques, His Royal Highness proceeded up the lawn to a marquee where he had tea with members of staff and medical users.

Completion of the scheme which, the Annual Report of March 1994 hoped, would provide The Evelyn with 'tangible evidence' of the success of its development plans by doubling its operating capacity, was announced in the following year's report as benefiting the Hospital by increasing the number of operations performed and by increasing bed occupancy. It was also apparent that creation of the Morland Suite had enhanced the Hospital's surgical performance overall, and it soon became common to find at least three and sometimes all four theatres simultaneously in use. The effect of this was noted in the Annual Report of March 1996, which recorded not only another year of growth and a record trading surplus, but also a record number of admissions (4,871) – of whom the majority (4,105) underwent surgery. That the surplus began to grow again as a direct result of the Third Theatre Project's completion was encouraging, not least because on its success hung the continuation of the Hospital's substantial capital expenditure programme.

Although the arrival of the Morland Suite allowed the Hospital to carry out greater numbers of operations, many of the surgical advances which were pioneered or saw some of their earliest manifestations at

The Duke of Edinburgh officially opens the Morland Theatre, 14 June 1995. He is accompanied by Julian Agnew, surgeon David Dunn and Sister Joyce Fraser.

The Evelyn took place in its older operating theatres between 1990 and 1994. This had been made possible by the Committee of Management's decision (reported with joy by the Medical Users Committee on 8 November 1990) to equip The Evelyn in general and its operating theatres in particular to 'the highest possible standard', one of the consequences of which was that 'the onslaughts of my superb surgeon' (as a patient put it) were assisted, first, by the installation of video cameras in the Gibson and Geoffrey Agnew Theatres and, second, by the acquisition of equipment which would enable laser-assisted surgery to be carried out. A video camera was an essential and the YAG laser a useful accompaniment to the minimally invasive surgery which The Evelyn was so keen to promote. On 22 September 1991, David Dunn performed the Hospital's first, and his third, laparoscopic cholecystectomy, one of the earliest to be carried out in the East Anglian region. The Evelyn patient was discharged forty-eight hours after surgery, a length of stay soon to be reduced by Mr Dunn to twenty-four hours and then to day-surgery proportions, a move which made the operation particularly exciting to nurses used to the ten-day stay of conventional gall bladder surgery and the attendant post-operative restrictions and discomfort of open abdominal surgery. By 28 November Mr Dunn had also performed three laparoscopic herniorrhaphies at The Evelyn, using, as the Executive Committee noted, 'techniques he has not yet practised at Addenbrooke's Hospital', while in February 1992 he performed Cambridge's first minimally invasive bowel resection in the Geoffrey Agnew Theatre, the patient being discharged six days later. In September 1994, the Morland Suite now being open, he performed the United Kingdom's first full operation using robotic assistance – the robot directing lights, cameras and instruments in response to light signals emitted by a headband worn by the surgeon. By the time of the Duke of Edinburgh's visit in June 1995, 450 minimally invasive surgical procedures had been performed at The Evelyn. The Executive Committee noted that, although the expensive disposable items used for this type of surgery put up the cost of medical and surgical consumables, the cost to the patient or to their insurance company was not materially affected because of the much shorter stay in hospital. Added to this, kudos accruing to the

Hospital was considerable, and patients were attracted to The Evelyn from far and wide.

Not all the schemes so optimistically listed in Mr Swindlehurst's Site Development Plan came to fruition as satisfactorily as the Morland Theatre. An example of a department which was re-equipped but not, as hoped, enlarged was Radiology, which continued to flourish (as the Annual Report of March 1991 noted), with 7,924 examinations being carried out in 1990/1, though – as Mr Swindlehurst noted in the Site Development Plan – the department's accommodation had become insufficient for current demand in less than the ten years originally allowed, chiefly because of the marked increase in orthopaedic surgery. The Executive Committee's meeting on 28 January 1993 agreed with Mr Swindlehurst's suggestion that X-ray be expanded along the ground-floor corridor, but the earmarked area was adapted for pharmacy use instead, the demands on the oncology service having become so great that creation of an isolator room dedicated to the preparation of cytotoxic drugs had become essential. Money was therefore spent on replacement of radiological equipment which was either nearing the end of its

natural life or had been overtaken by technological advances.

Although both the X-ray and the Health Screening Departments were affected by the recession, the latter in particular because of its foundation at the start of a difficult economic era, both were able to ride out the storm with the new contracts and returning clients of the one benefiting the other in terms of referrals for radiological examinations. By March 1995, as the Annual Report for that year noted, X-ray had resumed 'its habitual pattern of growth' and Health Screening had achieved 'an extraordinary result, some 50% higher than … the previous year'. The Health Screening Unit, unlike X-ray, *was* able to expand – although the establishment of new screening programmes in April 1994, which brought 460 new clients to the department within a very short space of time, meant that until an adjacent area of Agnew House was converted and equipped for clinical work, the unit functioned in very cramped conditions.

Further projects which Mr Swindlehurst wished to include in his Site Development Plan, such as the erection of a large outpatients department along the Hospital's Trumpington Road frontage and the creation of a day-surgery unit, were postponed *sine die* because planning permission was refused or because no suitable space could be found for them within the footprint of The Evelyn's enlarged but still restricted buildings.

A department whose upgrading was not envisaged in Mr Swindlehurst's Site Development Plan but whose reorganisation was drastic was that of Hotel Services in May 1993. The initial stimulus arose from the need to reduce the nurses' workload, much expanded by the 1989 extension of the Hospital's geography. Up till then, the first task of the day for the sister or staff nurse in charge of a ward had been the distribution of the day's menu to each patient and the taking of their order once a choice had been made.[1] Although the nurse did more than merely mark up the menu sheets – she was at the same time made aware of patients disinclined or unable to eat and why, and so was able to suggest a suitable remedy or tempt jaded appetites with promises of specially prepared food – the procedure *per se* was a waste of valuable nursing time. It was therefore decided to delegate it to non-nursing personnel, albeit with nurses remaining in overall charge of patients' nutritional needs. The second stimulus was economic,

Mr Swindlehurst expressing dismay that the cost of food per patient per day was excessively high: in part because items were purchased from local suppliers at full market price, in part because standing orders were fulfilled whether the items were required or not, and in part because there was an uncontrolled outflow of food items from the Hospital and unregulated consumption of items within it. His business plan therefore promised an early review of the 'working practices of the Hotel Services Department with a view to making improvements'.

An immediate change in working practices was brought about by the appointment of a Catering Manager in 1993. Following his arrival, reforms in the ordering of foodstuffs – a result of negotiations with local suppliers and use being made of London markets from which first-class produce could be bought at discounted prices – reduced the cost of food per patient per day, overstocks were streamlined and stock turnover improved, standing orders ceased, portion control was introduced, and the consumption of beverages was regulated by the purchase of dispensing machines. As a result of these measures, inspectors from the local Environmental Health

1. The floor sister's list of duties of 1938 included the following:

> Diets and meals:
> go round to each patient with menu for the day and write diet list;
> inform Matron of any special diets;
> order amount of milk required for the day;
> enter all extra meals for patients' visitors;
> check all meals as they arrive from the kitchen

Very little had changed in the intervening fifty years.

The Evelyn catering staff, 14 June 1995.

Office expressed their general satisfaction with the Hospital's foodstock policy. Essential upgrading of the main and ward kitchens was also carried out under his supervision in order to comply with new EEC directives on the storage and presentation of foodstuffs.

His efforts soon paid off. At a meeting held in December 1994, attended by the principal Environmental Health Officer for the City of Cambridge, the award to the Hospital of a Food Hygiene Certificate of Merit was confirmed and The Evelyn was nominated a Grade B catering outlet, rather than a Grade A (the highest risk category) which, as a hospital, it would be expected to be. A further compliment was paid in 1995 when The Evelyn was notified by the same authority that it was to be treated as a 'showcase' point of reference for other food outlets.

The Catering Manager's dictum that 'we are only as good as the last meal served' heralded the arrival of another change: food described by patients as being of 'excellent quality, plentiful, varied, and exquisitely presented … served hot and on hot plates'. A typical menu offered home-made soup or fresh fruit juice; followed by a main course with a

choice of meat (beef Stroganov, fricassee of veal), fish (grilled plaice, salmon salad) or vegetarian (mushroom risotto, spinach quiche) dishes, with fresh vegetables or a side salad; and a selection of desserts: ice cream, cheese and biscuits, yoghurt, apple and cinnamon slice, and the very popular fresh fruit platter. Patients who preferred a snack were offered a choice of sandwiches on white or granary bread. Children benefited from the institution of a special menu served in smaller portions on

decorated china. By September 1993, the Hospital had won its first Heartbeat Award for healthy eating. The medical users, noting the change in style of the refreshments provided in theatre, expressed their gratitude for the 'healthier diet they are now receiving' but some 'unhealthy but popular' items – as the Catering Manager put it – such as chips reappeared in the staff dining room in response to vociferous requests! Healthy eating also received a temporary setback during the Gourmet Week held in November 1993 to reward the staff for their forbearance during the renovation of the Aston Webb Wing, when dishes offered included poussin stuffed with paté and sultanas, crayfish, jacket potatoes with sour cream and caviar, cream cornets, trifle, tiramisu, and profiteroles. In December 1994, it was proudly noted that only twenty other local catering outlets had either the Heartbeat Award or the Food Hygiene Certificate of Merit – and only 4 out of the 1,207 in the city had both. Of the latter, The Evelyn was one.

Proud recipients of the Heartbeat Award and the Food Hygiene Certificate of Merit, the cooks and chefs of The Evelyn, June 1995.

CHAPTER 24

So many Leading Practitioners

FURTHER DEVELOPMENT of the Hospital's site did not, however, give rise to a concomitant increase in staff, for at the same time as work on the various projects took place moves were afoot to reduce their numbers. In contrast, therefore, to decisions made in the prosperous 1980s that a reduction in numbers was unacceptable because it would adversely affect standards of care, but as a direct result of the financial consequences of that decision for the Hospital's fixed cost base, in the economically unsettled 1990s the need arose to reduce expenditure on its most expensive resource. The 'significant reduction' in nursing and support staff numbers did not, however, take place immediately. Senior nurses strongly opposed cuts in staffing ratios, claiming that The

Evelyn's reputation for first-class care rested on its maintaining higher staffing levels than its competitors, and that any reduction in the level of care would increase the risk of accidents and hence of claims against the Hospital. They were supported in this by their knowledge that the Hospital's single rooms and extended layout added 10 per cent to the minimum numbers needed on each shift, and that its paediatric and seriously ill patients increased levels of dependency overall.

Matters were complicated at this point by Mrs Donald resigning as Matron on 31 July 1994. Her resignation was accepted with regret by the Committee of Management, particularly as she had been responsible for the reorganisation and modernisation of the management of the nurses, a task she had undertaken, according to the Annual Report of March 1994, 'with exemplary tact, skill, and patience'. Her successor, Wendy Mendham,[1] taking up her post on 1 August, found herself with the unenviable task of continuing her predecessor's attempt to reduce the nursing budget's contribution to the Hospital's fixed-cost base. It having been agreed that the arrival of a new Matron would be a good time to continue the Hospital's review of cost-control measures in relation to the nursing budget, Mrs Mendham's report on the subject could not have been altogether welcome to those advocating a reduction in staffing levels overall and in nurse numbers in particular. The Evelyn, said Mrs Mendham, actually needed *more* rather than fewer nurses, giving as her reasons that:

a) although the average length of stay had dropped from 4.3 days in 1993 to 3.8 by mid-1995, day-case activity had increased from an average of 100 to one of 129 cases a month over a six-month period and showed no sign of decreasing;
b) new consultants were about to be appointed, joining colleagues whose Evelyn workload had already increased, and this would put even greater pressure on the nurses;
c) more and more acutely ill patients and a greater number of complicated medical and/or elderly patients were routinely admitted to The Evelyn;
d) the greater complexity of surgical procedures carried out on a regular basis required patients to be nursed on a virtually one-to-one basis in the early post-operative period.

Far from a *decrease* in numbers of nursing and nursing support staff, there ought therefore to be an urgent increment in all areas.

In support of a decision which was bound to be controversial, Mrs Mendham cited her and the medical users' awareness that changes taking place in nursing at a national level were liable to have a deleterious effect on patient care in Cambridge. Because fewer nurses were entering or completing training (in part because Project 2000 with its more academic approach to nursing deterred some who might otherwise have entered the profession) and more were leaving because they were disillusioned with pay and conditions, there were fewer nurses available to take up permanent positions at The Evelyn or to work

1. Mrs Mendham arrived at The Evelyn with over thirty years' nursing experience. Married with two children, she described herself as a 'people person' with a 'warm and friendly approach to nursing'.

there as bank or agency nurses, with the result that on occasion no staff from any source were available to make up a deficit. This also meant that there were fewer experienced nurses to take on the more complex tasks expected of nurses, now that their role had been extended to supervise invasive monitoring devices, to assist at procedures formerly carried out in theatre, to care for those high-dependency patients who – prior to Mrs Donald's arrival – would have been transferred to Addenbrooke's, and to carry out procedures previously carried out by doctors – for example, the administration of intravenous drugs.

That Evelyn nurses of the 1990s were rapidly assuming the mantle of junior doctors would have been no surprise to its medical users; on the other hand, the medical users might have expressed surprise at hearing themselves described as its most important resource. John Randle Associates' report, quoted earlier, left no doubt on that score: consultants, it said, 'are the true clients of an independent hospital even though it is their patients who are the recipients of the service provided'.

As their report and other documentation showed, most Cambridge consultants worked at The

The Consultants v. The Evelyn cricket match, on Parkers Piece, September 1993.

Evelyn, and most carried out the majority of their private practice there – not least because it was conveniently placed for early morning and late evening visits before and after their work at Addenbrooke's. Conversely, because the majority of consultants working at The Evelyn also worked at Addenbrooke's, the former continued to benefit from its proximity to East Anglia's only teaching hospital, the Annual Report of March 1995 noting that The Evelyn was 'fortunate indeed' to have 'so many leading practitioners in their various fields' working there. Fortunately too, the majority of the consultants working at The Evelyn were in their 40s or 50s and so were not due to retire for at least ten years, while those in their 60s were matched by more recent appointees in their 30s, many of whom were introduced to the Hospital by those they replaced.

Following earlier recommendations that the committee structure of the Hospital be revised to suit its new role, Mr Agnew had decided that it would be appropriate if medical input into the running of the Hospital were focused at the executive level. There remained, however, a widespread feeling among the medical users that management mechanisms failed to allow effective medical input into the Hospital's policy-making and strategy-devising processes, and that decisions affecting medical and surgical practice continued to be made without reference to those who were best placed to know how things ought to be done. In May 1991, therefore, a Medical Advisory Committee was set up, composed of representatives of the various specialties found at The Evelyn, its chairman being *ex officio* a member of the Committee of Management. This resulted in a consultant body noted to be 'firmly committed to The Evelyn, appreciative of its many good points, and eager to see them safeguarded and developed', and believing that it now played an active part in the running of the Hospital. At first the Medical Advisory Committee dealt mainly with problems concerning the development of medical and surgical services at The Evelyn, but it soon diversified to include issues of medical relevance in the widest sense, such as the institution of systematic reviews of clinical performance (medical audit), and changes in postgraduate training heralded by the Calman Report of 1993 which, it was thought, might affect the appointment of The Evelyn's resident medical officers. (Fortunately, it did not). Mr Swindlehurst's *Business*

Plan 1993 Onwards supported the activities of the new Advisory Committee by promising to ensure that all consultants were contacted at regular intervals to determine levels of satisfaction on services provided, and to help newly appointed consultants establish their private practices at The Evelyn. It also promised to further good relations with the NHS and GP fundholders in general, and with the Cambridge Area Health Authority in particular, in order to ensure that The Evelyn was included in their plans for the future.

CHAPTER 25

We have Come a Long Way Together

THE EVELYN NURSING HOME'S first patient was admitted on 25 July 1921. On 25 July 1991, The Evelyn Hospital celebrated its seventieth birthday with a garden party. This was followed five years later by the Hospital's seventy-fifth birthday, for which even more celebrations were planned. These included an Anniversary Dinner held at King's College and a charity event in the Hospital's main waiting room, at which experts from the BBC's *Antiques Road Show* gave their advice on a variety of objects – including a set of personal weighing scales bought sixty years earlier and presented to The Evelyn by William Wingate Pemberton. Julian Agnew's comment on the 'celebration of so important an Anniversary' for the institution, with which he had been associated for over twenty-five years and his family for four generations, was that The Evelyn had been fortunate in being 'in the right place at the right time, in a city with an extraordinarily talented group of surgeons and doctors' and in a period of unprecedented growth for East Anglia in general and Cambridge in particular. As Nursing Home and Hospital, it had also been fortunate 'in the personalities of those who supported it with their generosity and their skills over the past seventy-five years', and he personally looked forward 'to working with their contemporary counterparts as The Evelyn progressed towards the millennium and its centenary'.

The new millennium, unfortunately, began with another conflagration. At 2 p.m. on 24 February 2000, forty-eight years almost to the day (20 February)

NEWS

24.2.00.

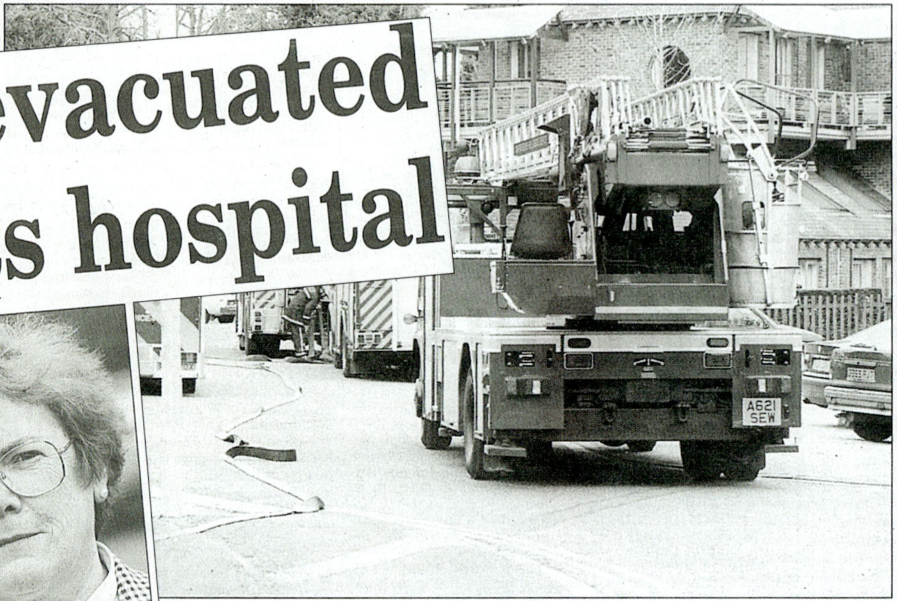

engines and crews on the scene at the Evelyn Hospital in Cambridge yesterday.

Patients evacuated as fire hits hospital

**Report by
HELEN POPPER
Pictures by
MATTHEW POWER**

PATIENTS were led to safety after fire broke out in a hospital ward.

Several operations were cancelled because of the blaze, which started in a bedroom block yesterday afternoon.

Ten patients, who were recovering from surgery, were wheeled out of the smoke-logged ward on their beds and taken to spare rooms as firefighters fought to bring the blaze under control.

More than 30 firefighters were called to the Evelyn Hospital in Cambridge where the fire started just after 2pm.

Staff at the private hospital said patients had not been in danger.

Marjory Rankin, chief executive, said the evacuation had gone according to well-rehearsed safety drills.

She said: "There was a lot of smoke in the building so we moved the patients to other rooms.

"They were moved very quickly and one told me they thought it was exciting.

"It has caused disruption. Some people were waiting for operations, which we cancelled. It throws everything out but we train and prepare for it."

Several bedrooms were badly damaged by smoke and will need redecorating. The fire started while workmen were using

Marjory Rankin . . . 'Safety drills paid off during evacuation.'

welding tools to repair piping in the roof, said Andy Watson, chief fire officer.

"There was a lot of smoke. We had to make sure there was no chance of it spreading to other parts of the roof," he added.

Firefighters used breathing apparatus and hoses to control the fire, and roof tiles were removed to make sure it was out.

The Trumpington Road hospital carries out all kinds of medical surgery, including treating cancer patients.

Smoke damage . . . firefighters get to work on the roof of the bedroom block where the blaze started.   Picture: Matthew Power

The report on the outbreak of fire at The Evelyn in the Cambridge Evening News, *24 February 2000.*

on which the 'Night Blaze at Nursing Home' made headlines in the local newspaper, a fire broke out in the suspended ceiling of an annexe to Newton Ward where a workman was using welding tools. The annexe, used as an extension to the ward, was undergoing radical alterations with the aim of turning it into a High Dependency Unit. Work had begun in 1999 and was, by the time of the fire, virtually complete; following the fire the new unit required such extensive repairs that its opening was delayed by six months. Not only this, but the fire, though quickly brought under control, broke out afresh in the roof farther along the Robinson Wing corridor. In spite of flames above her head, a courageous and conscientious nurse attending a post-operative patient in one of the affected rooms stayed with her patient until her colleagues, who had themselves braved a smoke-filled corridor in order to move patients to safety, came to her assistance.

Quite by chance, the *Cambridge Evening News* report of the incident was remarkably similar in tone and content to that of the *Cambridge Daily News* half a century before. Under the headline 'Patients evacuated as fire hits hospital', the report ran as follows 'patients were led to safety after the fire broke out … Ten patients were wheeled out … and taken to spare rooms as firefighters fought to bring the blaze under control … Firefighters used breathing apparatus and hoses to control the fire and roof tiles were removed to make sure it was out.' The Evelyn's Chief Executive told the newspaper that the evacuation had gone according to 'well rehearsed safety drills' and that patients were moved so expeditiously that some, not realising the danger, found the episode quite exciting. The nurses, shaken though they were by the sudden onset and rapid spread of the fire – but thankful that it had not happened, as previously, at night – collected themselves sufficiently to send a message to the firefighters of 'appreciation of their services'. Although very few operations were postponed or cancelled, fire and water damage to adjacent areas meant that some patients had to be housed for five months in a temporary building (the 'Garden Ward') on the lawn. This, and the fact that equipment and facilities lost or damaged in the fire had to be replaced or were unavailable until renovation work was completed, added to the inconvenience.

The desolation prevailing in the Robinson Wing was symptomatic, to some, of a wider malaise, for in spite of its busyness the years following The Evelyn's seventy-fifth birthday had not been altogether happy. An all-too-prescient depiction at that event of the bleak future facing stand-alone hospitals seemed, in financial if no other terms, to be coming true due to the drag effect of the recession and unremitting pressure from major health insurance companies. Added to this, loss of income following the fire resulted in further economy measures having to be taken. Changes in senior management and nursing staff added to the prevailing insecurity.[1]

Regeneration began with the appointment early in 1999 of a new Chief Executive, Marjorie Rankin, who set the Hospital some way along the road to recovery, but left early in the following year. At that time, too, a letter signed by Julian Agnew announced that on 1 April 2000 the Hospital's Board of Trustees, formerly the Committee of Management, would delegate responsibility for its management to the Hospital Management Trust (HMT)[2] whose executive director, John Randle, formerly head of John Randle Associates, had advised it in a personal capacity for ten years, the Board itself retaining ownership and the power of policy decision-making. The reason for this semi-arrogation of the Hospital's autonomy, continued Mr Agnew, was that with significant changes taking place in the NHS and the private healthcare sector, the Hospital's governing body – though determined to maintain The Evelyn's independence and ethos – nevertheless recognised the need for wider hospital management expertise than could be provided in-house. It had therefore asked the HMT to bring to bear on the Hospital its wider range of skills in this important area. To this end, a new Hospital Director would be appointed by the HMT to succeed Miss Rankin, supported and advised by an HMT management team. The Evelyn's new Hospital Director, Elizabeth Hayes, arrived shortly afterwards.

Alterations to the fabric of the Hospital continued unabated during this time, building works adding a physical dimension to the turmoil but at the same time providing material evidence of The Evelyn's continuing presence as a well-known and well-loved Cambridge institution. Although no new external structures were added to a site which had virtually exhausted its capacity for expansion, unless demolition of existing buildings took place, much internal alteration

1. Mrs Mendham and Mr Swindlehurst both left in 1999, the former being replaced by The Evelyn's fourth Matron in less than ten years, Gill Cockley, who had served The Evelyn as staff nurse and sister prior to her appointment.

2. The HMT, a like-minded charity established fifteen years earlier, was responsible for nine other hospitals and nursing homes. It was specifically created to support existing charitable hospitals and as a fall-back support for others in case of need.

occurred – some on a comparatively minor scale, some involving major adaptations of existing areas. It was, of course, conversion of one such area which sparked the fire that created so much 'disruption' at the start of the new millennium.

The High Dependency Unit – which eventually opened in October 2000, nearly seven years after the Medical Users Council's decision that it would be 'worth exploring' provision of such a facility – came about in response to Department of Health guidelines of 1996, which suggested that hospitals such as The Evelyn should contain a unit in which levels of care intermediate between ward and intensive care could be provided. The unit, situated adjacent to Newton Ward where all major surgery was now concentrated, contained three bed spaces where 1:1 or 1:2 nursing could be carried out, a nurses' station, and a small adjoining sluice.

Concentration of major surgical cases on Newton Ward formed part of the realignment of the Hospital's medical and surgical services instigated by Mrs Mendham in 1998. Prior to that, surgical cases were nursed on Newton or Chaucer Wards, patients being allocated to one or the other for reasons ranging from personal request

to surgeons' preference and room suitability. Chaucer also continued to house medical patients, a rather unhappy marriage of specialties remedied only partly by the ward's division into two areas: one, housed in the Robinson and Cooke Wings, continuing as a surgical unit; the other, housed in the Aston Webb Wing, being dedicated to medicine. A later reshuffling created a new ward situated in what had been Chaucer's Cooke Wing, housing medical and oncology patients.

Once established as a separate unit, Arthur Cooke Ward flourished under the care of oncology specialist practitioners and nurses whose interests lay in medical rather than surgical fields. Oncological treatment was provided to both inpatients and outpatients, the latter using a comfortable 'lounge' with adjacent rest and preparation areas. From a specialty too small to merit space of its own, The Evelyn's Oncology Service, the only private one in Cambridge, was to continue very actively even though chemotherapeutic drugs and regimes necessitating fewer admissions to hospital – combined with the comparatively few medical patients admitted to a Hospital whose activities were dictated almost entirely by its operating theatres – caused peaks and troughs in its workload which were difficult to predict and even more difficult to staff. Chaucer Ward, on the other hand, became The Evelyn's busy and successful Day Surgery Unit, later amended to the Short Stay Unit as some patients stayed overnight. The unit, opened in 1998, housed patients admitted for endoscopy, for minor surgery in all specialties, and for the alleviation of chronic pain.

Theatres too continued busy, 4,500 patients passing through in an average year. The number – a very far cry indeed from the six operations recorded by Miss Cracroft as having taken place in seventeen days in 1921, the two a day of the war years, and the average of a thousand a year immediately before the arrival of the NHS – topped the 3,500 which followed the opening of the Geoffrey Agnew and the refurbishing of the Gibson Theatres, but accurately reflected the smaller increase in activity (to just over 4,000 cases a year) which followed the opening of the Morland Suite. Slowing of the former exponential increase was due as much to saturation of the Hospital's forty surgical beds as to shortage of theatre staff (a national, not just an Evelyn, problem), the latter leading to

increased pressure on staff already in post, to the employment of expensive agency staff of unknown 'characters and powers', and to the rather more successful recruitment of nurses from abroad. Attempts to relieve the pressure by preventing surgeons from operating late into the evening were largely unsuccessful, given that on the 'product' of the operating theatres the Hospital's survival chiefly relied.

The Evelyn's abandonment of plans for expansion of its outpatients area beyond the Hospital's existing 'footprint' led to its having to decide where, within the footprint, it could position the extra clinic rooms urgently required by some thirty medical and surgical specialties. This resulted in the adoption of proposals made as early as 1990, namely that the majority of the rooms on the ground floor of the Aston Webb Wing (including those updated at some expense in 1993) be converted to clinic use. The conversion was duly carried out in 2000/1 and involved adaptation of larger rooms to consulting rooms and of former en-suite bathrooms to examination rooms. An orthopaedic treatment room at the far end of the corridor balanced the existing Physiotherapy Department at the other, with a small reception area and a sunny waiting room opening to the garden midway between them. In 2002, plans were also made to convert two large rooms into an ENT suite, with a dedicated waiting room and audiology booth across the corridor. The arrival of the ENT suite further increased the department's size by bringing the number of clinic rooms to fourteen.

Also noted ten years earlier was that because national trends showed the likelihood of increased demands on The Evelyn's outpatient and diagnostic services in the future, priority should be given to these at the expense of inpatient rooms. It was not, however, until the third millennium that the northern extension of 1976 underwent further and radical alteration in order to accommodate an extended and updated Radiology Department. (It was the necessity of installing a CT scanner for sophisticated cross-sectional imaging of all body parts that was the motive force behind the redesigning of the Hospital's radiological services, computerised tomography being now, as a 2002 Hospital newsletter called it, 'an indispensable part of modern imaging'.) Budgetary constraints and the exigencies of the site meant, first, that although the extension was so completely altered that all known

Redesign of the hospital's radiological services allowed the installation of the CT scanner in 2002.

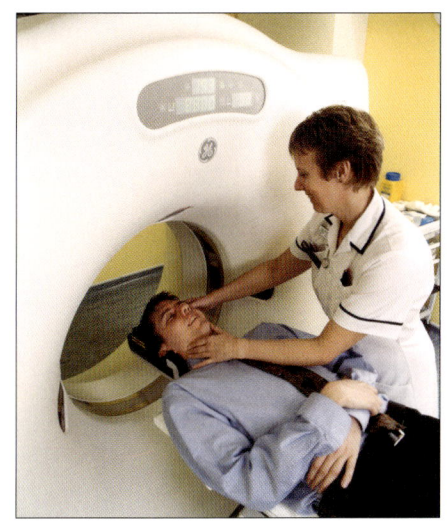

landmarks were obliterated, the new department had to be contained within the existing building's boundaries; and, second, that before expansion or rationalisation of the Radiology Department could take place, existing departments within the northern extension's envelope had to be removed. Repositioning the laundry services was easy: apart from patients' personal linen and a few other items, laundry was now dealt with off-site by a service provider and only a 'rump' of the former linen service had to be retained for the sorting and storage of clean supplies. Pharmacy also moved – indeed *had* to move before any other work could take place – into what was formerly the Radiology Department's office area. This resulted in Pharmacy's gaining an altogether more logical position relative to the rest of the Hospital, and much more space. The CT Unit, comprising the scanning room itself and offices for recording and reporting scans, opened two months ahead of the rest of the Radiology Department, building work continuing around it till March. The 'new' department in general and the CT Unit in particular were opened on 24 July 2002 by Professor Sir Alec Broers, Vice-Chancellor of the University, at the eighty-first birthday party of the institution founded by Morland Agnew, University alumnus.

In spite, however, of promises of building work planned for the near future because of the imminent need to implement conditions laid down by the Care Services Act of 2000, repeatedly postponed schedules of building, maintenance and redecoration suggested to those working there that something was lacking in The Evelyn's lifeforce – and this to such an extent that it appeared to have entered a kind of limbo from which only energetic measures could rescue it.

The reason for the Hospital's apparent inertia was revealed at a staff meeting held on 16 December 2002, at which Julian Agnew announced The Evelyn's impending withdrawal from the Hospital Management Trust as a result of its sale to Nuffield Hospitals. In coming to the decision to sell The Evelyn, said Mr Agnew, his principal concern was for its future. For a number of reasons, among which he listed the 'competitive and complicated world of private health care' and the arrival of the Care Standards Act with its implications for independent healthcare providers after April 2002, it was no longer sustainable for The Evelyn to continue as a stand-alone hospital. The new owner was not only a registered charity like The Evelyn – and so shared the same objectives and attitudes with regard to staff, patients and medical users – but was also, because of its position as the UK's largest independent healthcare provider,[3] better equipped to deploy the management skills (financial, investment, medical, legal and personal) needed to guarantee the Hospital's future. Lastly, Mr Agnew paid tribute to the 'excellent order' in which The Evelyn currently found itself, thanks to the quality of its staff, the reputation of its medical users, and the professionalism of its management team – who, he said, had made so many improvements to the functioning and financial position of the Hospital in recent years. The meeting concluded

3. Nuffield Hospitals already owned forty-three hospitals in the UK. The Nuffield praenomen was acquired in 1959 when Lord Nuffield suggested that the Nursing Homes Charitable Trust (as it then was) might benefit from the incorporation of his name in its title. Lord Nuffield, as William Morris, was founder of Oxford's Morris Motors; he had been a benefactor of an equivalent nursing home/hospital in Oxford, namely The Acland.

with the introduction of members of Nuffield Hospitals' management team and of the Hospital's new Manager, and with a short and moving speech from Peter Pemberton regretting the severing of his family connections with The Evelyn, connections which dated from his grandfather's having assisted Arthur Cooke at Evelyn's operation in Thompson's Lane in 1918.

The Nuffield Hospitals Group had, in fact, been associated with The Evelyn in an advisory capacity since 1968 in the guise of the Nuffield Nursing Homes Trust. Their formal union can therefore be seen as The Evelyn's progression from an institution founded, one might say, on a philanthropic whim to one on whose present success the NHG looked forward to building, this factor being reassuring to those at The Evelyn who had not been privy to the impending takeover (heads of department had received earlier intimations of the move, and the Medical Advisory Committee had actively supported it) and to patients who were reassured by letter that their care would not be adversely affected by the Hospital's change of ownership.

The Evelyn's last management meeting took place on Friday 10 January 2003. It concluded about the same time as The Evelyn's last major surgical operation took place in the institution (though not in the actual operating theatre) in which Arthur Cooke performed the first. Mr Agnew, sad at the ending of his family's long connection with the Hospital and of his own personal involvement with it for nearly thirty years, took a last walk in the garden to pay his respects to the memorial below which his great-grandparents' ashes lay. At 4 p.m. The Evelyn Hospital became the Nuffield Hospital Cambridge.

The Evelyn Hospital in the late 1990s.

Postscript

THE NAME EVELYN was not to disappear from the Cambridge scene. At the same meeting at which he announced the sale of the 'boon' given to the town by his great-grandfather, Mr Agnew looked forward to maintaining his family's connection with the area as head of the Evelyn Trust. The aim of the Trust, a newly created charitable foundation, was to further Morland Agnew's philanthropic intentions vis-à-vis the University and City of Cambridge 'and vicinity', and, as the 'pious benefaction' of a later generation, to benefit worthy medical causes in the locality. Thus, although The Evelyn as a Nursing Home and Hospital owing its name and existence to a lady with 'dyspepsia' did not survive to see its centenary, it was certain to have a role to play in Cambridge life in the new millennium in the shape of the Evelyn Trust.

Appendix

Senior Staff of The Evelyn Nursing Home / Hospital

Chairmen
1921–31	Charles Morland Agnew
1931–54	Charles Gerald Agnew
1954–81	Geoffrey William Gerald Agnew
1981–2003	Morland Herbert Julian Agnew

Administrators / Chief Executives
1975–84	Peter Finlayson
1984–92	John Allen
1992–9	Robert Swindlehurst
1999–2000	Marjorie Rankin
2000–3	Elizabeth Hayes

Matrons
1921–38	Edith Cracroft
1938–42	Nancy Puckle
1942–67	Margaret Quenilda Fynes-Clinton
1967–71	Morwenna Rendle-Short
1971–5	Helen McKay
1975–90	Peri Mundell (née Gwyther)

(no Matron March 1990 – Feb. 1991; Bridget Johnson, Deputy Matron, was Acting Matron)

1991–4	Jane Donald
1994–9	Wendy Mendham
1999–2003	Gill Cockley

Major Building Schemes of The Evelyn Nursing Home / Hospital

1920–1
Aston Webb building constructed

1923
Aston Webb building
extended/completed

1930–1
Airspace Wing (later known as Link
Building) built

1930–1
Major alterations to The Orchard

1935–6
Kitchen and Operating Theatre
extended

1936
'Night Floor' added to Airspace Wing

1947–8
Brookfield converted into Nurses'
Home

1951
'Night Floor' reconstructed following a
fire

1953
Kitchen enlarged and staff dining room
built

1955–6
X-ray department created from rooms
at east end of Aston Webb Building

1961–2
X-ray department converted into
Maternity Unit

1966
Installation of plumbing to all patients'
rooms in Aston Webb Building

1968–9
Conversion of Matron's flat in The
Orchard to consulting suite

1973
Maternity Unit reconverted to patients'
rooms

1975–6
Agnew House built

1975–6
Ancillary services area added to north
side of Link Building

1975–6
X-Ray Department established on
ground floor of The Orchard

1976
Consulting suite opened on first floor
of The Orchard

1976–7
Alterations to Link Building and Aston
Webb Building

1979–80
Geoffrey Agnew Operating Theatre
built on roof of Aston Webb Building

1982–3
Robinson Wing built

1984–5
Original Operating Theatre upgraded,
renamed the Gibson Theatre

1986
Conversion of rooms on first floor of
Link Building to clinic rooms
X-ray department extended

1989
Part of Agnew House converted into
Health Screening Unit

1988–9
Cooke Wing built

1993
Aston Webb Building's rooms
upgraded

1993–4
Morland Theatre suite built

2000
High Dependency Unit created

2000–1
Conversion of Aston Webb Building's
ground floor to clinic rooms

2002
Conversion of ancillary services area
into extended X-Ray (plus CT) Unit

Photographic acknowledgements

The author and publishers are grateful to the following for their kind permission to reproduce illustrations on the pages indicated:

Aerofilms Ltd: p.39;
J. Bartholomew: p.166;
Cambridge Evening News: pp.147, 198, 212;
Cambridge Newpapers Ltd: pp.80, 101, 116, 124, 152, 188;
Cambridgeshire Collection: pp.4, 12, 13;
C. Causton: p.217;
Commission-Air: p.220;
Hill and Saunders: p.31;
M. Holliday: pp.168, 178 (left), 180, 204;
Images: p.153;
J. E. Leigh: pp.129 (right), 156;
S. Mann: pp.vii, 11, 37, 39, 65, 67, 76, 96, 98, 109, 118, 121, 122, 126, 130, 135, 138, 146, 161, 179, 181 (top), 181 (bottom), 197, 198, 203, 207;
M. Manni: p.129 (left);
J. Pembrey: p.170;
Paul Raeside/Woolfson Communications: p.158;
Reeve Photography Ltd: pp.6, 32;
Royal Academy of Arts, London: p.8;
University Library, Cambridge: p.15.

Cover image(s): Evelyn Archives; Images

Every effort has been made to obtain permission for the reproduction of the illustrations and photographs in this book; apologies are offered to anyone whom it has not been possible to contact.

Index